The
FAIR DINKUM JEW

The
FAIR DINKUM JEW

THE SURVIVAL OF ISRAEL AND THE
ABRAHAMIC COVENANT

ALLAN RUSSELL JURIANSZ

iUniverse, Inc.
Bloomington

The Fair Dinkum Jew
The Survival of Israel and the Abrahamic Covenant

iUniverse books may be ordered through booksellers or by contacting:

iUniverse
1663 Liberty Drive
Bloomington, IN 47403
www.iuniverse.com
1-800-Authors (1-800-288-4677)

ISBN: 978-1-4759-0536-6 (sc)
ISBN: 978-1-4759-0538-0 (hc)
ISBN: 978-1-4759-0537-3 (ebk)

Printed in the United States of America

iUniverse rev. date: 05/01/2012

TABLE OF CONTENTS

INTRODUCTION

PART I: Personal History

PART II: Jewish History

PART III: Palestinian Arab History

PART IV: Conflict and Resolution

Dedication

This book is dedicated to our four children whose lives are a constant inspiration, and to my wife who challenges every thought that I voice to her.

Frontispieces: #1

(i) The LAND: Genesis 15:18 ". . . the Lord made a covenant with Abram, saying, Unto thy seed have I given this land, from the river of Egypt to the great river, the river Euphrates".

The IDF (Israeli Defence Force) must religiously secure and guard the LAND of Israel.

Frontispieces: #2

(ii) The TORAH: Exodus 25:1,8 "And the Lord spake unto Moses saying . . . . Let them make Me a sanctuary, that I may dwell among them".

(iii) The MESSIAH: Isaiah 9:6; 53:7 "For unto us a child is born, unto us a son is given, and the government shall be upon his shoulder; and his name shall be called Wonderful, Counsellor, The Mighty God, The Everlasting Father, The Prince of Peace . . . . He is brought as a lamb to the slaughter . . . ."

The Sacrifice by Abraham.
Painted by Rembrandt

PREFACE

I have always been interested in history despite my medical vocation. Had I become a historian or teacher of history I would have had a very satisfying life as well. I studied Ancient History and Medieval and Modern History as two separate subjects for my matriculation at Sydney University. For my Bachelor of Education degree at Avondale College I did Ancient History, Medieval and Modern History, British and Australian History, and Church History as separate tertiary subjects. The former three subjects were under the tutelage of Dr. Noel Clapham, easily the most knowledgeable and vibrant history professor I have had. He made history a vital part of life and made his students part of the past, teaching them lessons of life. Dr. Alwyn Salom taught Church History at Avondale College. He placed emphasis on doctrinal evolution. Naturally he gave us an insight into the development of elements of Christianity over 2000 years. He did not pay any attention to the doctrinal status of the Seventh-day Adventist Church (SDA) in its own evolution. (The SDA Church owns and operates Avondale College, a university accredited by the Australian Government). For that I attended a summer course of Denominational History taught by a fellow senior student. My insights into a deeper study of SDA Church History did not come till I encountered Dr. Arthur Patrick, a fellow classmate, who had become in my opinion the foremost SDA Church historian commencing in the 1990s. In summary therefore, my brain has been immersed in history most of my life.

Although recorded history is a personal view in its definition the comparative and relative study of it is a rich field. The neglect of the study of history has led to much woe in the world because of a loss in the contributions hindsight has to offer. The handling of problems of the present and expected future is difficult. Lessons are not learned and mistakes are repeated. The interpretation of history is difficult. History should be allowed to interpret itself. There is no substitute for learning these lessons whether religious or secular. History should be approached with a teachable open mind. Attention to consensus of recorders of history and archaeology often leads to better conclusions when variations are encountered.

My Judaeo-Christian heritage has bound me with the Jews with extraordinarily strong bonds. Recently I have discovered that there are Jewish genes in both my maternal and paternal ancestry. I have dedicated a chapter of the book to this discovery. The history of the Jews has been of paramount interest to me since I became aware of the world and my place in it, likely starting at the age of six years. The motivation for this book comes from the concern I have for the security of the Jews as a nation.

In the consideration of the security of Israel, apart from the Bible, three other books have greatly affected my thoughts: "Exiled" by Serpouhi Tavoukdjian, gave me a chilling education in the persecution, slaughter, and forced exile of the Armenian people from their homeland as experienced by Serpouhi; "Eichmann in Jerusalem-The Banality of Evil" by Hannah Arendt introduced me to the ravages inflicted on the Jews by the Nazis by an otherwise ordinary man; and "From Beirut to Jerusalem" by Thomas Friedman has given me insight into the precarious security of Israel. This last book has given me an understanding of the Middle East of recent times. It was first published in 1988 and revised in 1998. It needs a further revision to bring it up to date. Thomas Friedman's insights are so genuine in the main because he has experienced them in real life. I do not agree with all his conclusions and offered solutions to the problems he identifies, but his ideas are to be seriously considered. All three books discuss persecution and genocide. Serpouhi eloquently and graphically describes the Turkish inflicted genocide of the Armenians. I was twelve years old when I read that book. I was already aware of the persecution of the Israelites during their sojourn in Egypt, their Assyrian and Babylonian captivities, and the Roman induced decimation and diaspora that occurred in AD 70. These had been taught to me in my Sabbath School classes. I subsequently became fully aware of the Nazi Holocaust of the Jews. Reading the account of the capture, trial and execution of Eichmann almost destroyed my innocence and trust in humankind. As I became a more serious student of the Bible and world history, dreadful realities were thrust upon me, which scarred and hardened my innocent hopes for the world. The realization came to me that persecution and genocide have been the 'normal' happenings in the history of the human race. And it still goes on. The founding of every country has been at the cost of its indigenous people. Some take-overs are kinder than others. Some are most cruel.

The discussion of indigenous people is very relevant to Israel's claim to Palestine. When Abraham arrived on the scene there were several tribes occupying the land promised to him by God. He was instructed to evangelise it but the mission was not entirely successful and the effort to eradicate idolatry and establish monotheism was accomplished by his progeny through violence. The Tamils and the Sinhalese have been fighting over Sri Lanka, but both these peoples are themselves invaders from India who dispossessed, displaced and destroyed the Veddahs who were the indigenous people living in the island before them. This method of possession was no different to the methods most European countries were established by marauding tribes moving westward across Europe. In the modern era the current countries in South America, and the USA, Canada, Australia, and New Zealand were similarly established. In reality the Kingdom of King David was similarly established and there are no surviving indigenous people with a claim to Palestine other than the Jews. The empiric legality of their repossession of Palestine is that they are the original owners and historically the Arabs are relatively newcomers who arrived in Palestine after 600 AD. Arabization of the Middle East is a subject untreated as such by most historians. The spread of Islam went hand in hand with Arabization. In this book I refer to the splendid work of Dan Smith in his book "The State of the Middle East—An Atlas of Conflict and Resolution". He ignores the antecedent history of Palestine and begins his treatment of the Middle East from the Decline of the Ottoman Empire. As a result he relegates the history of the children of Abraham to an unrecognised quantity, and to my understanding vaguely describes it as the "magic and mystery of the region". His readers therefore get oriented to a jaundiced view of the history of Palestine. He does acknowledge that Palestine is the birthplace of Judaism and Christianity, and he introduces Islam as though it also arose in Palestine, and gives primacy to Islam: "The first is Islam . . . . Historically, the spread of Islam and the spread of Arabic from the Arabian peninsula to the borders of modern Turkey and through North Africa were a single process" (pages 8 &15). This totally misleads readers to the actual precedent Jewish history of the region. He does not adequately describe the Arabization of the Middle East. The Arabs never had a state in Palestine, as they did in Egypt and Libya.

As I look at the current state of the nations and the critically vulnerable status of Israel in a sea of surrounding rage, I am concerned for Israel's existence. If the United States of America is truly on the decline as the world's most powerful nation, who will defend Israel? Israel may have a nuclear arsenal as a deterrent to being attacked, but Israel is too divided against itself. Unity is vital since 'a house divided against itself' will not stand. That is why I ask the question: WHO IS THE TRUE JEW? Israel faces two major problems: Its viability as a nation and its religious disunity. This book is an attempt to address these two problems.

This book is not exhaustive of the subjects discussed and should be considered as a primer. I rely entirely on the Tanak for the positions I take in the book. I believe in God and in the Abrahamic Covenant. The future of Israel demands that the matter be seriously considered so that a vital solution may be politically found, whether it be MILITARY MIGHT or SPIRITUAL MIGHT or BOTH? Implementation is imperative. The children of Abraham are indeed a gifted people and have made a significant individual impression on the earth. But as a nation they have shown repeated failures and are yet to make a significant national impact on the planet. I take the attitude that all is not lost. Israel will survive. Israel will make its impact on the planet.

Allan Russell Juriansz

ACKNOWLEDGEMENTS

I am indebted to my parents, teachers, and the friends who have taught me. I am greatly indebted to the authors of the three books I have mentioned. I practiced urological surgery in Toronto, Canada, in a predominantly Jewish constituency and feel I have learned of the life experience of the Jews. I thank the many Jewish colleagues and patients for perspectives I had not envisioned before.

INTRODUCTION

This book is proffered as a definition and clarification of the Abrahamic Covenant. This is defined as the Call of God for Abraham to undertake a mission to secure Land, to be termed the Promised Land, to be inherited by Abraham's progeny, termed the Chosen People, with whom God had a close dialogue, and who he endowed with a mission. They would become as numerous as the stars of the firmament and would be instrumental in the blessedness of all nations. Abraham was thus entrusted to be the ancestor of the Messiah who would be the instrument to restore humanity to face-to-face communion with their God. The three great pillars therefore of the Abrahamic Covenant are LAND, TORAH, and MESSIAH.

The title of the book is 'THE FAIR DINKUM JEW, THE SURVIVAL OF ISRAEL AND THE ABRAHAMIC COVENANT'. This title has an Australian flavour. I migrated in 1954 under duress, from my birthplace Ceylon (Sri Lanka) to Australia. I utterly enjoyed living in Australia and absorbed much of the country's flavour and benefits. There are many Australian terms, which give the spoken brand of Australian English a delightful identity. This is less obvious today with the advancement of what could be termed as 'Americanization'. But fifty years ago it was prominent. The words Fair Dinkum have the meaning of being 'the purest reality of the truth'. To be a Fair Dinkum Jew is therefore the Jew who is closest to being the true Jew. Such a definition is not meant to be insulting in that it is not meant to imply that all other Jews are not true Jews. But it is meant to identify the Jew who is in possession of the understanding of the Abrahamic call of God in its original and purest identification. I would not presume to label any Jew as a false Jew for fear of being like Goering who stated: "I decide who is a Jew" (Cited in 'A History of Zionism' by Walter Laqueur). Every Jew must decide for himself/herself where he/she stands, as a part of God's chosen people.

The Jewish population throughout the world is composed of the genetic descendants of the Abrahamic lineage through Jacob (Israel) and all others who have become Jews by adoption and conversion. The Jews have always been an open and accepting society, anxious to reach out and contribute to the milieu in which they find themselves. Their distinctness results from their practice of Judaism, which at times has caused them to be ostracised. The Jews are very genuine socially and enter wholeheartedly into any open society, which they serve and enrich. For example, in the United States of America today the Jewish population is estimated at two percent. But their involvement in the elected political governance of the US is estimated numerically at seventeen percent. They have a tendency to prominence because of their willingness to be involved. Their gifts and talents bring them to the forefront in a proportion that is in excess of their numbers (See 'Israel's Lobby on the US' in Wikipaedia and also 'Jewsweek' July 22, 2002).

I want this book to identify the Abrahamic call of God in the original basic simple terms of LAND, TORAH, and MESSIAH. In these terms lies the security and strength of Israel. Israel's indelible history as a nation has been composed of persecutions, invasions, slaughters, captivities, diasporas, and returns to the homeland. In discussing these dynamics I am acutely aware of the threat to the security and perpetuity of literal Israel in the world today. I want to bring a awareness of the Tanak as Israel's guide to strength in its nationhood. I rely on my knowledge of the Tanak and dedication to it to achieve this end.

This book is divided into segments. Part I will introduce my identity and background. It will also define my place in the religious atmosphere in Judaism. My extreme desire to bring peaceful solutions to the current conflicts in Israel will then become apparent. Part II will trace a religio-political history of the Jews from Creation to Abraham and thence to the AD 70 diaspora. The following 2000 years of Jewish history proves the resilience of the Jews and the persistence of God to bring them back. The relevance of Judaism to Jewish existence and future in terms of the Abrahamic Covenant will be discussed. Part III will describe aspects of the Arab infiltration and occupation of Canaan (Palestine). In Part IV the current conflict between Jews and Arab Palestinians will be treated in terms of the post 1967 borders. Possible solutions will be identified.

Achievement of peacefulness in Israel and the Middle East will not only increase the tranquillity in the Middle East but I hope will lay the groundwork for what I believe is the eschatological vision of the Tanak. Israel needs to believe in and defend its integrity not only as a political and national identity but also in the religious milieu defined by the Tanak. A great reformation in this milieu in Jewry is needed to understand the Messianic Mission and to the realization of it.

PART I
PERSONAL HISTORY

A major part of my life has been lived as a devout Seventh-day Adventist. I considered myself a 'Spiritual Jew'. Sabbath keeping and some Levitical health laws were strictly obeyed. Seventh-day Adventism does not accommodate many of the Levitical health rules such as menstrual impurity, and Jewish Feasts, which are considered no longer applicable. Although homosexuality is considered an aberration of God's plan SDAs do not believe in stoning homosexuals. They leave that judgement up to God. Seventh-day Adventism is very strict about Sabbath keeping but does not believe in stoning Sabbath breakers. SDAs unofficially consider Moses was over-zealous in some of his ideas. SDAs have, in my opinion, a jaundiced view of history in the construction of their eschatology. They 'proof text' the rise of the SDA Movement and their importance into the Tanak and the B'rit Hadasha. Quite early in my involvement with the SDA Church I had rejected their pre 1948 prediction that the Jews would never return to Palestine. They are silent on it since but were very vocal about this belief in their pre 1948 proselytising evangelistic campaigns. I also rejected their doctrine of the replacement of the Jews as God's chosen people destined to carry out the Abrahamic Covenant. Their insertion of themselves into that position became presumptuous. Their eschatology is strained and fixed by their prophetess Ellen G White who interprets the Bible for them. Their scholars who reject her authority are ostracised. It is not my desire to make this book an analysis of the SDA religion. Let it suffice that in 1979 I broke with them rejecting their eschatology and the authority of their prophetess. My attention was applied to the Tanak and I became more sensitive to Israel's modern besetment. I remain sensitive also to the plight of the Arab Palestinians but am frustrated with Arab leaders and the lack of cohesion and generosity in the Arab world to help them achieve a peaceful settlement. The intent of extreme religio-political Islam to wipe Jews off the planet saps Arab energy and prevents them reaching reasonable goals. The desire to Judenrein the world does not coincide with the eschatology of the Tanak. My personal story demonstrates my own dedication to the Tanak and to God's plan of salvation contained in the Abrahamic Covenant. In Part I, I describe my personal history and orientation in the application of the Tanak.

CHAPTER 1
WHO AM I?

I was born in Colombo, Ceylon, now called Sri Lanka. Back then it was a British colony that had been shaped by 150 years of British influence. Colonialism is now a dirty word but in my opinion British colonialism in Southern Asia was responsible for placing Sri Lanka, India, Pakistan, Bangladesh, Malaysia, Singapore and Burma in the modern world, teaching them English, giving them great infrastructure, systems of health, education, social structure, and above all democracy. Westminster is the basic model in governance. Burma is currently a renegade under a totalitarian military regime, but thankfully the opposition party is democratic, though suppressed.

Underlying the British era in Sri Lanka were two other substantial colonial eras, which also in my opinion laid great foundations to modern nationhood. Both were European, the first being the Portuguese in 1505, and then the Dutch who supplanted the Portuguese in 1602. Britain took total control in 1802. All three colonial powers carried away much of the riches of the country to their homelands but it cannot be denied that they gave Sri Lanka its place in the modern world. To be sure Sri Lanka was not in the dark cannibalistic ages when the Europeans came. It has a rich civilized heritage from the advent of the Dravidian Tamils from south India and the Aryan Sinhalese from north India about 500 years BC. Their histories go back further than the highly civilised reigns of Asoka the Great and his son Mahinda. Both these men were converted to Buddhism, which originated with Prince Siddhartha Gautama, the Buddha. Mahinda brought Buddhism to Sri Lanka. Buddhism has given the majority Sinhalese a well thought out philosophy by which to live, and properly practiced can enrich life. The Tamils are mostly Hindus.

The three colonizing powers also bequeathed to the island their genes. A mixed race arose from intermarriage that did not exactly fit into the native Sinhalese or Tamil cultures, nor into the European mould. The mixed race that arose preferred to value their European roots and maintained a separate identity. The Portuguese who started the mixed blood gave them the name of 'Burghers', which in Portuguese means 'Inhabitants of Towns'. Indeed that is where the mixed blood was born. The colonizers mainly lived in the immediate hinterlands of the ports in the island where the trade and commerce were concentrated. Those Europeans who decided to spend their lives there took to themselves spouses from the native communities or in the main intermarried with each other in this new community or race of people. They became a force to be reckoned with in that they spoke the European language in vogue at the time, as well as developed facility in speaking Sinhalese and Tamil. They were therefore used by the colonial powers as the sub-governing class, the interface with the natives. Their loyalties were with the colonial powers and it was a mutually beneficial symbiosis. Their skin colours were varied but lighter than the natives and they were easily recognisable as a separate entity. They attended 'missionary schools' whose language of teaching was the prevailing European one and their mother tongue remained Portuguese, then Dutch, and finally English.

After one hundred and fifty years of British colonialism the Burghers considered themselves British and their mother tongue was English. They assumed British history as theirs and were totally loyal to the British Crown. They were the ruling class under the white British hierarchy and with their 'superior' British education commanded higher incomes and European standards of living. They also assimilated some of the native culture. They retained Christianity as their religion. The native Sinhalese and Tamils considered them as 'outsiders'. They were 'misfits' in the land of their birth. After the granting of Independence to the island in 1948, they were left high and dry by the departed British and were considered karapoththas (cockroach vermin) by the rank and file natives. Their privileged position disappeared. The new law of the independent Sri Lanka enshrined Buddhism as the state religion and Sinhalese/Tamil as the state languages. The Burghers were at an impasse as they had omitted learning to read and write Sinhalese/Tamil although they could speak these languages. They were no longer able to retain their government jobs. Much more significantly, they strongly considered themselves British and refused to 'go native'. They wanted out and initiated their own diaspora. They were strangers in the land of their birth, a self-inflicted circumstantial estrangement.

My father was "more British than the British" in his outlook and attitude. When I questioned him about my race he informed me that I was a Burgher.

But when I asked what my ancestry was he told me that my ancestors were Dutch. Our Juriansz name came to the island in 1786 when Jacobus Juriaansz arrived aboard a Dutch sailing vessel. He was born in Antwerp when it was still a part of The Netherlands. He married a mixed blood woman with the Dutch name Petronella Bougart and my father was descended from that liaison. My mother's maiden name was Ondatje and that name came to the island when Michael Jurie Jurgen Ondaatje arrived in 1657 via a short sojourn in Tanjore, India. He was born in 1635 in Utrecht, The Netherlands. He first married a mixed blood woman with the Portuguese name Magdalena De Cruz. She died of tuberculosis. Subsequently he consorted with an unknown Sinhalese woman who bore him a son named Philip Jurie Jurgen Ondaatje from whom my mother had descended. The lineage has been traced carefully from these two Dutchmen down to my parents. There is an admixture of Dutch, Portuguese, Tamil, Sinhalese, Danish and German in my father's lineage. And in my mother's lineage there is an admixture of Dutch, Portuguese, Sinhalese, Tamil, German, Irish and English.

And so I was born with a mixed colonial ancestry with the presumed Dutch name of Juriansz. I seemed to belong everywhere but nowhere. I realised my mind was strongly British, like my father's. I decided then that I did not belong anywhere else other than in the British world and I was extremely happy to be British. I had a British heritage and high school education in the private Anglican St. John's College in Colombo, and I was deeply loyal to the British Crown. Many of my family on both sides were veterans from World Wars I and II. Some of them fought for Britain in the Boer War.

It was one of the happiest days of my life when my father decided to ship me off to Australia. It was a day of destiny. I have written extensively about my family in my book titled 'Colonial Mixed Blood—A Story of the Burghers of Sri Lanka'. I eventually became an Australian citizen, despite the 'White Australia Policy' and was proud to belong to the British Commonwealth. I found I had no emotional ties to the land of my birth. I first enrolled in Avondale College in Cooranbong, not far north of Sydney, where I obtained a Bachelor of Education degree. I then attended Sydney University Medical School and began my medical life. I married an Australian of Irish ancestry, and have a lovely family of three sons and a daughter. Exciting times, more of them, were still ahead.

Australia provided me with a country, a home, a tertiary education, a wife and a great sense of belonging, and I was in the British Commonwealth. Seeking specialization in urology I went to Toronto in Canada and qualified as a Fellow of the Royal College of Surgeons of Canada. My wife and I then spent three years in the Far East (Hong Kong and Thailand doing 'missionary work') before settling down to a urology practice in Willowdale, Toronto. We raised our four children there. I was still in the British Commonwealth.

It is of interest to look at the status of the Burghers in Sri Lanka in more detail. They were a mixed race that grew out of the intermarriage of basically five races: The European races were the Portuguese, Dutch, and British. The native races were the Sinhalese and Tamils. During the colonial period from 1505-1948 they developed a separate identity as a community. They were Christians and worshipped in churches and they were oriented as missionaries spreading Christianity to the natives. They were the predominant users of the European oriented educational systems. With Portuguese as their mother tongue they worshipped as Roman Catholics. Then they were changed to the mother tongue of Dutch and a very strong Martin Luther Reformation Dutch Reformed Christianity. Their greatest European orientation was accomplished by the British occupation which was much more intense and pervasive. English became their mother tongue. The Church of England became dominant in the religion realm. The education system was highly developed and modelled after the British high school and university culture, standards, and traditions. And they became heirs of the benefits of the Industrial Revolution. Westminster democracy was established and the British were responsible for laying down a modern infrastructure. The Burghers adopted the English language as their mother tongue and their English medium high schools followed the English curriculum. At the same time the British made vernacular schools free, which greatly benefited the natives. The Burghers became British in their thinking and developed a great fondness for and loyalty to the British Crown. All these benefits spilled over to the native Sinhalese and Tamils who desired them. The Burghers became predominantly the civil servants. They were the bosses under the British ruling hierarchy. They had the command of the English system and were also able to speak the native languages. But they neglected to read and write the native languages. When Sri Lanka gained its independence in 1948, the situation changed dramatically. The Burghers lost their privileged class status. They refused to 'go native' and became misfits in the land where they were born. They were swept aside by the native nationalism, which they refused to embrace. With their European loyalties and their fluency in English they created their own diaspora into the English speaking countries of the world: Britain, USA, Canada, and New Zealand, and belatedly Australia, after the White Australia policy was abolished.

The Sri Lankan nationals generally despised the Burghers for being of mixed race. But there was no element of ethnic cleansing in their departure. They were looked upon as 'second class Europeans', who had lost their privileged status. They could have learned to read and write the native languages and they could have embraced the native culture and nationalism but they did not choose to do this.

CHAPTER 2
SPIRITUAL ISRAEL

With my father's Dutch ancestry he also inherited the legacy of Martin Luther's Reformation theology. Essentially, Martin Luther, a German Roman Catholic priest challenged the corrupt Roman Catholic Church of the time, which sold indulgences to obtain leverage in getting eternal life, a future in God's hereafter. Martin Luther contended that based on the Bible, eternal life as defined in Christianity came as a free gift of Grace, provided by the life and death of Jesus Christ, the Son of God. My father's Dutch Reformed affiliation was not nominal. Both his parents were devout adherents of the Dutch Reformed Church and instilled Reformation theology in all their children, four boys and two girls. My father did not attend any church after he married but remained a self-admitted 'sinner' all his life and was totally dependent on the provision of Grace as defined by Martin Luther. He died in that hope.

My mother's Dutch ancestry also bequeathed her the legacy of Martin Luther's theology. There were several in her Dutch ancestry who were Dutch Reformed ministers and her father was a strict Dutch Reformed adherent. He was a lawyer, educated in England, who later became a judge. But after he married Alice Pate, from an Irish family living in England for generations, he never attended church but continued to maintain his membership in the Wolvendaal Kruis Kerk Dutch Reformed Church in Colombo, in Sri Lanka. He supported that church financially and in his will he requested a Dutch Reformed burial, which was carried out. Alice Pate his wife was an ardent Baptist and brought my mother up to be an ardent Baptist. And so my mother brought up her entire family as Baptists, that is, until just prior to my birth. I was her unexpected eleventh child, born four years after the previous one. I have five older brothers and five older sisters.

About the year 1932 my father found that he was having increasing difficulty supporting his large family with his wage as a stationmaster in the Ceylon

Government Railway. There was an aggravating factor to this situation. He had started gambling. The sought for financial help in the hope of winning in gambling was adding to the gravity of the situation. It came to a crisis when he lost his job because of his gambling. After two years of desperate financial circumstances he finally found another job, but he had built up a large amount of debt, which he could no longer manage. "So he went to [his Aunt] who lived over the way".

Ellen Sophia La Faber was of Jewish lineage. Her immediate ancestors had arrived from France and settled in South India as traders. They had mixed with the Chetty people. The Chettys were Tamils who had intermarried with Europeans and because they were rich and of mixed blood they lived as an elite society, aloof from ordinary Tamils. Some of them had a Syrian Christian ancestry. The latter considered themselves converts of St. Thomas, the disciple of Jesus. They worshipped in the Syriac Liturgy in the Aramaic language. The La Fabers had intermarried with the South Indian Chettys who were Nasrani Sabbath keeping Syrian Christians. Despite the presence of a Jewish community living not far away they had strayed from their Jewish heritage into a comfortable but less stringent living as Sabbath keeping Syrian Christians. Ellen's grandparents had migrated to Sri Lanka and settled culturally and socially into the Burgher Community and continued their trade and commerce, which had made them wealthy. Ellen La Faber had married Alfred Jacob Baptist of Portuguese and Dutch ancestry. Alfred Jacob Baptist's sister, Elizabeth Margaret Baptist happened to be married to Peter John Juriansz and they were the parents of Benjamin John Juriansz, my father. The wealthy Ellen Sophia La Faber, who was Jewish was my father's aunt by marriage. So my father went to Ellen hat in hand for a loan to consolidate his debts and start anew. There was one problem in the way.

Ellen Sophia La Faber had recently been converted to Seventh-day Adventism and was a rabid proselytising convert. She was willing to lend the money so my father could consolidate his debts and pay her back monthly. But she requested his attendance with the family at the SDA Church for just one occasion as a condition of the loan. But that one visit was fateful and resulted in the conversion of my mother and the family to the Seventh-day Adventist Church. My father remained Dutch Reformed. But the rest of my family became SDAs.

9

SDAs are first and foremost seventh-day Sabbath keepers as are the Jews. They are extremely strict in their observance of Sabbath hours from sunset Friday to sunset Saturday. They consider the Sabbath "The Seal of God" which they bear invisibly in their foreheads, and which sets them apart as God's chosen and destined 'to be saved'[1]. They also adhere to the stringent Levitical clean and unclean food laws, significantly abstaining from pork and seafood. Apart from following Kosher rules SDAs are almost indistinguishable from Orthodox Jews in their religious observance. As their name implies their next important tenet is their belief in the physical bodily return of Jesus Christ, which is called The Second Coming. Originally, led by William Miller, they believed this would happen in October 1844, a date set by their interpretation of Daniel's prophecies. In Daniel's vision of the he-goat's 'little horn' recorded in Daniel chapter 8, Daniel hears a conversation between two heavenly beings called "Saints". In the vision the "daily" (sacrifice) of the Temple is desecrated and discontinued by the "little horn" of the he-goat who magnifies himself against God. One "Saint" enquires of the other: "How long shall the daily ... be trampled under foot?" In Daniel 8:14 the answer comes "Unto two thousand three hundred days; then shall the sanctuary be cleansed". William Miller interpreted the two thousand three hundred days would end in October 1844 by the return of Jesus to eradicate sin from the earth. When Jesus did not return as predicted the "Great Disappointment" occurred. The prophecy was subsequently reinterpreted in terms of the "Heavenly Sanctuary". The event was reinterpreted in terms of the earthly Jewish Temple service. Jesus who had been in the Holy Place of the Heavenly Temple since his ascension to heaven, had moved into the Most Holy Place to perform the Day of Atonement Service in October 1844. This service in the Most Holy Compartment was one of "Investigative Judgement" to determine who was worthy of salvation. Jesus then offered his own shed blood to God, himself the sacrifice and High Priest. The records kept in heaven of the lives of humans were to be examined and judgement passed on those saved and those damned. When that Investigative Judgement is concluded, then Jesus would return to earth. So, according to SDAs that judgement is still in progress since 1844, and will soon be concluded. Then Jesus will come.

As devout Christians, SDAs also consider themselves 'Spiritual Jews' and heirs of the Abrahamic Covenant[2]. They take Paul the apostle of the B'rit Hadasha very seriously when he said: "If ye be Christ's then are ye Abraham's seed and heirs according to the promise"[3]. They consider that God rejected the Jews as his chosen people and has chosen them instead as his new chosen people and given them the heritage he had previously offered the Jews[4]. They claim the point of God's rejection of the Jews occurred with the stoning of Stephen by the Pharisees and Sadducees (including Saul/Paul) in B'rit Hadasha times[5]. They trace a lineage of Sabbath keeping Christians from Stephen's stoning, through the ages to themselves. SDAs believe in a stringent healthful life style and in an intense proselytising endeavour. They predict a latter day 'Time of Jacob's Trouble' (see Daniel 12:1) when the 'Apostate Church and State' single them out for a Nazi-like Holocaust and set a date for their annihilation. They will then seek refuge in the hills and mountains. Deliverance comes with the return of Jesus Christ to take the resurrected and living saints to heaven for a thousand years. At the end of this millennium their final eschatological event will occur and is based on the B'rit Hadasha book of Revelation (Chapter 21). A 'New Jerusalem City' descends down from heaven on the Mount of Olives in Israel. There will be a battle for it with the resurrected 'wicked' who will then be wiped out by 'Fire and Brimstone'. The Messiah will then reign with the redeemed from the New Jerusalem in an 'Earth Made New' for ever and ever.

And so apart from my father Benjamin John Juriansz the rest of the family became strict Seventh-day Adventists. That is how I became enrolled at Avondale College. But when I left there in 1957 I met Desmond Ford who became a reformer in the SDA Church pointing out doctrinal flaws in their interpretation of prophecy[6]. SDAs take the Tanak very seriously and have interpretations of prophecy, particularly in the Book of Daniel, from which they build a significant eschatology. It was over this crisis that I left the SDA Church in 1979 since I felt they are mistaken. I have no connection with denominational Christianity since then.

Despite a spiritual identification with Jews SDAs sometimes had difficulty adjusting to physical Jews. It is important to mention the German Seventh-day Adventist Church's relationship with the Nazi Party and the holocaust. Roland Blaich, an SDA professor in one of the American SDA universities has researched this dark chapter. Anxious to maintain separation of church and state, a non-combatant role in the military, 'proper' Sabbath keeping, and cooperation with the regime to prevent being banned as a denomination, the German SDA Church leaders made compromises. These compromises were utterly unchristian and not the general views held by worldwide Adventism. The German SDA Church leaders failed to protest the persecution of the Jews, and even expelled Adventists who had a Jewish background from church membership. These were despicable acts. Many German Adventists however gave private and individual help to Jews, including hiding them from the Nazis[7].

My self-identification as a spiritual Jew had its physical side. I remember in my childhood that a Jewish gentleman in Colombo converted to Adventism. My Jewish aunt by marriage, Ellen Sopia La Faber, had something to do with that conversion. Close contact with Jews started in my tertiary education. At Avondale College I looked with awe on Dr. Alwyn Salom, who it was whispered was a convert from Judaism. In the close contact I had with him as my teacher of the subjects of 'New Testament Epistles' and 'Church History', never once was his Jewishness ever broached. I held in awe my friends who were classmates with Jewish genes. Pam Ion's family had converted from an assimilated Jewish family, and Edith Bradbury's mother was also from an assimilated Jewish family. She had converted to Seventh-day Adventism when she married her Christian husband. I spent a summer at the Bradbury home and experienced unbelievable love, inclusiveness and hospitality. I have kept in touch with them ever since Avondale days. Edith and Pam are both still in Adventism. Since discovering my few Jewish genes we now exchange "Next year in Jerusalem!" when we see each other. Singing with the Avondale Symphonic Choir was memorable, particularly Richter's "Creation" and Gounod's "Babylon's Wave". The latter is a rendition of Psalm 137, which captures the agony of the Babylonian Captivity. I also remember my mother sang to us at bedtime. One song, which is etched in my memory is "Is It Far to Canaan's Land". I still hear her voice. Hymns we sang in church also gave me connection. Hymns like "Jerusalem the Golden", and "We're Marching to Zion" always made me feel a spiritual Jew. In medical school I was very close to my several Jewish friends. I played squash with Tim Blashki, now a respected psychiatrist practicing in Melbourne. My chemistry, biochemistry, and physiology laboratory partner was David Kaplan. Both Tim and David were practicing orthodox Jews who went to synagogue each Sabbath. Sydney University sometimes scheduled written examinations for the Sabbath. For these, Jewish and SDA classmates were sequestered at an SDA pastor's home where we observed Sabbath hours and wrote the examinations after sunset. In my internship year I was very close to Eddy Loebel and Marica Moser. Both are Hungarian Jews whose parents had migrated to Australia. Marica was not strict as I discovered after the fact, that I had hungrily devoured tasty Hungarian pork gulash at her home. Marica and her mother apologized and I believe the incident brought some changes in their home.

Did God reject the Jews and discard them as participants in the Abrahamic Covenant? There is no evidence in the Tanak that can be used to prove this, either in a declaration or cocooned in a prophetic utterance that can be interpreted to prove this.

God's promises to Israel in the Tanak had the prerequisite of obedience to the Torah. He repeatedly punished Israel for idolatry and then brought them back to his bosom. How many times can he do this? He will do this as often as he likes. The Book of Hosea abundantly declares his eternal love for his people Israel. Hosea forgave his wife five times for her unfaithfulness. God used this as an illustration of his forgiveness and longsuffering. God will punish Israel when necessary but he always forgives and reclaims them. He will never forget his promise to Abraham. With God, the best future of Israel is yet to come. David sang of it in the Psalms. Isaiah showed the price God was willing to pay in the Messianic vision to reclaim his people. Is Israel as a nation willing to return to God? Will they understand his promise of LAND, TORAH and MESSIAH?

NOTES

[1]   See ASSURE—Seventh-day Adventists Believe . . . 'The Sabbath' Chapter 19

[2]   See 'Daniel 8:14—The Day of Atonement and the Investigative Judgement' by
      Desmond Ford for a full explanation of the prophetic beliefs of SDAs.
      See AllExperts, Seventh-day Adventists, Tom Norris speaks for SDAs
      See John Lomacang and Wilfredo Hepolongca: 'Why the SDA Church emerged
      from the Foundation of the Jewish economy (its predecessor) to become
      'Spiritual Israel', Ministers, SDA Church
      See also SDA Bible Commentary Volume 4 pages 25, 26, 33 and 'Christ's Object
      Lessons' by Ellen G. White page 305 (Quoted in Replacement Theology on line
      by Dr. Jack Gent)
      "The rejection of Jesus by the leaders of Israel meant the permanent irrevocable
      cancellation of their special standing before God as a nation" and "Accordingly,
      what he proposed to do for the world through Israel of old He will finally
      accomplish through His Church on earth today. And many promises originally
      made to Israel will be fulfilled to His remnant people [SDAs] at the close of
      time". The SDA Bible Commentary Volume 4: 25,26,33
      In contrast read Jeremiah 23:36, Ezekiel 36:24-32, 39:27,28, Amos 9:8,9, Isaiah
      4:2-6, 59:20,21.

3   Saint Paul's Epistle to the Galatians 3:29 (B'rit Hadasha)
4   'Conditionalism: A Cornerstone of Adventist Doctrine' by Tim Crosby
    (Ministry Magazine, August 1986)
5   See ASSURE—Seventh-day Adventists Believe … 'The Doctrine of Last
    Things', Chapter 23: 'Christ's Ministry in the Heavenly Sanctuary'
    The 2300 Day Prophecy of Daniel 8:14: The pivotal date is AD 34 when
    Stephen was stoned. God rejected the Jews as his 'Chosen People'
    See also 'The Crisis Ahead' a compilation by Robert Olson from the Prophetess
    Ellen White's writings about the 'End Time' Chapters 2-21.

6   See Good News Unlimited: Desmond Ford—'Daniel 8:14—The Day of
    Atonement and the Investigative Judgement' 1980. Available online
7   Roland Blaich: 'Nazi Race Hygiene and the Adventists', Spectrum 25, September
    1996
    See also Corrie Schroder: Seventh-day Adventists, Pro-Seminar Papers
    See also Zdravko Plantak, 'The Silent Church: Human Rights and Adventist
    Social Ethics', New York: St. Martin's Press, 1998, page 20

Chapter 3
The Fair Dinkum Me?

My curiosity about my ancestry was aroused while I was practicing urology in Toronto, Canada. I was privileged to care for a Jewish migrant from Riga, Latvia. This man had bladder cancer and I operated on and followed him for many years fearing a recurrence. He died 10 years after I first met him from a heart attack. He and his family and I became friends. On one of his visits to my office he asked me the origin of my name Juriansz. I told him it was a Dutch name and he disagreed. He told me that he thought my name originated from a Jewish name in Riga, Latvia. Since I was fairly confident that my name originated in The Netherlands I dismissed the suggestion as being far-fetched. I thought no more about it until my retirement from surgical urology. Since I had lots of time on my hands when I retired I decided to research my ancestry. The motivation came from my mother's constant request for me to write the story of the family. She wanted this for a religious purpose. She had a lifelong American friend from Texas, the wife of a former SDA missionary to Ceylon. This woman was a writer for the Church's journals and was impressed that all my mother's children at the time were SDAs although her husband was not. She wanted to write my mother's story as a triumph of her religious strength in raising all her children as SDAs. But I had not been able to do so for lack of time. Both my mother and her friend had passed away when I retired but the motivation for writing the story of the family remained with me. The religious circumstances had changed as well and five of the surviving ten children in the family had left the SDA Church over Desmond Ford's doctrinal revelations. My desire had changed to researching the family's roots.

During my research I discovered the origin of my mother's maiden name-ONDAATJE. With the aid of Kate Monk's Onomastikon I discovered that her name had come from the ancient Frisian name of ONTJE. It had been "Dutchified" by the addition of two letter 'a'-s with the linguistic addition of convenience of the letter d. Ontje became Ondaatje. One of my mother's recent

15

ancestors had dropped one letter a from his name and his descendants spelled their name as ONDATJE. The addition of 'aa' was a common practice in The Netherlands. Friesland was a large ancient country in Europe and a part of it had become one of the provinces with that name in the federation that became The Netherlands.

I next discovered that my name Juriansz had originally been JURIAANSZ. There were several variations of that name in The Netherlands. The root name for it was JURIE. In Holland the name had been "Dutchified". I discovered that the name Jurie in Poland was spelled Jure. Both Jurie(s) and Jure(s) had migrated from Riga, Latvia where the name was Shure, or Schure (with several more variations), in the 1400s. They were all Jews who had left Latvia because of persecution by the German Princes who controlled Latvia at that time. Intermarriage with the Dutch and changes of religion occurred and the Juries lost their Jewish heritage. My ancestor Jacobus Juriaansz who migrated to Sri Lanka in 1786 had his name written in the Groot Kerk in Galle (The Dutch Reformed Church), where he had been married, as Jacobus Juriaansz but in the Sri Lankan Dutch Archives as Juriansz. I concluded that dropping one of the letters 'a' occurred in Galle, Ceylon. The circumstances of this spelling change appear clerical.

My next surprise was that the full name of my mother's first ancestor to migrate to Sri Lanka in 1657 was Michael Jurie Jurgen Ondaatje. Researching the name Jurie incorporated into his name I found out that it was his mother's maiden name. The Juries had intermarried with the Ondaatjes in The Netherlands, and the Ondaatjes also had Jewish roots. So I had a name, which was derived from the Jewish name SHURE and my mother had Jewish genes from the same Shure source. The Shure family in Riga, Latvia had been there since the AD 70 diaspora. Recently I located a family named Shure living in Tel Aviv, but have yet to discover whether they are migrants from Latvia to Israel.

To be specific I cannot claim that there are only Jewish genes in my blood. My Sri Lankan ancestry traced from the two Dutch immigrants to Sri Lanka reveals that there was intermarriage with Sinhalese, Tamils, Portuguese, English, German, Danish and Irish before I came along. Nonetheless I do have some Jewish genes in both my mother's and father's ancestries, and my name is a "Dutchified" Jewish name. I have accepted this with trepidation and honour and am prepared to follow wherever that may lead. My acceptance into the

Jewish fold is up to others. Do I qualify as a physical Jew with some Jewish genes and a name that was originally Jewish? Am I a fair dinkum Jew?

My identity is in crisis. I have referred to the fact that while a boy in Sri Lanka I had the feeling I belonged 'everywhere but nowhere'. I did not have an allegiance to the land of my birth. Sir Walter Scott's poem Patriotism: "Breathes there a man with soul so dead, Who never to himself has said: This is my own, my native land . . . ." did not produce any pangs in me with regard to Sri Lanka. I had found a haven in the British Commonwealth and a 'home and native land' in Australia. I had adopted a country, which gave me pangs. I continue as a 'Royalist'. And now I have been undergoing a metamorphosis since I rejected being a 'Spiritual Jew'. I have not qualified with my few Jewish genes for aliya. But the Abrahamic Covenant has now absorbed me completely into its ramifications.

PART II
JEWISH HISTORY

An important benefit of Seventh-day Adventism was my Sabbath School classes.

Bible study is one of the great strengths of SDAs. Throughout my childhood and youth until I graduated from medical school, every Sabbath day found me in a Sabbath School class appropriate to my age with a prescribed syllabus, which I was to study every day of the week. I was taught the Seventh-day Adventist interpretation of the Bible. SDAs are very knowledgeable about the Bible and I became proficient in the details of Jewish history recorded in the Tanak. This is a rather rigorous regime for a person to go through as a child, youth and young adult. The religious intensity in the family under my mother's influence could be measured by the fact that of my five brothers, four became ordained ministers in the SDA Church.

In Part II I try to portray my revised views of the Tanak since leaving Adventism. I try to look at the Tanak through Jewish eyes. In these chapters I have portrayed the simple story of the Jews and the Abrahamic Covenant; I have related the Tanak to the denouement of Jewish history, which is embodied in all the books of the Tanak. In the Pentateuch Moses laid the foundation of Judaism. One of the most exhilarating recent experiences of my life has been the reading of 'The Year of Living Biblically' by A J Jacobs. He does not claim to be a trained theologian but his insights are refreshing and very practical for today. The Tanak is not a difficult book to digest and he has made it enlightening and has strengthened my conviction of its sacredness. But I go a little farther by seeing the huge significance of the Abrahamic Covenant. A J Jacobs is silent on this in his book but I feel certain he has his views, which are no doubt challenging and inspiring. Jewish history in the Tanak is not difficult. It is repetitive in that disobedience and idolatry are followed by loss of Jewish nationhood and sense of mission. I want to be faithful to the desire I have to see a solid Jewish future, which is loyal to the Abrahamic Covenant. I want to see a reformation.

Highlights of Jewish history start at the Creation story and the lost Eden. God's plan to rescue the lost perfect status is overwhelming to me. The story of Noah's flood is sad. But God made a covenant with Noah signified by the rainbow that he would not destroy civilization by a flood ever again. Then Abraham comes to the rescue of God's plan. Jacob's dedication and Joseph's rescue of Egypt and his own family from starvation are outstanding. But prosperity is often associated with idolatry. Moses was chosen by God to perform marvellous deeds and place Israel on a secure foundation. The possession of the Promised Land by David and Solomon is the brightest chapter of Jewish history. But it is downhill all the way from them, culminating in the AD 70 crushing by the Romans. Over this elapse of time Israel could not focus for long on the Abrahamic Covenant. Two thousand years later Ben-Gurion made AD 1948 a stupendous time for Jews to be alive. And now Israel is faced with a time of religious confusion and loss of focus on the Abrahamic Covenant. This is hampering their future and another dark chapter may be written. This should not be allowed to happen. In this section I skip a focus on the period of the development of the Babylonian and Jerusalem Talmuds. I also skip the European Yeshivas where persecuted Judaism survived marvellously. Both periods demonstrate the resilience of the Jews as well as God's tenacious hold on them. I briefly refer to the rise of Zionism and the valour of people like Theodor Herzl, Chaim Weizmann, Vladimir Jabotinsky and Max Nordau. One of my most erudite and admired surgical teachers was University of Toronto Professor Martin Barkin. We enjoyed many discussions of religion. He was quite intrigued with a 'gentile' who kept the seventh day Sabbath and was stricter than he was about the dietary rules. When discussing the matter of being Jewish, he told me in a moment of utter frustration: "I wish God had chosen some other race". But God did not. And since that night at Jabbok when Jacob had God in his tight embrace, God has clung on to Israel much more tenaciously than Israel has clung to him (Genesis 32). At one dramatic moment of God's despair, God exclaimed "Israel slideth back like a backsliding heifer . . . . Ephraim is joined to idols, let him alone" (Hosea 4:16,17). Hosea makes the call to repentance: "Come, and let us return to the Lord: For He has torn, but He will heal us; He has stricken, but he will bind us up". (Hosea 6:1)

CHAPTER 4
IN THE BEGINNING

Judaism today is a very complex, multifaceted system of religious philosophy. This is an important state of affairs that has evolved over the history of the Children of Israel. The plurality of thought has a great deal to do with the current status of Israel and this will be dealt with in very great detail later on in this book. The situation was simpler in the beginning. Moses who was responsible for the initial systemization of all things important in Judaism reached back in time to the beginning, way back before Abraham, to the creation of the Universe ("the heavens and the earth"). He was a very astute leader for doing so because he revealed the link between God and the Jews. No other people are interposed between the Divine and the particular status for which God would call Abraham[8].

The Creation Week as outlined in the Book of Genesis contains many scientific facts but it is not considered a scientifically accurate document in the world today[9]. Even some very religious Jews regard the Creation Week description as literary form. The creation account constitutes a marvellous piece of literature. Nonetheless it contains the basic foundation of what is considered the very holy and vital essentials of Judaism: A MONOTHEISTIC GOD, Creator, in eternal existence, titles himself as 'Us', thus assuming multiple expressions of himself. The Planet Earth is placed in the solar system, in the Milky Way. Life is created, expressed in vegetable and animal kingdoms, culminating in humans, the pinnacle of God's creativity. The Sabbath rest is instituted as the acknowledgement of creation and provides time for worship of the creator and rest from labour[10]. So in the very beginning God took satisfaction with that perfect state of affairs, and himself gave THREE GREAT GIFTS: First a piece of LAND (the Garden of Eden), second the original 'primitive' TORAH, which was communication with their God. The third great gift was eternal life by the correct use of FREE WILL.

The primitive Torah requires definition here. The word 'primitive' is used to mean the first utterances of God to humans. God commanded (law) that Adam and Eve take care of the Garden (work), eating the fruits thereof (sustenance). He commanded that they live as husband and wife, thus initiating marriage, the home and children. The Sabbath was to provide celebration of creation, rest from labour and time for worship. And the final piece of this primitive Torah was the commandment to refrain from eating of the Tree of Knowledge of Good and Evil, which was a test of free will. The primitive Torah contained the rules for the great bond that was to envelope the Creator and his creatures. But the primitive Torah also contained the consequences of disobedience to God's command: "In the day that thou eatest thereof, thou shalt surely die"[11]. Primitive Judaism wholeheartedly embraces the creative act of God, his endowment of existence by the breath of life, and the three great gifts: LAND, TORAH, and FREE WILL. But events did not go on in perfect fashion and will power was not exercised as advised by God. The knowledge of evil was embraced by humanity, the commandment in the primitive Torah was broken, and so death passed upon all mankind. The primitive Torah was not a written document at this stage. It had been communicated by the voice of God in God's face-to-face presence with Adam and Eve. The disobedience of humanity was now to be a wall of separation from God, and God's future communication with humanity was veiled[12]. God would keep talking but humanity's perceptive powers were diminished. The Torah would expand and be given detailed utterance and finally be written down. Prophets would be sent from God to deal with unfolding events in their history. The application of the Torah would be magnified. It would have the potential for interpretation and commentary. It would have the potential also to get confused and complicated.

The consequences of disobedience to God soon became obvious. The original gift of LAND was lost. Eden was removed, and humanity was left to wander upon the face of the earth, which was now blighted[13]. WILL POWER became difficult to exercise in keeping God's commands. The new reality was that death passed upon all mankind. A hopeless situation ensued. God then proffered his fourth great gift. In cursing the serpent God issued the great "enmity between thy [the serpent's] seed and her [Eve's] seed. He shall bruise your head and you shall bruise his heel"[14]. Here is the great enunciation of the redemptive MESSIAH. The Messiah would attack the serpent's head, which was lethal. But the serpent could only retaliate with the non-lethal bruising of the heel. The shedding of the blood of a sacrificial animal, symbol for the Messiah, brought forgiveness and remission for sin in lieu of God's redemptive plan. Abel the second son of Adam and Eve is the first recorded human to offer a lamb as a propitiation for sin. The lamb's shed blood was a symbol, required as an offering for sin. It was a symbolic substitution for the blood of the coming Messiah. He would eradicate sin and prevent eternal death. Why else would God require blood for the forgiveness for sin? The intricate service of the temple reflected what God required. Leviticus chapter 9 describes the beginning in Israel's nationhood of the Aaronic priesthood and the sacrificial system. It had already existed since Eden. "Moses said to Aaron: Take for yourself a young bull as a sin offering and a ram as a burnt offering without blemish, and offer them before the Lord". Aaron did this and the blood was sprinkled on the horns of the altar and poured at the base of the altar. The same was then done for the people. Those were the main sacrifices but others were also made. For now, the shedding of innocent blood would symbolically pay for their transgressions[15].

The Creation story including the loss of Eden is also an allegory signifying the repetitive history of Israel. LAND, TORAH, and ETERNAL LIFE are lost with disobedience to God (the wrong use of the will). This has happened repeatedly. Israel is standing again in a very vulnerable spot in history. Some LAND has been reclaimed and must be retained. The TORAH is in confusion and needs to be cleansed. It has become a divisive enemy, which is internally rupturing the strength and unity of Israel. The authentic Torah must be identified and retained and magnified. The MESSIAH must be defined and he will restore eternal life. The original Torah must identify the Messiah.

Israel cannot exist as a purely secular state that does not recognize these verities. Israel's strength lies on the foundation of Land, Torah and Messiah. The history of Israel shows that Land can be lost, Torah can be confused, and The Messiah not identified.

Israel desired a monarchy but the Prophet Samuel was reluctant to give them one. God said to him "They have not rejected you, they have rejected me". Rejection of the Torah (God's will) leads to trouble. Samuel gave them a monarchy, which distracted them from their mission[16]. A theocracy at that time was more relevant. A monarchy without democracy deteriorated into a dictatorship with corrupt monarchs. A secular state for Israel that ignores Land, Torah and Messianic expectation spells trouble and crumbles. It is not founded on what is important to God. Today a democracy is advocated. Democracy can work well if Israelis recognize and understand the Abrahamic Covenant, if their democratic decisions from the grassroots accommodate its requirements. The ideal would be that every Israeli be a religiously oriented citizen who is true to the Abrahamic Covenant and dedicated to the accomplishments it entails. A "theocracy" is not being advocated except as an acknowledgement of God in their lives. A succession of inspired and powerful prophets would be necessary to make all vital decisions in a theocracy. In their absence a powerful religious hierarchy would determine the direction of government. A situation as exists in Iran today would result. Rather, Israel must vote to make the central pillars of the Abrahamic Covenant the foundation on which they organize the state, the principles by which the citizens live. Personal piety and dedication will prevent the necessity of the mixing of church and state. If they do that as a nation they will achieve the great power that will confound their enemies. This calls for all Israelis to recognize and obey the call of God in their lives. They must be true to their heritage, which is what brought them together out of the diaspora.

NOTES

[8]   The Exodus from Egypt occurred about 1445 BC. Moses wrote Genesis about 1405 BC. He was a scholar educated in the universities of the Egypt of the Pharaohs. Literary experts are of the opinion that the Book of Genesis has had four authors because of the different literary styles in the writing. In my opinion this can be explained on the basis of four editors, who came after the original writing by Moses.

[9]   Genesis 1:24 "Let the earth bring forth living creatures according to its kind" 1:26 "Then God said: Let Us make man in Our image, according to Our likeness .... So God created man in His own image ... male and female". 2:7 "The Lord God formed man of the dust of the ground and breathed into his nostrils the breath of life and man became a living being". These texts are scientific in themselves but assume the power of God to originate life.

[10]   Genesis 2:1 ". . . He rested on the seventh day from all His work .... Then God blessed the seventh day and sanctified it . . . ."

[11]   Genesis 3:3-7 ". . . but of the fruit of the tree which is in the midst of the garden (of Eden) God has said you shall not eat of it nor shall you touch it lest you die".

[12] Genesis 3:8-22 "... Then the Lord God called to Adam ... Where are you? So he said: I heard your voice in the Garden and was afraid because I was naked ....". They had hidden themselves because they had lost their innocence.

[13] Genesis 3:23 "Therefore the Lord God sent him out of the Garden of Eden to till the ground from which he was taken".

[14] Genesis 3:15 "I will put enmity between you and the woman, between your seed and her Seed. He shall bruise your head and you shall bruise His heel".
4:1 "Now ... Eve ... conceived and bore Cain and said: I have acquired the Man from the Lord."

[15] Genesis 4:1-15 "... Cain brought an offering of the fruit of the ground to the Lord. Abel also brought of the firstborn of his flock .... And the Lord respected Abel and his offering, but he did not respect Cain and his offering ...."
Leviticus chapter 9 outlines the beginning of the Aaronic Priesthood and Temple Services.

[16] 1Samuel 8:6 "... for they have not rejected you but they have rejected Me, that I should not reign over them ... they have forsaken Me and served other gods ...."

CHAPTER 5
GOD COMMUNICATES

Torah is the garb and record of God's communication with humanity. It is humanity's tangible connection to the Divine. In the Garden of Eden there was no communication problem. God talked to Adam and Eve FACE-TO-FACE. The primitive Torah, the spoken commands of God were clearly enunciated and easily understood[17]. According to the creation story humans were created on the sixth day. And God saw that everything he had done was perfect. The seventh day he declared the Sabbath. It is not known how many cycles of weeks took place in the perfect state. Adam and Eve clearly enjoyed this face-to-face communion with God as they worshipped him in the time spent with him. According to the story God called on them in the Garden. "And they heard the sound of the Lord God walking in the Garden in the cool of the day"[18]. It was his custom to chat with them. They had heard his footsteps often enough to recognize them. They worked in the Garden to tend it. God came along as the sun was low in the heavens to enjoy their company. It was on one such visit that he could not find them because they were hiding from him, having discovered that they were naked. They had disobeyed the primitive Torah, his commandments for their wellbeing. They had eaten of the Tree of Knowledge of Good and Evil[19]. So they were expelled from the Garden. Face-to-face communication with God was lost[20]. Veiled messages got through and the redemptive process came into being. They would make animal sacrifices to atone for their sins. The shedding of blood of a sacrificial animal would bring them remission. The Torah would be committed to memory till Moses wrote it down. It would be expanded and explained by God's special spokesmen in the future. Eventually the Tanak would be written down in its entirety.

With the loss of Eden and their perfect state God was no longer visiting with and personally advising them one on one. His glory would have destroyed them on the spot had he done so. Now his person and glory were veiled and the understanding of his will and requirements became difficult. The gulf between God and man had widened, not because God wanted it, but because humanity distanced itself from him by their disobedience. God conversed with Cain with a veiled face after Abel's murder by Cain. Cain was jealous that God had accepted Abel's sacrifice of a lamb whose blood was shed for the remission of his sins. But Cain's offering of fruit was rejected because his substitute concoction did not involve the symbolic blood that was to be shed to procure forgiveness[21]. It did not point to the Messiah. After that conversation Cain declared he would be hidden from God's face. "Then Cain went out from the presence of the Lord".

Thereafter it was God's hidden face but audible VOICE-TO-EAR communication that took place, for want of a better terminology. There were exceptions, as with some of the Patriarchs such as Enoch with whom God had a special relationship. God liked him so much that he took him up to glory[22]. Noah was the last recorded antediluvian Patriarch to have had a close relationship with God[23].

The communication gulf between God and humans widened further because the heart of mankind became grossly iniquitous to the point that they did not recognise God's existence, let alone listen for his voice. God saw that "every intent of the thoughts of man's heart was evil continually. And the Lord was sorry He had made man on the earth, and He was grieved in His heart"[24]. And the great gulf widened even further until God decided to destroy mankind. They had become totally idolatrous and multiplied gods of wood and stone unto themselves. But NOAH found grace in the eyes of the Lord and God made a covenant with him. Noah would build the Ark in preparation for the destruction of the civilization around him. He and his family were saved. Noah still had the primitive Torah and continued communication with God. On exiting the Ark Noah built an altar and offered a sacrifice to God. Unfortunately the civilization that followed Noah replicated the evil conditions and idolatrous living of the antediluvian world[25].

ABRAHAM was the most prominent person after Noah and enjoyed a very close relationship with God[26]. Then there was JACOB who wrestled with the presumed Angel, but realized it was God with whom he was wrestling. God loved him so much he was in God's bodily embrace. God changed Jacob's name to Israel. He had seen God face to face[27]. MOSES was next in importance and

27

was to implement the forgotten Abrahamic Covenant and organize the nation of Israel to worship God[28]. God called SAMUEL when he was a child. God gave him specific instructions concerning Israel[29]. God talked to ELIJAH face to face as He took him up to glory in a chariot of fire[30].

Analysis of God's methods of communication reveals FACE TO FACE, 'VEILED FACE TO FACE', 'VOICE TO EAR', and MIND TO MIND modalities. Sometimes when God communicated, there was a 'friendship' and/ or 'physical companionship' between God and the person being accessed by him. Then came communication by VISIONS and DREAMS. Latterly, God used a third party for communication, eg an Angel. The person being accessed by God would be termed 'inspired'. Torah kept coming from God through his chosen human channels by these methods. Humanity has unfortunately become distant. When Messiah is found, God will take human form and dwell again with humanity.

God gave Abraham the Promised Land, the Land of Israel. He possessed it by promise. His dialogue with God continued. At times there was a teasing quality to their friendship. The request for the sacrifice of Isaac seems to hint at that quality although it had deep spiritual significance. The requirement for the shedding of blood for the remission of sin was well understood by Abraham. But this time God was asking for human blood, the blood of Abraham's preferred son. The human sacrifice ritual had been practiced in the idolatrous world of Abraham and his ancestors. It came as a surprise to Abraham. He should have baulked at it. Abraham had already destroyed all the idols in his father Terah's house. Here was the hint, nay, the very strong statement that the Messiah, the very Son of God was to be the sacrifice. The Messiah would sacrifice his own blood to eradicate disobedience from the universe. This incident on Mount Moriah was the promise of the Messiah and was also to be the foundation for the (first) Temple, the worship of the one and only true God. Mount Moriah became important in recognition of the Messianic Sacrifice. This was all a reiteration of the primitive Torah. It was a revelation of God's will and plan for mankind entrusted to Abraham.

In summary, God talked to mankind originally face-to-face. After the disobedience God had to hide his glory to protect mankind from succumbing to his awesome presence. So he spoke to them voice-to-ear. And then he spoke in visions and dreams. He speaks mind-to-mind through the study of the

Torah, in quiet contemplation and in prayerfulness. Having given the Tanak he talks to us through the Tanak. The authors of the Tanak are therefore labelled INSPIRED. Inspiration means a God-directed 'closeness' to God, close enough to receive a message direct from God. He also talks to us more distantly in the experiences he sends us and in the lessons life has to offer. This book takes up the challenge to define how God's will, having been received and understood can be accomplished.

God has spoken to mankind, and his Torah was given to the Patriarchs from Adam to Malachi. The Tanak contains the written Torah. The Tanak is closed and constitutes the only tangible Torah that has been given to humanity. What authority closes the canon with the Tanak? The Tanak contains the Abrahamic Covenant and it is the completeness of the Abrahamic Covenant that has closed the canon. God's complete plan for Israel and the whole world is contained in the Abrahamic Covenant.

NOTES

[17] Genesis 2:15 ". . . and the Lord God commanded the man saying: Of every tree of the Garden you may freely eat but of the Tree of Knowledge of Good and Evil you shall not eat, for in the day that you eat of it you shall surely die".

[18] Genesis 3:8-9 ". . . and they heard the sound of the Lord God walking in the Garden in the cool of the day. And God called to Adam: Where are you?".

[19] Genesis 3:10 "So Adam said: I heard your voice in the Garden and I was afraid because I was naked: and I hid myself".

[20] Genesis 3:24 "So God drove man out of the Garden".

[21] Genesis 4:3-16 ". . . So the Lord said to Cain . . . Where is Abel your brother? Cain said: I do not know, am I my brother's keeper? And God said: What have you done? The voice of your brother's blood cries out to Me from the ground . . . . And Cain said: My punishment is greater than I can bear . . . . I shall be hidden from your face . . . . Then Cain went out from the presence of the Lord".

[22] Genesis 5:21 ". . . Enoch walked with God, and he was not, for God took him".

[23] Genesis 6:9 ". . . Noah walked with God".

[24] Genesis 6:5,6 "And God saw that the wickedness of man was great on the earth. And the Lord was sorry He had made man on the earth".

[25] Genesis 6:13-22 "God said to Noah: The end of all flesh has come before Me"

[26] Genesis 12:1-13:18 The Abrahamic Covenant.

[27] Genesis 32:22-32 ". . . For I have seen God face to face and my life is preserved"

28 Exodus 3:1-22 "... God called to Moses from the burning bush and said: Moses, Moses. And he said: Here I am ...."
Exodus 20:18 "So the Lord spoke to Moses face to face, as a man speaks to his friend".
Exodus 34:29 "... When Moses came down from the mountain ... the skin of his face shone while he talked with God".
Deuteronomy 34:10 "But since then there has not arisen in Israel a prophet like unto Moses whom the Lord knew face to face".

29 1Samuel 3:1-19 ".... Speak Lord, for your servant hears ....".

30 2Kings 2:11 "... and Elijah went up by a whirlwind into heaven".

CHAPTER 6
THE ABRAHAMIC COVENANT

W ho was Abraham? He was the son of Terah, born by the name Abram. They were Semites, descendants of Shem the son of Noah through the line of Arphaxad. After the cleansing of Noah's world by the Flood there was a return to the worship of Noah's God. The first thing Noah did on getting out of the Ark was to make a sacrifice of thanksgiving and a burnt offering for sin. Terah was not far removed from Shem but the family had become utterly idolatrous. We are not informed in the Tanak of the beginning or cause for Abram's aversion to idolatry but tradition has it that Abram as a youth was asked to tend his father's shop. His father was an idolater and bought and sold idols. Abram took a hammer and smashed every idol in the shop except the largest and placed the hammer in the hands of the largest idol. On his father's return, his father viewed the mayhem and was told by Abram that the idols got into a fight and the largest was victorious. To this his father replied that the idols had no life and could not do this. Abram then asked his father why he worshipped them (this account is from the Talmud). The cleansing of his father's house of idolatry has been left as a monument to posterity. He reinstituted the worship of the one true God. This was a very forceful act and was not resisted by his father and grandfather. Monotheism was re-established. The Patriarchs from Adam to Noah were indeed aware of and worshipped the one true God. They communicated with that God. Abram was merely re-establishing this verity. Nonetheless he is remembered as the great insister on Monotheism and gave the world two great people who are steeped in monotheism—Isaac and Ishmael, the forebears of the Israelis and the Arabs. These descendents of Abram have given the world three major religions.

Here is the Abramic Covenant:

> Now the Lord had said to Abram:
> Get out of your country,

From your family
And from your father's house,
To a land that I will show you.
I will make you a great nation;
I will bless you
And make your name great;
And you shall be a blessing.
I will bless those who bless you,
And I will curse him who curses you;
And in you all the families of the earth
Shall be blessed.

Genesis 12:1-3

After Abram had cleansed his father's house of idolatry God said to him, voice-to-ear: Leave Ur of the Chaldees and go to a land that I will show thee, extending from the river of Egypt to the great river, to the River Euphrates[31]. So the original tract of land God gave and was won in battle by King David was much bigger than the post 1967 borders. Modern Israel is not greedy. Abram was offered a package deal. In offering the deal God changed his name to Abraham: "For I have made you a father of many nations". Abraham already had Torah in the primitive terms of God's will for mankind. He was aware of Adam and Noah and the Patriarchs between them so he had taken Torah seriously. He had cleansed his father's house of idols. And now God was saying that he wanted to give him a particular tract of land where his progeny would prosper and become as the stars of the firmament[32]. The Messiah would come through him. Abraham offered animal sacrifices, which prefigured the Messianic mission on altars he built along the way to the land of Canaan[33]. But he did not realise the connection God had with the Messiah till he got to Mount Moriah. Abraham was childless at this time but had immense faith in God and like his ancestor Noah took God at his word and acted on it. As a shepherd he mustered his animals and marched to Canaan. We can question God's decision to ask him to leave the environs of the thriving metropolis of Ur of the Chaldees, deep in Sumerian Mesopotamia, sitting on a sea of oil, which would bring immense wealth to its inhabitants of the future. But God had chosen the strategic tract of land that occupied the junction of the trade routes between the East and the West, between three continents. It was the hub of communication and travel in that and eras to follow. It was a land flowing with milk and honey and had all manner of nourishing fruit[34].

Another Semite was already in the Promised Land. He was Melchizedek the "King of Salem". He is also referred to as the "King of Righteousness". He was not an idolater but a worshipper of the one true God. He was a guru to Abraham as evidenced by the fact that Abraham treated him as a superior priest and paid tithes to him[35]. The only logical conclusion here is that God put the two men in touch for the same mission: Magnification of the primitive TORAH; occupation of a splendid piece of LAND; and establishment of the line through which he would send the MESSIAH. Here were the vital three items again—Torah, Land, and the Messiah. A great and significant act of Melchizedek the King of Salem was the bequeathing of the site he owned, the future capital of Israel, JERUSALEM. Moses recorded this for posterity. The Children of Abraham need to be aware of it. The Torah would be magnified in time, the Land was still to be possessed, and the Messiah would come. Abraham had great faith in his God.

The Abrahamic Covenant was not to be just between Abraham and God, but between all Abraham's descendants and God. No Jew can excuse himself from the Abrahamic Covenant and remain a Jew. Circumcision became the sign that every male Jew was a signatory to the Covenant[36]. God was very serious about the Abrahamic Covenant.

Abraham did not understand the significance of the giving of the Messiah as a vital part of the Covenant till he had a son and was on Mount Moriah. What happened on Mount Moriah? By this time Abraham had had the miraculous son of his old age, Isaac, the pride and joy of his life and heir to the promise God had made to him. "Take your only son and sacrifice him as you would a lamb as a burnt offering to me". Human sacrifice was what some heathens did. This was a highly unreasonable request and some say it happened only in symbolism. But nevertheless Abraham was willing to do it. Isaac carried the wood, wondering that he was the sacrifice in the absence of the preparation of a lamb. This became crystal clear when Abraham bound him. He cooperated fully with the dreadful act to be carried out. But as the knife was drawn to kill the innocent lad God stopped Abraham from carrying out the dreadful and unreasonable deed. "Abraham, I will save your son, BUT MY SON MUST DIE, FOR BY THE SHEDDING OF [HIS] BLOOD THERE IS REMISSION". The Messianic gift was prefigured on Mount Moriah[37]. God emphasized to Abraham that through his seed "all nations of the earth would be blessed". Gods' gift of the Messiah to Abraham would result in the blessedness or happiness of all nations. The Messiah will restore Eden. This has made Mount Moriah the epicentre of the world and in humanity's limited knowledge, the epicentre of the Universe (Multiverses).

In his book 'Beirut to Jerusalem', Thomas Friedman cites the astronaut Neil Armstrong's visit to Israel. It was after the moon landing. Neil Armstrong was taken on a tour of the Old City of Jerusalem by Israeli archaeologist Meir Ben-Dov. At the Hulda Gate, which is at the top of the stairs leading to the Temple Mount, Armstrong asked Ben-Dov whether Jesus walked there. When told it was highly likely since these very steps led to the Temple, Armstrong was electrified: "I am more excited stepping on these stones than I was stepping on the moon". Not only is Mount Moriah the epicentre of the Universe for Jews but also the epicentre of the Universe for all Christendom.

The story of Abraham and Isaac on Mount Moriah has to be the core of the Abrahamic Covenant with God. It was of seismic significance. It was where the two plates of heaven and earth meet, and the epicentre of all spiritual earthquakes. On Mount Sinai God extolled the Torah. On Mount Moriah he extolled the Messiah. In the Israel Museum grounds in Jerusalem today there is a model of Solomon's Temple, which was in the Old City of Jerusalem in Solomon's day. Israel has its duty to rebuild the new Temple on Mount Moriah. Its western wall is already there. The Messiah will be proclaimed from the Temple in Jerusalem. The LAND, the TORAH, the MESSIAH are intertwined in one on Mount Moriah.

God has not endowed any other ethnic people in history with a covenant in which he commissions Land, Torah and Messiah. A discussion of these three core elements in the Abrahamic Covenant follows in this book.

NOTES

31   Genesis 12:1-3 "Now the Lord said to Abram: Get out of your country . . . ."
      Genesis 15:1-21 ". . . . On the same day God made a covenant with Abram,
      saying: To your descendants I have given this land, from the river of Egypt to the
      great river, the River Euphrates—"
      Genesis 17:1-27 ". . . and God talked with him, saying No longer shall your name
      be called Abram, but your name shall be Abraham . . ."

32   Genesis 15:4,5 ". . . Look now toward heaven and count the stars if you are able to
      number them . . . . So shall your descendants be".

33   Genesis 12;7,8 ". . . And there he built an altar to the Lord . . . ."
      Genesis 13:3,18 ". . . to the place of the altar which he had made . . . ."

34   Joshua 5:6 ". . . . a land flowing with milk and honey".

35   Genesis 14:18-24 "Then Melchizedek King of Salem . . . the priest of God Most
      High . . . blessed Abram and said: Blessed be Abram of God Most High . . . Who
      has delivered your enemies into your hands. And he gave him a tithe of all".

36   Genesis 17:9-16 ". . . As for you, you shall keep My Covenant, you and your
      descendants after you throughout their generations . . . . And the uncircumcised
      male child . . . has broken My Covenant.

37   Genesis 22:1-18 ". . . . Then God said: Take now your son, your only son Isaac
      whom you love and go to the land of Moriah and offer him there as a burnt
      offering . . . . Then Isaac said: Look the fire and the wood, but where is the lamb
      for a burnt offering? And Abraham said : My son, God will provide for Himself
      THE LAMB for a burnt offering . . . And Abraham built an altar there and
      placed the wood in order. And he bound Isaac his son, and laid him on the altar,
      upon the wood and Abraham stretched out his hand and took the knife to slay
      his son . . . . Then . . . the Lord called to Abraham . . . and said: By Myself I have
      sworn . . . because you have done this thing, and have not withheld your son,
      your only son—blessing I will bless you, and multiplying I will multiply your
      descendants as the stars of the heaven and as the sand on the seashore; and your
      descendants shall possess the gate of their enemies. IN YOUR SEED ALL
      THE NATIONS OF THE EARTH SHALL BE BLESSED, because you
      have obeyed My voice".
      See IJS Israel and Judaism Studies, The education website of the NSW Jewish
      Board of Deputies: Abraham and the Covenant.
      See also My Jewish Learning: The Binding of Isaac—By Rabbi Louis
      Jacobs—The dramatic story of the binding of Isaac is central to Jewish liturgy
      and thought, and has perplexed many generations of commentators. ('The
      Akedah' See: 'The Jewish Religion: A Comparison', Oxford University Press)
      See also About.com—'Jews and Jerusalem: The Source of the Bond' from Lisa
      Katz

CHAPTER 7
THE LAND

It matters not whether the account of the creation is allegorical or real. The beginning of life on the planet is certainly practical. In the beginning God created. The first piece of land given to Adam and Eve, the first ancestors of the Jews was the Garden of Eden. God had planted it with his own hand. It contained the 'Tree of Life' and the 'Tree of the Knowledge of Good and Evil'. Their future in it had no end as long as they obeyed the Torah (God's will). They were to be sustained eternally by the Tree of Life. Their abstinence from the Tree of Knowledge of Good and Evil prevented death. They were to tend the Garden and live off it. They also had access to the rest of the earth, which their descendants were to occupy as they became fruitful and multiplied. Their extended jurisdiction was to replenish the earth. Disobeying God (rejecting the Torah) was the cause of their 'first diasporic captivity', a captive estrangement from God. They were cast outside the Garden of Eden and could never return to eat of the Tree of Life. They had become mortal and now had to find a livelihood in an earth that would only respond to "the sweat of their brow". Eking out a livelihood and no longer having access to the Tree of Life they would all grow old and die. But God had a plan to restore the LAND and immortality.

LAND is a priority to God. It was the first thing he did in his original project: "The Lord God planted a garden, eastward in Eden"[38]. He had just made the heavens and the earth and he pre-planted Eden for the first couple. It was a beautiful and luxuriant botanical garden. Similarly after he chose Abraham and Sarah, the new substitute couple, he chose another garden, the Land of Canaan. It was no Eden but they were to make it one. So in the Abrahamic Covenant LAND was chosen first. The land became sacred where they were to be the keepers of the Torah and the channel of Messianic blessedness for all nations. God had redemption for mankind in mind.

After Adam and Eve, the earth, as the early inhabitants knew it, became populated with idolatrous people and Noah was chosen to bring about a reformation. Idolatry had supplanted the worship of the one true God. After 120 years of Noah's preaching to them, the hardness of their hearts persisted. God then destroyed the idolatrous people and provided a new cleansed land for Noah's progeny to inhabit the earth and carry out his will as outlined by the Torah. But after Noah the earth's inhabitants again became idolatrous and lost touch with God. God's face-to-face verbally delivered Torah was lost until Abraham cleansed his father's house of idolatry and reorientated it to monotheism. A great responsibility was placed on Abraham's shoulders: "In thee shall all Nations of the earth be blessed". Abraham was to provide happiness (the state of being blessed) for all nations. Abraham became the channel to receive the messianic salvation to be provided, to restore the Edenic perfection.

A partnership to restore the TORAH was first planned. Melchizedek, descended from Noah's son Shem, was still bearing the torch of worshipping the true God in Canaan. He is described as The King of Righteousness. He was also the King of Salem, the strategic location on which Israel's capital forever, Jerusalem, would be located. Here was another Semite who was a monotheist who worshipped the true God in a wild land full of wickedness and idolatry. Once in the land, Abraham forged ties with Melchizedek and supported him financially by paying tithes to him by which he undertook the partnership with Melchizedek to cleanse the land of idolatry. David the Psalmist understood the part played by Melchizedek and sang about it[39]. Melchizedek was a symbol of the Messiah to come, a High Priest and a King.

What was so special about the new tract of LAND offered Abraham? Had he remained in Ur of the Chaldees his descendants would be living today in an oil-rich country. Exploration has revealed that Israel is sitting on one of the biggest deposits of natural gas known. An ocean of oil also lies beneath them, still untapped[40]. Israel has the potential to be a energy giant. But at that time one has to ask what sense of logic would motivate God to offer Canaan (Palestine) as the better piece of property. As already mentioned Canaan was the centre of the then known world and central to all the trade routes involved between the continents of Europe, Africa and Asia. Israel would exert a special influence from that central piece of land. What could it be other than the propagation of Abraham's monotheistic influence, the worship of the one true God, the restoration of the Torah, and the promise of eternal life through the Messiah?

The Messiah would eradicate death caused by disobedience. He would usher in world government fulfilling the promise that in Abraham all families of the earth would be blessed. The Messiah would atone. The sins of the whole world are to be forgiven on this land. The Messiah would declare his kingdom there and bring a new world order. There was far-reaching logic in this Covenant. As a sacred vehicle for the Torah and the Messiah the Land will become again the centre of civilization.

The LAND is very special, a great and enduring gift from God. Jerusalem will one day be Eden restored with a Tree of Life in it, and of great strategic importance in the changed world order. Before the entire land was delivered to Abraham he bought a foothold. He built an altar in Hebron and made a sacrifice to God, in confession of his sins and in thanks to God for his arrival there[41]. Hebron became the birthplace of the new nation where King David the Bethlehemite, then a shepherd boy, Israel's greatest temporal monarch, was anointed by Samuel to be king. Hebron was bought as a burial place for Abraham and his wife Sarah. The Cave of Machpelah contains the bones of Abraham and Sarah, Isaac and Rebekah, Jacob and Leah, and Joseph. Hebron and the Cave of Machpelah should be valued as much as Jerusalem and always possessed by Israel as a memorial to the great gift of God to Abraham, the founder of the Nation of Israel. Abraham was counting on his bones being resurrected. He believed in a restored immortality, which would be provided by the Messiah[42]. The Cave of Machpelah is vital to Israel. It is a shrine for all who worship the one true God.

Jerusalem is the eternal city, important as the possession of Melchizedek, Abraham's partner in God's plan. Jerusalem is where Abraham was given his son Isaac. Its central and holiest spot is Mount Moriah where Abraham was asked to sacrifice Isaac. And this is where Solomon's Temple was built. It is the seat of Jewish history, a gift from God to Israel. Solomon's Temple was to be the seat of the Torah and the place of promise of the Messiah and immortality. Solomon's Temple contained the Ten Commandments, the essence of God's will for mankind. God and humanity are reunited in Jerusalem. It is the city where the Messiah will live and reign forever.

Idolatrous tribes inhabited Canaan when Abraham arrived there. They were the Moabites, Ammonites, Amorites, Phillistines, Jebusites and the Gibeonites. There were other tribes as well. Sodom and Gomorrah were typical of the morally bereft land[43]. It would be a while before complete possession of the land occurred. Isaac and Jacob looked at the land and dreamed of its possession but the descendents of Abraham had not yet multiplied and achieved numerical strength. Isaac's son Esau turned idolatrous and was rejected by God. The birthright passed to Jacob who remained monotheistic and a worshipper of the one true God. His patriarchal witness was immense and he wrestled with God to become Israel, by which name the nation of his progeny would be called. The great patriarch Joseph would save the children of Abraham and Egypt from starvation. Freedom from hunger and prosperity in Egypt exposed Israel to an idolatrous nation. They behaved as if Egypt was the Promised Land. This disastrous influence caused them to lose sight of the mission of the Abrahamic Covenant. Their prosperity in Egypt's land of Goshen made them forget their God-given birthright of the LAND, the TORAH, and the promise of the MESSIAH. Goshen was a corner of the land God had given to Abraham, but they forgot their mission there. God allowed them to be in Egypt for 430 years, some of it spent in luxury and idolatry but most of it in slavery. Moses was then raised by God to bring them out of Egypt, out of idolatry and slavery. Moses was the great restorer of the Land, the Torah and the promise of the Messiah. He would not only document and explain the Decalogue but would enunciate the great story of Creation, the beginning of the human race and mankind's dialogue with God.

The extent of the piece of land promised to Abraham is identified in God's original words: ". . . from the river of Egypt to the great river, the River Euphrates . . . ."[44]. The land possessed at the time of King David and King Solomon included a considerable part of what is modern Syria, and all of Jordan. Its current reduction to the 1967 post Six Day War boundaries of Israel is so much smaller. It is a partial repossession and a gift from God and won again in modern battle. It is a minimal return. The Jews possessed it before the Arabs. They have now taken it back in battle.

The land was originally obtained by Israel in battles climaxing in the glory of Israel at the time of David and Solomon. God had commanded annihilation of the idolatrous tribes living in it after they proved resistant to conversion and rejected Israel's witness of the one true God. A case may be made for patience in obtaining the land by conversion of the idolatrous tribes to the worship of the true God. But they outlived God's patience and did not turn from idolatry. These tribes refused the benefits of the Abrahamic Covenant including eternal life offered by the Israelites. Therefore the wiping out of these idolaters occurred by the sword. This has been labelled as genocide. Every time Israel was evicted from the land that was their home, it was done in battle and by genocide inflicted on Israel by her enemies. This is the general history of the whole world. Nations have come into existence similarly throughout history. How does the United States of America maintain its territorial national status? It is by past battle against the North American Indians and Mexicans. The Red Indians were slaughtered by every possible means. There can be no reversal of the sovereignty of the US. Consider Australia where the gentle Aborigines were poisoned and gunned down by the thousands and there are still thousands isolated in reservations. Are the European settlers renouncing their sovereignty? Consider the country called New Zealand. The European settlers did not honour the treaty with the Maoris. The Maoris are in a condition of acquiescence and are being assimilated. Are the European settlers renouncing their sovereignty?

Land is an integral part of the Abrahamic Covenant. How will Israel solve this problem of land ownership? This will be dealt with later in the book.

NOTES

[38]   Genesis 2:8

[39]   Psalm 110:1-4

[40]   Anne's Opinions: Gas, oil and sun-meeting Israel's new energy needs. Posted 26 July 2011 by anneinpt
         Seeking Alpha: Israel's Huge Oil and Gas Discovery (leviathon project). Posted by Ian Cooper.

[41]   Genesis 23:7-20 "... If it is your wish that I bury my dead ... give me the Cave of Machpelah ... at the full price as property for a burial place ....".

[42]   1Samuel 16:12,13 ".... Then Samuel took the horn of oil and anointed David in the midst of his brethren ..."

[43]   Genesis chapters 15 to 24.
         Exodus 3:17 "And I have said I will bring you ... to the land of the Canaanites and the Hittites and the Amorites and the Perizites and the Hivites and the Jebusites, to a land flowing with milk and honey".

[44]   Genesis 15:17-21 "To your descendants I have given this land, from the river of Egypt (the Nile) to the great river, the River Euphrates—"

CHAPTER 8
THE TORAH

The word Torah was originally used as a name for the Pentateuch, the five books of Moses[45]. Basically it was put forward as the messages from God through Moses his recognized messenger. God was the source and Moses was the vessel to put it into human context. The connection between them would be termed inspiration. Moses was inspired. I have introduced the term 'Primitive Torah' in this book. It is meant as the original communication from God in the history of Judaism. So the Torah is defined as the revealed will of God for Israel and the whole world. The primitive Torah was given at Creation in the Edenic setting. The written Torah came in the garb of the humanity of Moses.

Torah then developed to mean the Tanak (Genesis to Malachi), which is the Bible (Old Testament) in Judaism. Several human beings were inspired and expressed messages from God. The current or modern concept of Torah has broadened exceedingly in Judaism and contains the whole body of Jewish law and teachings[46]. Modern day Torah has come to include the Talmud. Some scholars have used the halacha synonymously with Torah.

God the Creator had a plan and way of life for humanity. Moses coopted the original Edenic will of God for the founding nation of Israel. With the developing patriarchal denouement of Jewish history, insight into the revealed will of God showed an evolution. The patriarchs each added their own inspired personal colour, spiritual experience, and connection with God in the enunciation of the will of God. We are entirely indebted to Moses (the author of the Pentateuch and the Book of Job) for the recording of the patriarchal pronouncements of the spoken will of God in the founding of the nation of Israel[47]. It is the basic, solid foundation part of the Torah that we possess. It is assumed that his recording of the will of God constitutes the first time the spoken will of God was supplemented by the written will of God. The word of God continued to be in spoken communication: 'face-to-face' and 'voice-to-ear'. It began also to

41

be communicated in 'visions and dreams' and finally it included 'mind-to-mind' revelation. The perception of the will of God was frequently 'situational' and described in the happenings of everyday life. The communication of God's will to Moses at the burning bush is an example of this with its supernatural element[48].

The great primitive Torah expanded into the first written Torah at Mount Sinai. Mount Sinai is now believed to be in the Negev and not as previously thought in the Sinai Desert[49]. God made Moses prepare the Israelites for that dramatic encounter by the ritual of sanctification. Then God came down onto Mount Sinai, which almost took the form of an active volcano. Moses spoke and God answered requesting him to come up to the summit. The mountain was fenced to prevent people from getting too close so that they would not die from seeing God's fiery majesty. Then God spoke the words of the Ten Commandments. He forbade them in detail not to make and worship idols. Instead they were to build altars of stone for the sacrificial animals. Multiple laws, both moral and ceremonial were then given. God also gave instructions for the structure, furnishings, and symbolic functions of the services of the Tabernacle. The Levitical priesthood was installed[50]. The Ten Commandments were written on two tablets of stone by the finger God[51]. In the short space of time while Moses was in the mountain with God, in full view of the awful manifestation of God's glory, the Israelites got into a idolatrous heathen frenzy and worshipped the golden calf. In virulent anger Moses dashed the tablets of the Ten Commandments written by the finger of God, breaking it in pieces at the foot of the mountain. He ground the golden calf idol to powder, sprinkled it in the water and forced the Israelites to drink it. Three thousand men died as punishment[52]. Subsequently he took another two tablets of stone and God wrote again the Ten Commandments on them[53].

Until the time of Moses there was no written sample of the revealed will of God. The written will of God became the method par excellence by which we now have the knowledge of God's will preserved for us. Moses is dated 1300 BC. Moses planned and executed the return of Israel from Egypt but because of the hardness of their hearts, they wandered in the desert for 40 years, succumbing to their appetite for the fleshpots of Egypt and their yearning for its idolatry[54]. Moses died on Mount Nebo. Joshua was the great leader who led them from this wilderness of their perverted minds into the Promised Land[55]. After Joshua, the will of God was declared and recorded by the Judges in Israel. After the Judges there was a special channel recorded in the experience of Ruth, a very important gentile who embraced the Jewish Monotheistic God and the Jewish faith[56]. As a convert from idolatry she became the beacon for the entry of gentiles into Judaism. What was important with her was that by conversion she typified an authentic method of entry into Judaism of those not born Jews. This is absolutely remarkable as it defined the channel for the inclusion of gentiles by conversion into the House of Israel. The revealed will of God coming to us via a woman born a gentile who contributed her experience to the written Torah proves that Judaism is not a closed society. By this method Judaism is open to entry to all mankind. Moses' wife was famously a black Midianite gentile woman[57]. This in no way castigates the importance of Moses to Jewish history. Israel will not countenance racism. Because of this Jews can never be justly accused of being racist and can never be justly accused of being a closed society.

After Ruth the Royal Line of David (Ruth was David's great grandmother) became channels for receiving Torah, the revealed will of God. David and his son Solomon, Israel's most powerful monarchs added the Psalms, Proverbs, Ecclesiastes and the Song of Songs to the Torah. The experiences of other kings in the books labelled 'Kings' and 'Chronicles' contained Torah as well. Another woman came to the fore. During the Persian period of history Esther found favour in the eyes of the Lord and bore witness to the role of the Jews in the history of the world. Esther is the prototype for diasporic Jews who contribute by their witness to the safety of Israel. American Jews are functioning in the role of Esther. Esther's story became part of the Torah[58].

Since Moses we are indebted to the scribes of Israel for the recording of Torah and preserving for all mankind the revealed will of God. The recording of the experiences of the prophets from Eli and Samuel to Malachi completes the envelope of the written Torah. Israel has closed the written Torah. The universally accepted Torah, the Tanak, is the written will of God. Did God stop talking to the Jews and the rest of mankind after Malachi? Did he close the matter of his requirements for Israel after Malachi? Is there sufficient in the written Torah, the Tanak, to determine all God has to say to the Jews and the rest of mankind till the end of the world? Suffice it to say that nothing further is needed to convince Israel of the authenticity of the Abrahamic Covenant and its meaning as explained in the Tanak. The Tanak is a complete plan.

Landmarks of the Development of TORAH (Tanak)—The Revealed Will of God are:

Torah (The Law): the Pentateuch, the 5 books attributed to Moses was recognised as Jewish Scripture about 450 BC

Nebhiim (The Prophets): recognised as Jewish Scripture about 201 BC

Kethubhim (The Writings): It is difficult to date acceptance of this collection of books as part of sacred Jewish Scripture, but its acceptance as such by the Qumran Community and Yochana Ben Zakhai's Jewish Rabbinic School at Yavneh dates its acceptance to not long after the Nebhiim was accepted.

The Tanak became the body of sacred scripture, which was considered 'closed' in Roman times. The Tanak constitutes a collective term for the revealed will of God and is applied synonymously as the TORAH. Therefore the body of writings, the Tanak, is the pure and final TORAH, the closed canon of Judaism[59].

In 250 BC these writings, the Tanak, were translated into Greek and labelled the Septuagint. It was translated in Alexandria in the diasporic community of Jews living there who used Greek as their everyday language. It is said that 72 Jewish translators took part, but Judaism only accepts the Pentateuch translation as authentic[60]. The rest of the Septuagint is not regarded as an authentic and reliable translation. The Vulgate is a 4th Century AD Latin translation of the Bible.

In conclusion, any other inclusion as Torah confuses, desecrates and pollutes it.

NOTES

[45] Judaism 101 (Tracey R Rich)

[46] Ibid.

[47] The Talmud appears to credit Moses with the authorship of Job. This is not definite but highly likely. Job was the son of Uz, the son of Nahor, Abraham's brother. See 'Job in Rabbinic Literature'

[48] Exodus 3:1-22 "... And the Angel of the Lord appeared to Moses in a flame of fire from the midst of the bush ... the bush was burning with fire but the bush

was not consumed . . . . Then God said: Do not draw near this place. Take your sandals off your feet, for the place you stand is holy ground . . . ."

49 See 'Har Karkom' by Emmanuel Anati, an Italian-born archaeologist whose Jewish parents lived in Florence, Italy. Mount Har Karkom is in the Negev and situated halfway between Kadesh Barnea and Petra. Leon Cohen in his book 'Is Mount Sinai in the Negev?' discusses the findings of University of Wisconsin's Harry Jol who is more convinced as is the Vatican. Professor Israel Finkelstein of The University of Tel Aviv is not convinced. He does not see connection between 3000 BC findings at Har Karkom and the Exodus story, which happened several centuries later (the Jerusalem Post 6th January 2011). The Exodus is dated to have taken place in 1313 BC.

50 Exodus chapter 19: Arrival at Mt. Sinai and the consecration of the people Exodus chapter 20: The Ten Commandments spoken by God Himself. Exodus chapters 21-23: Multiple Ceremonial and Moral laws were enunciated. Exodus chapter 24:1-8 The laws were all written down by Moses since the record says: He took the Book of the Covenant and read in the hearing of the people . . . . And Moses took the blood and sprinkled it on the people, and said: This is the blood of the covenant which the Lord has made with you . . . ."

51 Exodus 32:15,16 ". . . the two tablets of stone were in Moses' hand. The tablets were written on both sides . . . the writing was the writing of God engraved on the tablets."

52 Exodus 32: 19-35 Three thousand people were killed for worshipping the golden calf.

53 Exodus 34:1,2 "And the Lord said to Moses: Cut two tablets of stone like the first and I will write on these tablets the words that were on the first tablets which you broke . . . ."

54 Numbers 14:20-35 ". . . your carcases shall fall in this wilderness. And your sons shall be shepherds in this wilderness forty years . . . ."

55 Deuteronomy 34:1-12 ". . . So Moses . . . died in the land of Moab . . . and God buried him in a valley in the land of Moab, opposite Beth Peor."

56 Ruth 1:—22 ". . . . Your people shall be my people, and your God my God . . . ." Ruth 4: 18-22 Ruth married Boaz and had a son Obed who had a son named Jesse who was the father of King David

57 Exodus 2:16-21 ". . . and he gave Zipporah his daughter to Moses . . . ."

58 Esther 2:15-18 "so the king Ahasuerus . . . made Esther queen . . . ."

59 The Tanak: The Complete Jewish Bible—Chabad.org Library

The 24 Books of the Hebrew Bible—torah.org

The Written Law-The Torah—Jewish Virtual Library

See also 'Origin of the Bible—Chapter 5: The Books of the Old Testament, The Canon'

60   The Septuagint—See Rabbi Tovia Singer

CHAPTER 9
THE CONFUSED TORAH
OF MODERN TIMES

This is a daring title. To call the current 'Torah writings', so reverently held in the synagogues confused, is anathema. It is accusatory and calls for retaliation and dismissal by many of those who hold their religious views so close to their hearts and lives. They live by it.

In discussing the status of Judaism as a religion during the early 19th Century AD in his book 'The History of Zionism', in the chapter titled 'Out of the Ghetto', Walter Laqueur mentions the Talmud several times, but not once does he refer to the Tanak. Here is an admired man of considerable stature as a Jewish scholar, an authority on Zionism, who appears to see the Talmud and not the Tanak as the basis of Judaism. The Talmud (the word Talmud means study) became an entity after 70 AD when Israel was without a homeland and without the Temple. The Talmud is a record of RABBINIC DISCUSSIONS pertaining to Jewish law, ethics, philosophy, customs, and history. It has two components: The Mishna (dated about 200 AD) and the Gemara (dated about 500 AD). There are two distinct works known as Talmud: The Yerushalmi (Jerusalem Talmud) developed by the Jews in Palestine, and the Bavli (Babylonian Talmud) developed by the Jews in the Babylonian captivity since the 6th Century BC. The Bavli appears to be regarded as having greater authority and is quoted more often in Judaism.

Traditionally the Talmud has come to be considered the SUPREME SOURCEBOOK OF JEWISH LAW. It purports to take the rules listed in the Tanak and describe how to apply them to different circumstances. But in doing that it has become the ultimate source that is used to decide all matters of halacha or Jewish law. The simplicity and primitive authority of the Tanak has been virtually nullified. The date of the 'closure' of the Talmud is difficult to arrive at, but it is considered 'closed'. It appears to have not been added to since about 500 AD. There continues to be a steady stream of publications by revered rabbis and scholars, which their followers are pushing with great authority as being of 'Talmudic status'.

Today's 'Torah' in synagogues contains far more than the Tanak. No one has attained enough authority to have his thoughts and writings incorporated into the Tanak.

It is boldly pointed out that the Talmud[61] has replaced the Tanak as Israel's religious focus and unauthorized expanded Torah. And here lies the great weakness of the Jewish faith as viewed in Israel's recent history. The Talmud is basically the writings of commentary and interpretations of great teachers and religious leaders. It should not be included in the Tanak or referred to as Torah. The disciples of these Talmudic leaders take their opinions so seriously that it has become the leading cause of disunity in Israel. This disunity is seen in the plethora of branches in Judaism. It is seen in the Knesset. Because of this disunity Israel is unable to present a united front to her enemies. Religious division in the Arab world is their weakness. Sunni, Shiite, Alawite, etc. are warring branches of Islam, which has led to their disarray. The Jews must look inward and realise their own resultant disarray, confusion and vulnerability. They must return to focus on the closed canon, the Tanak. Their resolute will must be found there. The Tanak embodies what the Patriarchs presented as the will of God. Abraham obeyed it in its verbal primitive state. Jacob wrestled God for it. Joseph's life embodied it. Moses defined it. David sang it. Solomon opined on it. Isaiah wept about it and gave his life for it. These Patriarchs were imbued by the primitive will of God, an enduring witness. They had no Talmud. They gave the Jews the Tanak. The Talmud has caused Judaism to be confused. The enormous Talmudic minutiae have confounded the message of the Tanak. The baggage carried by the various Jewish sects is massive. The deafening din of the religious Babel in Israel prevents her unity, confuses her allies, and is fodder for Israel's enemies. The Talmudic interpretation and practice of Judaism has driven many Jews to become secular. Their distaste and disgust for the minutiae of extreme Judaism has driven them to lose faith in their religion. It is for these reasons that the Talmud is called into question as the great usurper of the authority of the Tanak.

Thomas Friedman is outstanding in his description of the religious confusion in Israel. In his book 'Beirut to Jerusalem' his colourful and insightful description of the religious life in Israel is extraordinary and unsurpassed. Though not exhaustive, it is the best description of the religious divide in Israel today to my knowledge. As an American he was able to look at it from outside Jewish thinking. As a Jew he has excellent understanding of it from the inside. His book does not define and describe the Torah, but he describes a scene that in my opinion has resulted from a confusion of the understanding of the current 'Torah'. The Talmud, the 'interpretive writings' and 'writings of commentary' now "incorporated into Torah" are divisive and rendering Israel irrelevant as a nation. These writings have been taken too seriously. Resultant warring religious factions are directly responsible for confusion and disunity in Israel.

Friedman describes four religious divisions in Israel[62]. There are more and others will be added without being exhaustive. At the outset, labelling of religious diversity as confusion must be viewed as an attack on pluralism. Pluralism of belief is a mark of freedom and in particular, religious freedom. Nonetheless, pluralism can run amok and be so divisive that it can be a detriment to any system of belief or plan of action. What is desirable will therefore be arbitrarily stated: There should be "UNITY IN ESSENTIALS and pluralism or DIVERSITY IN NON-ESSENTIALS". In all religious and secular bodies there are centrists, left-wingers and right-wingers. This is acceptable. But in order to have the power of action these three 'factions' must come together in agreement in basics for action and the demonstration of unity and power. This is not happening in Israel today and is resulting in weakness. Today Israel needs a leader who will be inspired to make strong decisions and inspire the nation to follow him. He must come from the centre of Judaism.

Thomas Friedman gives us four categories of strong religious thought in Israel today. The following is a quotation from page 288 of Friedman's book:

> "In fact, each of the four main schools in the great Israeli identity debate was so convinced that the others would wither away that as a group they were never willing, or able, to sit down and hammer out a consensus about the meaning of the state of Israel and the land of Israel for the Israeli people. As a result the different visions grew side by side. Israel became more secular and more Orthodox, more mundane and more messianic, all at the same time. Far from

having built a 'new Jewish identity,' or a 'new Jew,' Israel seems to have brought out of the basement of Jewish history every Jewish spiritual option from the past three thousand years; the country has become a living museum of Jewish history."

This is extremely well stated.

The cause for this deplorable status is the poor clarity in the comprehension of what is the true God-given Torah. IT SHOULD BE EXCLUSIVELY TANAK.

Thomas Friedman says rightly: "Jews in Israel are not differentiated by synagogue affiliations as much as by how they relate to the land of Israel and to the state". This has come about because of a lack of understanding of the will of God for Israel. There has to be a correct understanding of the ABRAHAMIC COVENANT. There has to be a proper unity of meaning, and affinity and loyalty to LAND, TORAH, and MESSIAH.

Friedman outlines four broad divisions of Jews[63]:

1. Secular and non-observant Jews: For this group ". . . being back in the land of Israel, erecting a modern society and army, and observing Jewish holidays as national holidays all became a substitute for religious observance and faith . . . For them, coming to the land of Israel and becoming 'normal' meant giving up religious ritual as the defining feature of their Jewish identity. Science, technology, and turning the desert green were their new Torah". This group constitutes about 50% of the population.
2. Religious Zionists: These are ". . . the traditional or modern Orthodox Jews, who fully support the secular Zionist state but insist that it is not a substitute for the synagogue . . . they serve in the army, celebrate Israel's Independence Day as a new religious holiday, and send their children to state-run religious educational institutions". This group numbers about 30% of the population.
3. Messianic Zionists: The Gush Emunim number about 5% of the population. "For them the rebirth of the Jewish state is not simply a religious event; it is the first stage in a process that will culminate with

the coming of the Messiah . . . That means, in particular, settling every inch of the land of Israel".

4. The Haredim: The ultra-Orthodox, non-Zionist Jews are about 15% of the population: ". . . those filled with the awe of God . . . content to live in the land of Israel . . . because they can fulfil more of the Jewish commandments there, and in order to be on hand when the Messiah arrives".

A fifth group, the Messianic Jews, should be added. Thomas Friedman himself adds two others together, the Reformist and Conservative Jews:

5. Messianic Jews: Estimated at about 30,000 Jews living in Israel (and 500,000 worldwide) they believe that Yeshua of Nazareth the son of Mary was the fulfilment of the Messiah. They live as religious Jews, celebrate all the Jewish festivals, and keep the Jewish Sabbath. They however are looking forward to the second coming of Yeshua and the resurrection of the dead. They differentiate themselves from Christians. But they accept the B'RIT HADASHA (the New Testament) as inspired and part of their expanded Torah. Messianic Jews hold the Abrahamic Covenant as the basis for Jewish identity. Whether they understand it correctly is difficult to know[64].

6. Reformist and Conservative Jews: See below.

To summarize the above categories of belief:

Here indeed is a plurality of belief, which largely finds 50% of the current inhabitants of Israel having no regard for Torah. They are totally imbued by a secular state. Another 30% of the population believe in Torah but without proper definition of Torah. The Messianic Zionists and the Haredim are more correctly classified as sects and follow interpretive and commentary writings as their collective 'Torah'. The tiny segment of Messianic Jews appears to be embracing the Jewish Torah of the Tanak but have interpreted it as predictive of Yeshua of Nazareth as the Messiah. They honour the Sabbath, celebrate the Passover and Yom Kipper, and rejoice in redemptive salvation by their Messiah. They look forward to his return and a new world order.

Add to this religious plethora the Reformist and Conservative movements, which at the time of Friedman's publication had just arrived from America into

Israel. According to Friedman they were not really welcomed by the Orthodox Jews[65].

Plurality is good, but when it creates warring factions, it is disunity and confusion. It is no longer plurality among friends but battlefields of enemies. The word plurality then cannot be used to describe the situation because it lacks agreed harmony.

With such a confusion of religious division how can there be consensus as to what is the will of God for Israel as contained in the Tanak? This will be a major undertaking. How can the State of Israel fulfil the Abrahamic Covenant in the basic Torah of the Jewish Bible—the Tanak? The Arabs individually are much more serious about their religion than the vast majority of Jews now in Israel. Arab factions are so rigid that they kill each other to achieve their religious goals. How can the strength of Israel be found and grounded in the Torah and harnessed to confound their enemies? Will another slaughter of Israel and another diaspora of the remnant be necessary?

An analysis of how 50% of the inhabitants of modern Israel have come to disregard their birthright having arrived in the land of Israel is necessary. The Land by itself is not the entire birthright. The Torah and the Messiah are also in the envelope. We should look at previous experience, indeed extract "history from the basement", to find out why God chose to turn his back on the Jews in the past. An examination of the causes and conditions of the Almighty's protection being withdrawn from them is vital.

The "current Torah" (which includes Talmud) in Jewish practice is certainly too wide, too confused, too packed with minutiae, and utterly divisive. Many of the Zionist leaders in Europe were opposed to the Talmud and to ultra-Orthodox halacha. They referred to it as a fossilized religion that had been built up by the well-meaning rabbis over the centuries. Walter Laqueur is right when he guardedly refers to the malaise, which the extreme right wing rabbis had achieved among the Jews as a Talmudic malaise. See the chapter titled 'The Forerunners' in his book 'A History of Zionism'. He credits the Enlightenment that followed the French Revolution with the rise of the intellectual awakening and the development of conditions that led to Zionism. Laqueur unwittingly bears witness to the inevitable confusion that results from leaving the Tanak as the central and only foundation of Judaism. In his chapter titled 'The Interregnum'

Laqueur cites Ahad Ha'am (Asher Ginzberg) who hailed from Skvira, near Kiev and represented the Eastern European bloc, and Martin Buber, born in Vienna, who represented the Western European bloc. Both were marginally active in the Zionist Movement but fancied themselves destined to preserve Judaism. But neither of them based their brands of Judaism on the Tanak. Ahad Ha'am spent his energies trying to "rescue . . . Judaism as a spiritual entity" by creating a cultural centre in Palestine based on Judaism—a Judaism not based on the Abrahamic Covenant. Martin Buber's thought processes originally "advocated a return to the origins of Judaism", but then got lost in the "somewhat intangible philosophical-theological" ideas of pantheism. The Patriarch Moses describes the only authentic origin of Judaism in the Tanak. Wandering away from the Tanak as these men did only increase the confusion in Judaism. The Talmud is the greatest wandering away from Judaism. Judaism has no foundation for a spiritual entity outside the Tanak.

Rabbi Jacob Petuchovski in his 1966 book 'Zion Reconsidered' makes a surprising assessment of Jewish religious observance. He assesses the legal concepts in the Mishna, Midrash and Talmud as being borrowed from a non-Jewish environment, and alleges the Jewish holidays are borrowed from the Canaanites. He lists three: Shavuot, Passover and Sukkot. The latter two are from Moses in the Tanak. Shavuot celebrates the giving of the law at Sinai, but its origin is not a command in the Tanak.[66] These holidays celebrate vital events in Jewish history. Moses received an Egyptian university education and probably studied Hammurabi's Code. The Pentateuch likely reflects Moses' background. I accept Rabbi Petuchovski's attitude to the Talmud but he 'throws the baby out with the bathwater'.

The Tanak has application to all eras and civilizations. Its application is to be found contextually and must be used practically. A J Jacobs in his book 'The Year of Living Biblically' strikes a balance in the practical application of the Tanak for this present generation. He achieves an understanding of the Tanak that is faithful to the spirit of the law rather than the letter. His book is not exhaustive of all that is in the Tanak and he leaves much of the vital parts untouched. His book is recommended reading for serious students and devotees of Judaism. He appears to hold the Tanak as the pure Torah and he regards the Talmud as valuable commentary but not Torah.

NOTES

[61]   See "The Talmud-The Jewish Home in Exile" Commentary by Dr. Gerhard Falk
jbuff.com See also FAQ archives "what is the Talmud?"

See Views of Jewish Law: Practices and Beliefs. Haredi Judaism, Wikipedia

[62]   See 'Beirut to Jerusalem' by Thomas Friedman, page 288 and on.

[63]   See 'Beliefs of Messianic Congregations' by Rabbi Mottel Boleston: "The
Abrahamic Covenant—The Basis for Jewish Identity"

See also B'rit Hadasha Messianic Jewish Synagogue.

Torah and Messiah, Nazarene.net: B'rit Hadasha.

The Orthodox Jewish B'rit Hadasha, AFI International, Translated by P.E.
Goble

[64]   See 'Beirut to Jerusalem' pages 470-474

[65]   Ibid.

[66]   A History of Zionism' by Walter Laqueur, Schocken Books, New York

CHAPTER 10
THE MESSIAH

Israel's greatest legitimacy comes from the Abrahamic Covenant, which is linked by Moses, Israel's greatest guru, to the creation of the Universe. In a discussion of the inordinate attention that is paid to the Israeli-Arab Palestinian question by the US and the rest of the world, Thomas Friedman quietly but aptly describes Israel's legitimacy. I quote: ". . . the Palestinians simply are not part of the BIBLICAL SUPER-STORY through which the West looks at the world, and it is the SUPER-STORY that determines whose experiences get interpreted and whose don't, whose pain is felt and whose is ignored" (Emphasis mine)[67]. Friedman is using the SUPER STORY simply to differentiate Jews from Arabs and not to define Israel. He is making a case for the Arab Palestinian pain being ignored. It is my belief that God does not ignore anyone's suffering and it is difficult to explain people's suffering in terms of God's interference or lack of it. The exercise of free will may have something to do with people's suffering, but a discussion of this topic, much as I like to enter into it, is beyond the scope of this book. After punishing Israel for 2000 years with absence from their homeland culminating in the most dreadful Nazi extermination of 6 million Jews God has finally brought Israel back. Will God now allow anyone to endanger Israel's existence? No Nobel Prize should titillate the negotiators who might be tempted to compromise secure borders for Israel. It is Israel's destiny to return to the Abrahamic Covenant and to re-establish her legitimacy. It certainly is the super-story. And that is why Israel needs a REFORMATION. This must come in a return to the simple covenant that they have forgotten. There has to be a clarion call to the Jewish people of all religious stripes to return to a correct contemplation of their part in that covenant. And what is their part?

Over and over in this book thus far an examination has been made of the Abrahamic Covenant between God and Abraham as recorded by Moses. In simple terms it was a business arrangement in a redemptive religion: You will have LAND, and TORAH and you must tell the world of the MESSIAH and that his blood brings remission. It is the remission that will bring you back to the Edenic state, which is where mankind was placed before they disobeyed God. And that involves a proper understanding of the MESSIAH. The LAND is Israel. The TORAH is the Tanak and the Tanak reveals the MESSIAH. Every Jew must arrive at an understanding of Messiah from the Tanak and realise the Messiah cannot be a solely secular leader. No other writing or witness must be used to decide and define the Messiah. The Talmud is good for discussion and guidance. Only the Tanak can be allowed to define Messiah. One might argue that there are different interpretations of the Tanak, which lead us to a plurality of thought. For avoiding plurality the interpretation of the Tanak must stay simple. We have no difficulty defining the land. At present it is the post 1967 Six Day War borders but future negotiations may change this. We have just defined the Torah—it is the Tanak. The Tanak is universally accepted by the Jews as God's will for all. Israel's mission, morality and hope derive from it. And now the Tanak must define the Messiah. The change to this ideation is the reformation desperately needed by Israel.

The earliest promise and pronouncement of the Messiah occurred in Eden. It is described in the serpent metaphor as 'the ENMITY between the serpent (disobedience) and the woman (Eve representing mankind), between thy seed (all acts of disobedience) and HER SEED" (the Messiah who brings redemption) (Emphasis mine). All humanity has representation in the Messiah. The Messiah would bruise the serpent's head (a lethal wound) but the serpent would only succeed in inflicting a heel wound (non-lethal wound). A major description of the Serpent is present in the book of Job[68]. And when Eve gave birth to Cain she proclaimed: "I have begotten the Man-Child from God"[69]. She thought Cain was the promised Messiah. The function of the Messiah was defined outside the gates of Eden when all hope was lost. They were required to offer an burnt animal sacrifice for sin, prefiguring what the Messiah would do since the shedding of his blood would bring remission. From Creation to the AD 70 destruction of the Temple and Jerusalem, the burnt offering of the 'lamb without blemish', whose shed blood signified the remission for sin prefigured the Messiah. Abel's offering of a lamb was accepted. Cain's substitute was rejected[70]. We cannot concoct a substitute for the Messiah. There are several concocted definitions of Messiah being paraded around today by Israel's religious leaders.

The next explicit reference to Messiah comes in the Abrahamic Covenant. "In thy seed shall all nations of the earth be blessed"[71]. The Messiah would come from the seed of Abraham. Again the sacrifice of a 'lamb without blemish' is required, but before that happens, the very connection of God to the Messiah is wonderfully defined, it will be God's Son, Messiah will be deity. So God says to Abraham to emphasize this: "Take thy son, thine only son", and shed his innocent blood, and burn him on the altar. Again the emphasis is made on the fact that the Messiah's blood must be shed for remission. But now the Messiah gets powerful definition as the Son of God and it is clear that the blood of deity is the requirement. So Abraham takes his son who willingly cooperates and carries the wood to his impending death. But as Abraham raises the knife to carry out the dreadful deed God calls out to him "Stop it!". God says to Abraham "I will save your son but MY SON MUST DIE". The Messiah is deity (the Son of God), the Messiah is human (the seed of Abraham), and his volunteered shed blood will provide remission[72]. Deity created humanity in a perfect state and deity will restore that perfection. The Messiah will restore the Edenic state. Israel! O Israel! there is a glorious future before you and through you for the whole world! That is the gist of the Abrahamic Covenant. "[Abraham], in thy seed shall all nations of the earth be blessed", "your seed will number as the stars of the firmament". Mount Moriah is the most sacred spot on earth and Israel must one day SOON rebuild the Temple on that spot. Jerusalem will not be complete till the Temple is rebuilt on Mount Moriah. It is the duty of every Jew to bring that to pass.

The leadership of Moses was dedicated and unwavering. His 'mistake' of leadership was to strike the rock rather than speak to it as he was asked to do by God[73]. The water that gushed out from that rock would quench the thirst of Israel. I would not have held that mistake against him. But God did not allow him to enter the Promised Land as a punishment for that mistake[74]. God relieved Moses of the job of leading Israel into the Promised Land. But Moses had already recorded his greatest achievements: he had rescued the Israelites from slavery in Egypt, and he had interceded with God on their behalf when God threatened to destroy them for worshipping the golden calf[75]. At that point Moses preserved the Abrahamic Covenant as applying to all Israel of all time. Moses himself was therefore a figure or type of the coming Messiah. Moses prophesied about the Messiah in Deuteronomy 18:18,19: "The Lord your God will raise for you a Prophet like unto me from your midst, from your brethren. Him shall you hear . . . ." Then God reinforces what Moses has just said with his own voice: "I will raise up for them a Prophet like you (you who has saved your people from my anger) from among their brethren and will put my words in his mouth and he shall speak to them all that I command him.

God used the night they left Egypt to institute the great Passover feast. They ate roast lamb, unleavened bread and bitter herbs, standing up and wearing their sandals, all ready to quickly depart. Here is the great proclamation of the Messiah in Egypt. The lamb they used signified the Messiah. They ate the flesh of that lamb. The lamb's blood was splashed on the doorposts and on the lintels of their houses. When the Angel of Death passed by at midnight their firstborn did not die. The angel saw the splashed blood. "I will pass over you when I see the blood". The great Passover festival was instituted to point to the Messiah's blood that saves[76]. The Messiah's blood must be shed. His blood must be splashed on the lintel and doorposts of every Jew's life. Yes, on the life of every human, to escape eternal death.

The Day of Atonement[77] is another mighty pointer to the Messiah. It was instituted at Mount Sinai. Once a year the High Priest took the blood of the sacrificial animal, which was slaughtered for all the sins of all the people, into the Most Holy Place of the Tabernacle (Temple) and sprinkled it on the Golden Altar, Ark of the Covenant and the Mercy Seat. It was a sacrifice that cleansed them all collectively from all their sin. The High Priest himself represented the Messiah who presented the blood to God. Symbolically the Messiah presents his sacrifice to God. It is too bad that the sacrificial system did not survive past AD 70 as it is a wonderful witness to the plan of God to bring back the Edenic state. As part of the Abrahamic Covenant it is the duty of Israel to tell the world about the promised Messiah, identify him, and draw attention to the plan that saves mankind. The Day of Atonement must be celebrated forever."[78].

The Talmud credits Moses with the authorship of the Book of Job. Job lived in the land of Uz, which was in proximity with Midian where Moses dwelt in self-exile for forty years. The Book of Job, which is about the life of Job in nearby Uz, was his first writing. I would not be dogmatic about it. In the story Job proclaims the Messiah: "For I know that my Redeemer liveth and that he shall stand at the latter day upon the earth; and though after my skin worms destroy this body, yet in my flesh shall I see God . . . ."[79]. Job and Moses both firmly believed in restored immortality by the Messiah. There is hope for the bones interred in the Cave of Machpelah. Judaism is redemptive indeed.

Isaiah waxed eloquent in his identification of the Messiah: "For unto us a Child is born, unto us a Son is given; and the government shall be upon His shoulder. And His name shall be called Wonderful, Counsellor, the Mighty God, the Everlasting Father, the Prince of Peace. Of the increase of His government and peace there will be no end. Upon the throne of David and over his kingdom to order it and establish it, with judgement and justice, from this time forward, even forever"[80]. The Messiah is no ordinary person. Isaiah establishes the Messiah's deity with the Godhead. He is one with the Mighty God. He is one with the Everlasting Father. He is born human as Abraham's seed but he is divine. Monotheistically he is Jehovah. He will sit upon the throne of David in Jerusalem. He will be Israel's darling. He will order and establish the kingdom of David and establish judgment and justice forever. This great proclamation of Isaiah occurred in Jerusalem, the heart of Israel.

The Prophet Daniel introduces the Rock, which strikes and grinds the image of Nebuchadnezzar's dream of history in the days of the feet and toes. It then grows to fill the whole earth. He interprets the dream: "And in the days of these kings shall the God of heaven set up a kingdom which shall never be destroyed . . . ."[81]. This is the Messiah's kingdom. Later, Daniel makes multiple references to the "Son of Man" which are references to the Messiah. The fiery furnace into which Shadrak, Meshach and Abednigo were thrown for not worshipping Nebuchadnezzar's golden image showed their daring act. Here the "Son of Man" joins them in the furnace and protects them from being consumed. Four men are seen unsinged in the furnace, the fourth is "like unto the Son of God". The Son of Man becomes synonymous with the Son of God. Only three men walk out of the furnace. Again: "I Daniel saw in the night visions, and behold, one like the Son of Man came with the clouds of heaven and came to the Ancient of Days . . . and there was given him dominion and glory and a kingdom, that all people, nations, and languages should serve him; his dominion, which shall not pass away and his kingdom which shall not be destroyed". In his Seventy Weeks Prophecy Daniel outlines events in relation to Messiah[82]. Here are trumpet declarations of the Messiah's featuring in the fulfilment of the Abrahamic Covenant.

David the Psalmist waxed lyrical in the Messianic enunciation of the Twenty-third Psalm. Consider the redemptive experience credited to the Messianic Shepherd in the beautiful words: "Yea though I walk through the valley of the shadow of death I will fear no evil, for thou art with me.... Surely goodness and mercy shall follow me all the days of my life and I shall dwell in the house of the Lord forever". The Messiah destroys eternal death and bestows life forever, and forever is a long, long time. Then David prophetically looks forward to end times in Psalm 24: "Lift up your heads O ye gates and be ye lift up, ye everlasting doors, and the King of glory shall come in. Who is this king of glory? The Lord strong and mighty, the Lord mighty in battle, the Lord of hosts". He was visioning the entry of the Messiah into Jerusalem.

The prophet Zachariah also dreamed of the Messianic entry into Jerusalem: "Rejoice greatly, O daughter of Zion; shout, O daughter of Jerusalem; behold, thy King cometh unto thee. He is the righteous Saviour, and he shall speak peace unto the heathen". Zachariah 9:9-10.

In summary: The Messiah was proclaimed by God outside the Gates of Eden to bring humanity back to face to face communion with him. He was proclaimed to Abraham in Ur of the Chaldees in the Covenant and again in Hebron at the mouth of the Cave of Machpelah. Moses proclaimed the Messiah as Job's hope of resurrection and eternal life. Messiah was proclaimed on the dark night in Egypt when the Passover was instituted. Messiah was proclaimed by Moses at Mount Sinai, in the institution of the Day of Atonement. Isaiah waxed eloquent in Jerusalem about the Messiah's government. Daniel and his companions proclaimed the Messiah in Babylon. And David the shepherd boy sang about life forever bestowed by the Messianic Shepherd. The Messiah is the central subject of the Tanak. The Tanak would make no sense without the Abrahamic Covenant, which embodies Land, Torah and Messiah.

There are many other references to the Messiah in the Tanak. Those presented are some of the powerful ones[83]. The Tanak abounds in Messianic utterances and predictions. The listing and discussion of them could fill a book. Jewish scholars in Israel today should be challenged to turn their attention to the Messiah, restricting the scope of their studies to the revelations in the Tanak. The identification of the Messiah must be drawn from the Tanak. It is an urgent matter indeed as the Messiah is the salvation of Israel and the nations of the world.

Reformation and revival in Israel can only come with singleness of mind and utmost reverence to LAND, TORAH and MESSIAH. This is a mighty task, which requires unity and dedication. It has to be discussed in the synagogues, revered in the Knesset, and taught in the schools[84]. In every Jewish home the Tanak should be the central discussion. The Tanak must be uplifted throughout the land of Israel. It must be taught to strangers. Israel's large number of tourists should be given the opportunity to enter the discussion of LAND, TORAH and the MESSIAH. The Yad Vashem Holocaust Centre is a wonderful monument in Jerusalem. The tears I shed there were unabashed. I wept for the sufferings of Israel. The Yad Vashem is a magnificent presentation of and monument to the sufferings of Israel, which must never happen again. It is a good educational and informational centre visited by young Israelis, Jews from all over the world, and gentile tourists. Israel needs a similar centre called YAD BERITH. The education of all Israelis, diasporic Jews and tourists about the Abrahamic Covenant and the three most important aspects of it—LAND, TORAH and MESSIAH should be the prime aim of the state of Israel. These three should be the guiding light of all political discourse and international negotiations. Considerations of Torah and Tanak are neglected by at least 50% of the population of Israel who order their lives as part of a purely secular state. They give not a thought to the great heritage of Israel that has brought them back together in the Holy Land. They cannot be forced to worship God but they must be shown the better way. Israel cannot escape the claims of Abraham and his God.

Particular reformation is needed in the observation of the Sabbath. This is a memorial of creation. This is Israel's rest in the accomplishments, which the Messiah fulfils. The minutiae of current ultra-Orthodox Sabbath keeping is wrong[85]. It makes the Sabbath a burden and most unattractive to young people. It was meant for rest, both physical and spiritual. They are to rest in what the Messiah is to accomplish for them, the banishment of the fear of eternal death. The Sabbath should be a delight[86], a joyous celebration where worship and rest from labour occurs and the Tanak is discussed. Joyous coming together for mutual celebration of happiness with relatives, neighbours and friends should occur. There should be no burdensome rules and regulations where people are castigated. Rules for Sabbath keeping must not incite loathing. Let Israelis meet and dance and revel in the streets on the Sabbath rejoicing in the freedom and safety provided by the security of the land of Israel and Messianic salvation. Let them revel in dealing bread to the hungry and bringing the poor that are cast out to their houses[87]. The laws of the minutiae of Sabbath keeping imposed by the extreme right wing is a curse to Israel and the pleasure of worshipping God is lost.

A great reformation is needed by many in Israel and world Jewry, but most by the 50% of Israelis and 90% of American Jews who are satisfied in being a part of a secular state and see no need to truly honour their heritage. They are modern day idolaters. Their idols are the modern comforts of life with all the titillations, and their money in the bank. And if they do not have riches already they are in a sweat striving for riches. That is a form of idolatry. No one would object to comfortable living but that is not the end of life in itself. Israel must not forget the worship of their God and they must seek him and honour him more than worldly goods. Worldly goods become idols if the people who have them forget God. The extreme segment of religious Jews in both divides must sharpen their acumen. A clear vision of LAND, TORAH and MESSIAH should emanate. This will unify Israel and world Jewry. Abraham's Covenant with God will be kept. Yad Berith is eternal.

Moses has uttered the warning: ". . . but [when] you shall cross over the Jordan and possess that good land, take heed to yourselves, lest you forget the covenant of the Lord your God which he made with you, and make for yourselves A CARVED IMAGE IN THE FORM OF ANYTHING, which the Lord your God has forbidden you. For the Lord your God is a consuming fire, a jealous God. When you beget children and grandchildren and have grown old in the land, and act corruptly and make a carved image in the form of anything, and do evil in the sight of the Lord your God to provoke him to anger, I call heaven and earth to witness against you this day, that you will soon utterly perish from the land . . . and the Lord will scatter you . . . among the nations . . . But from there you will seek the Lord your God, and you will find him if you will seek him with all your heart and all your soul" (emphasis mine)[88]. The scattering has happened before. It can happen again.

Reformation in Israel can only come at a price. That price must be paid by the world's Jewry, but principally by the six and a half million American Jews and the five and a half million Israeli Jews. They are poles apart in their thinking. American Jews are too lax religiously. Reform and Conservative Jews who predominate in the US must look deeply into their religious lives and have a better understanding of the Torah and the Abrahamic Covenant. The Orthodox and ultra-Orthodox Jews must lose their confusion in the minutiae of halacha, and their extreme opposition to the Reformists and Conservatives. They must come to a meeting in the middle with emphasis on LAND, TORAH and MESSIAH. Politically, the American Jews must admit that a two state settlement has already taken place. But it will be a difficult proposition to maintain Israel's current borders. Unilateral withdrawals and land for peace deals have not brought permanent peace yet. The Arabs state they want all of the land. Hamas admits nothing less will satisfy. In any future settlement the world must realise Israel's borders must be secure and that Jerusalem is indivisible as the Messianic seat of government. Israel has no alternative but to keep negotiating in good faith.

NOTES

[67]   Beirut to Jerusalem, by Thomas Friedman, page 445.

[68]   Genesis 3:14,15. Also see Job chapters 1 & 2.

[69]   Genesis 4:1

[70]   Genesis 4:3,4

[71]   Genesis 12:1-3

[72]   Genesis chapter 22

[73]   Deuteronomy 8:15

[74]   Deuteronomy chapter 34

[75]   Exodus chapter 32

[76]   Exodus chapter 12

[77]   Leviticus chapter 16

[78]   Leviticus chapter 16

[79]   Job 19:25,26

[80]   Isaiah 9:6,7

[81]   Daniel chapters 1&2

[82]   Daniel 3:25 ". . . I see four men loose, walking in the midst of the fire: and they are not hurt. And the fourth is like unto the Son of God".
Daniel 7:13,14 : Daniel's night vision.
Daniel 9:21-27 Timeline to Messiah the Prince

[83]   References to Mashiach in Judaism: Judaism 101 on IDEAS-Messiah: Isaiah 2,11, 42; 59:20; Jeremiah 23,30,33; 48:47; 49:39; Ezekiel 38:16-23; Hosea 3:4,5; Micah 4 (vision of Earth's Golden Age); Zephaniah 3:9-20 (vision of unity); Zechariah 14:9-21; Daniel 10: 14-21 (vision of the latter days)

[84]   Israel: In Search of an Identity, by Nissim Rejwan in his chapter on Israel as an Open Society quotes Zalman Aranne, Minister of Education: "We respect religion, because religious faith in its pure form elevates man. We adopt the Jewish tradition which embodies both the national and religious elements because it epitomises the glory of former times and ancient glory never wanes . . . ." But his curriculum did not teach the Abrahamic Covenant.

[85]   Judaism 101 Shabbat: In one list of prohibited works there are 30 categories of 'work' listed that may not be performed. Other lists number in the hundreds.

[86]   Isaiah 58:13,14 ". . . and call the Sabbath a delight . . . ."

[87]   Isaiah 58:6,7 and 61:1-3

[88]   Deuteronomy 4:22-29. *See also* Isaiah chapters 61 and 62

CHAPTER 11
THE CAPTIVITIES OF ISRAEL

G od allowed Israel to be punished many times by their enemies for their waywardness and indifference to the Abrahamic Covenant. Idolatry in its various forms beset Israel. But there is no evidence that God gave Israel up totally. For the purposes of discussion an arbitrary assignment of their captivities to four major estrangements from God is outlined:

Egyptian Slavery
About 1875 BC Joseph was sold into Egypt. Israel's sojourn in Egypt lasted 430 years according to Moses (Exodus 12:40). A major part of that period was spent in slavery.

Assyrian Annihilation
About 722 BC the Assyrian annihilation was inflicted. Shalmaneser V took the Northern Kingdom captive to Assyria. He then resettled Samaria with Babylonians. The 10 tribes lost their identity and never returned. They succumbed to assimilation.

Babylonian Captivity
About 588 BC Nebuchadnezzar II inflicted the Babylonian Captivity on Judah. Only the poor Jews were left behind. He destroyed Solomon's Temple.

The Roman Conquest
Rome subjugated Israel for about a hundred years before the Emperor Titus finally destroyed Jerusalem and the Temple, slaughtered many and created the diaspora in AD 70.

The captivities of Israel were near annihilations. (The northern kingdom was totally annihilated). The diaspora of the remnants who were not slaughtered was devastating. It is amazing that Israel recovered. The survival of the remnants of Israel has been miraculous. It cannot be denied that God who determined a place and witness for them was always ready to bring them back. Four hundred and thirty years in Egypt was a long time. The AD 70 destruction of the Jews with a diaspora of those who escaped slaughter has taken 2000 years to recover. Modern Israel must consolidate this recovery.

The period of slavery in Egypt is highlighted by the slaughter of the Hebrew firstborn, accomplished by a Pharaoh who did not remember Joseph. It is the only lethal infliction by the Egyptians that was recorded. Moses was the only firstborn Israelite male infant to be saved[89]. The survival of Moses was miraculous. The period of slavery was a living hell. There was immense suffering. Why did God allow slavery to happen? The immediate progeny of Jacob who went into the land of Egypt were privileged. Joseph had achieved fame and prominence and had vaulted them into prosperity in the land of Goshen, considered as one of the most fertile parts of Egypt.

Their birth rate and prosperity were soon recognised as threatening factors to the Egyptians and to a new Pharaoh, who did not remember the salvation from starvation provided by Joseph. He enslaved them[90]. There were other factors, mainly the idolatry of the Israelites. They absorbed the religion of the Sun worshippers and forgot their monotheistic jealous God. Moses jolted them out of idolatry and slavery. Some of them resisted his liberation movement, and he had to reorientate them to the Abrahamic Covenant and the mission entrusted to them. It is recorded that even when freed they hankered after the fleshpots of Egypt[91] and the idols they left behind, while journeying towards the Promised Land[92]. The spoken Torah was disregarded and forgotten. They had serious attachment to Egypt despite being freed. Many Israelites, despite the wondrous deliverance from Egypt had turned their backs on the God of Israel. Intermarriage and idolatry had drained a large number who remained in Egypt and who did not choose to follow Moses.

The next great slaughter and diaspora occurred after Israel had settled in Canaan. But first contemplate the glory of Israel under the leadership of Joshua as they entered the Promised Land. View the fall of the walls of Jericho[93]. Understand the leadership of Samuel[94]. The surrounding idolatrous tribes were destroyed for rejecting Israel's God. This enabled possession of the land. View Samuel's weakness in allowing a theocracy to be replaced by a monarchy, and the disastrous result of the actions of King Saul. View the anointing of David in Hebron and the glory that followed in his reign and in that of Solomon. View Solomon's glorious Temple[95]. Let the achievements of Israel impress you as you see what follows obedience to the Torah. Can a parallel be created today?

Trace the history of Israel from David and Solomon to the Assyrian Captivity that occurred in 722 BC[96]. It was downhill into idolatry. The monarchy had made a mess of Israel, which was divided into two kingdoms, the ten tribes of the north and the two tribes (Judah and Benjamin and elements of Levi) of the south. Baal worship was everywhere. The Torah was disregarded. During this period the prophets Hosea and Micah repeatedly called for Israel's repentance, but to no avail. So God allowed the Assyrians to destroy the northern kingdom. The ten northern tribes were lost subsequently with the land being taken again by idolaters. There was no return for them.

The southern kingdom called Judah found favour with God by the righteous acts of King Hezekiah[97]. But when his son Manasseh took the throne idolatry returned. Manasseh was so evil he had the prophet Isaiah put to death[98]. He built altars for Baal in the temple Solomon built. He was carried away captive by the Assyrians but he repented and was allowed to return to the land of Judah. How can God allow the murderer of the great prophet Isaiah to return? It was because he repented. But then his son Amon transgressed again against the Lord. He filled the land with idols. He was so wicked that his servants assassinated him. When Josiah his son came to the throne there was a return to the worship of the true God. Hilkiah the high priest found the long forgotten Torah in the Temple and it was shown to Josiah. He was determined to return to the worship of the true God. Josiah said: "Go ye and inquire of the Lord for me, and for the people, and for all Judah, concerning the words of this book that is found [the Pentateuch]; for great is the wrath of the Lord that is kindled against us, because our fathers have not hearkened unto the words of this book . . . ."[99]. However after Josiah idolatry flooded again into the land of Judah. God longed for his people: "Neither will I make the feet of Israel move anymore out of the land which I gave their fathers, if only they will observe to do according to all that I have commanded them, and according to all the law that my servant Moses commanded them. But they hearkened not . . . ."[100].

This was followed by the third major slaughter and diaspora of the children of God by the Babylonian Nebuchadnezzar II in 586 BC[101]. It was at this time that Daniel and his three companions found themselves in Babylonian captivity. They were worshippers of the true God and found favour in the eyes of their captors. Jehoiachim was king of Judah when they were carried away to Babylon. But as the Prophet Jeremiah had prophesied some of the Jews were allowed to return and rebuild Jerusalem after 70 years of captivity. "Behold I will gather them out of all countries to which I have driven them in mine anger, and in my fury, and in great wrath; and I will bring them again unto this place, and I will cause them to dwell safely"[102].

The repeat transgression of Israel because of idolatry was disastrous. Their disregard for the Torah was blatant. Yet again the Israelites took a downward path and by the time the Roman occupation occurred they had built up a confused Torah, just as confused as today. The Scribes and Pharisees had built up a false system of worship. The temple Herod built for them became the site of apostasy. Money was their god and the Temple was desecrated by a greater regard for monetary gain. The sacrificial system instituted for the expiation of their sins had been turned into a venue for money making. Israel had lost sight of the idea that the shedding of the blood of the sacrificial animal was for the forgiveness of sin, pointing to the Messiah's mission. Instead the shedding of blood became the opportunity to make a monetary profit. The Temple became the site of marketplace. The interpretation of the Torah was a shambles. And so God allowed the Romans to destroy the Temple and the city of Jerusalem in AD 70. There was a great slaughter and the final diaspora occurred.

It would take two thousand years 'in the wilderness', the pogroms of Eastern Europe, the selfless and inspired efforts of Theodor Herzl, Chaim Weizmann, Herbert Samuel, Louis Brandeis, Vladimir Jabotinsky and others, the Nazi Holocaust and the muscle of David Ben Gurion to enable a return to Israel as a nation. The terrible suffering of European Jews motivated Herzl. He saw it in diabolical contrast to the light of the Enlightenment sweeping Europe after the French Revolution. The suffering of the Jews in Eastern Europe is typified by the Kishinev pogrom. This is recorded in the Complete Diaries of Herzl, Volume 4, page 1501, and quoted by Walter Laqueur in his book 'A History of Zionism' page 123: "Only a few months earlier, between 6 and 8 April [1903], a pogrom had taken place in Kishinev in the course of which 50 Jews had been killed, many more wounded, and many Jewish women raped. The feeling in the Jewish community was one of horror, but also of terrible shame that Jews had been beaten and killed like sheep without offering resistance. 'Great is the sorrow and great is the shame', Bialik wrote after the massacre:'And which of the two is greater, answer thou O Son of Man?'. The grandsons of the Maccabeans—they ran like mice, they hid themselves like bedbugs and died the death of dogs wherever found'". The suffering of the Jews and the prayers of Herzl and Chaim Nachman Bialik had reached to high heaven.

Israel declared itself a nation in 1948 and in 64 years what has happened? The most significant thing is that over 50% of the population of Israel has no regard for the Torah and are again worshipping idols. The main idol is money and a comfortable living in a land they call the land of their fathers. Money and comfort are not evils in themselves but when there is disregard for the Torah they become blatant idols. Chaim Weizmann gave idolatry a very wide definition. In a speech at the Seventeenth Zionist Congress he was making a plea for restraint from violence by Jews, which was being advocated against the British Mandate. He was called a demagogue. In anguish he replied: "... I warn you against bogus palliatives, against shortcuts, against false prophets, against facile generalisations, against distortion of historic facts .... If you think of bringing redemption nearer by un-Jewish methods, if you lose faith in hard work and better days, then you commit idolatry and endanger what we have built. Would I had a tongue of flame, the strength of prophets, to warn you against the path of Babylon and Egypt. Zion shall be built in Judgement—and not by any other means"[103]. The majority in Israel today are happy with a secular state and a release from worshipping the true God. There is a great need for repentance and turning to the Torah and Messianic expectation, to prevent another annihilation.

The Abrahamic Covenant needs to be back in focus. There must be no halting till the LAND and TORAH become their primary concern and the age of the MESSIAH is ushered in. The idols of modern living and trust in a secular state must be cast down and the God of Israel given his rightful place. The Temple must be rebuilt and the worship of the one true God must be central. The Tanak must become enshrined as the pure Torah. Otherwise the next great slaughter and diaspora of Israel will take place.

NOTES

[89]   Exodus 2:1-10 "... and behold the baby Moses wept. So the Egyptian princess had compassion on him and said: This is one of the Hebrews' children ...."

90   Exodus 1:1-22 "... the children of Israel were fruitful and increased abundantly, multiplied and grew exceedingly mighty, and the land was filled with them ... So Pharaoh commanded all his people saying: Every son who is born you shall cast into the river ...."

91   Exodus 16:3 "... Oh that we had died by the hand of the Lord in the land of Egypt when we sat by the pots of meat ...."

92   Exodus chapter 32: "... make us gods that shall go before us; as for this Moses who brought us out of the land of Egypt, we do not know what has become of him ..."

93   Joshua 1:6,7 "Be strong and of good courage, for to this people you shall divide as an inheritance the land which I swore to their fathers to give them. Only be strong and very courageous that you may observe to do according to all the law which Moses My servant commanded you, do not turn from it to the right hand or to the left .... This Book of the Law shall not depart from your mouth, but you shall meditate in it day and night, that you may observe to do all that is written in it".

94   1Samuel chapter 8 ".... Give us a king .... Heed the voice of the people ... for they have rejected Me, that I shall not reign over them ...."

95   1Kings chapters 6-9 ".... Then the word of the Lord came to Solomon saying: Concerning this Temple which you are building, if you walk in My statutes, execute My judgements, keep all My commandments, and walk in them ... then I will dwell among the children of Israel, and will not forsake My people Israel".

96   2Kings, chapter 17. Note that the King of Assyria brought people from Babylon to settle in Samaria instead of the children of Israel (see verse 2).

97   2Kings chapters 19,20.

98   2Kings chapter 21

99   2Kings chapters 22,23

100   2Kings 21:8

101   Daniel chapter 1

102   See Jeremiah Chapter 32.

103   Quoted in Silverberg, 'If I forget Thee, O Jerusalem', pages 344-345. This has been quoted in my source 'A History of Zionism' by Walter Laqueur, Schocken Books, New York, pages 575, 576

CHAPTER 12
THE RETURNS OF ISRAEL FROM CAPTIVITY

There were many mini punishments inflicted by God on the Jews through their enemies for their waywardness. Why does God punish, sometimes so cruelly? Why do we inflict such heart-wrenching disappointment on him? Both are good questions. Or are the calamities or good things that happen the result of personal and/or collective free will, the choices made? That is a question to ponder. Israel's history is an excellent example of what happens to a nation as a result of collective decisions made. If that is the case God may be innocent of the bad things that happen. The plan of redemption is then his initiative to restore humanity to the original perfection.

There were several mini recoveries by small groups of Jews allowed back from captivity. The recoveries from the major captivities are discussed below. As a people they dreamed of nationhood and longed to return. Zionism was alive among them. The fire of Judaism burned in their hearts. They could not continue living in a foreign land. As a people they would not assimilate. There were many who did. Despite punishing them there is no evidence that God gave them up totally. He never forgot his covenant with Abraham and his promise of LAND, TORAH, and MESSIAH. Every return was motivated and driven by Zionist efforts.

1. The Return from Egypt:

The great deliverance of Israel from slavery in Egypt shows God's great love for his people. It is awesome to consider the way God led them out. The Moses-inspired majority of them longed for freedom from slavery. Their suffering had reached to high heaven and God repented of ignoring them for so long. God waited for Moses. Moses was a remarkable man and considered the greatest of the prophets in Israel till the Messiah. He laid the foundation for the permanence of the Jewish state despite the interruptions that would occur in the future. Moses gave them the resilience and desire to return. There is no doubt that he battled anti-Zionist detractors in order to motivate his people to leave Egypt. He left them a template and if they departed from it there would be suffering. They can be in trouble again today if they ignore the template.

The manner in which the Israelites exited from Egypt was dramatic. The plagues were inflicted on Pharaoh and his nation as a punishment for the ill treatment of Israel[104]. Look at the great lessons that Israel was taught. Look at the great and dramatic night of the flight from Egypt. They were packed and ready to leave. They left behind all the nonessentials. They 'borrowed' golden jewellery from the Egyptians, which God allowed them as a small token payment for all the hard years of labour. The most massive event was the Passover Feast. They ate it standing up with shoes on their feet, ready to leave. They ate roast lamb, unleavened bread and bitter herbs. The roast lamb was from the burnt offering for their sins and in thankfulness as a sweet savour to God. The blood of that lamb was sprinkled on the doorposts and lintels of their dwellings. This was a sign to be recognized by the Angel of Death as he passed by: "I will pass over you when I see the blood"[105]. Here was the great foreshadowing of the Messiah whose shed blood for their sins provided eternal deliverance. Here was the great deliverance from slavery and sin in their lives. The Angel of Death passed by at midnight and seeing the blood on the entrances of their houses spared their firstborn. But the Egyptians firstborn were all destroyed. There was no saving blood on their houses. Picture the streaming of the Israelites out of their homes toward the Red Sea after Pharaoh gave the command for them to leave. Watch the dramatic pursuit by the armies of Pharaoh after he changed his mind. Watch the crossing of the Red Sea and the drowning of the Egyptian Army[106].

How marvellous were the pillar of cloud by day and fire by night as God protected his chosen prize[107]! See the manna fall from heaven that nourished them in the desert[108]. Behold the water flow from the rock to quench their thirst[109]. How marvellous the protection God provided for the care of his beloved people!

Israelis see a modern day parallel in the conduct and outcome of the 1967 Six Day War when God delivered Israel from their surrounding enemies who had vowed to annihilate them. Witness the airplanes on the airfields of the enemies, all in flames from the pinpoint discomfiture inflicted by the Israeli Air Force. Israelis see a marvellous deliverance and victory.

Yet, after leading them out of slavery in Egypt, they were stiff-necked and God let their carcases fall in the desert in the forty years of wandering in the wilderness. Their complaining, idolatry and disregard for the Torah were the causes for their being barred from the Promised Land. How bad were they? Just look at Mount Sinai! While Moses was up on the mount receiving the most important document of the Torah, the Ten Commandments, they forced Aaron to melt their gold and make the golden calf, which they worshipped[110]. So great was their attachment to idols that God said to Moses: "Separate yourself from them and I will destroy them, and make of you a great nation". How angry was God? He was very, very angry. But Moses would have none of it. "If you do not save them, then blot me out with them" was his reply[111].

Is there a parallel today with modern Israel? Fifty percent of Israelis are secular Jews with no regard for Torah or Messiah. They are worshipping the golden calf of secularism, comfort, complacency, and neglect. There is need for a leader like Moses to turn them from their modern idolatry. Where is the prime minister who will call it as it is and declare the non-negotiables to both Israel and her enemies?

2. The Return from Assyria:

There was no return for the ten tribes who had been carried away by the Assyrians.

". . . Hoshea king of Israel . . . did evil in the sight of the Lord . . . . For so it was that the children of Israel had sinned against the Lord . . . . they built for themselves high places in all their cities . . . sacred pillars and wooden images on every high hill and every green tree . . . . they served idols . . . . Yet the Lord testified against Israel . . . saying: Turn from your evil ways and keep My commandments and My statutes according to the law which I commanded your fathers . . . ." Israel worshipped Baal. God allowed the king of Assyria to take Samaria and carry Israel away captive[112]. The king of Assyria then resettled Samaria with Babylonians[113]. The northern kingdom was lost. They chose not to return. There was no collective Zionism to stir their souls. They preferred assimilation. They ignored the Abrahamic Covenant. God clung tenaciously to Judah and Benjamin, still situated in the Homeland.

3. *The Return from Babylon:*

But Judah and Benjamin made troubles for themselves in their departure from Judaism. Jehoiakim, king of Judah did evil in the sight of the Lord[114]. God allowed Nebuchadnezzar, king of Babylon to make Jehoiakim his vassal. His son Jehoiachin did evil in the sight of the Lord. He was carried away captive to Babylon. Nebuchadnezzar made Zedekiah a puppet king in Judah. But he rebelled. The total rout of Judah was then accomplished, and the temple was destroyed. The valuables were taken. Daniel came into prominence during the Babylonian kings' reigns as well as in their Persian conquerors' times. Zionism became a powerful force in Babylon. Cyrus then conquered Babylon and was favoured by God[115]. Ezra was the great Zionist who took the leadership to motivate the return. The Book of Ezra chronicles the waves of the returns of Jews from Babylon. Jeremiah had prophesied of it[116]. Cyrus' declaration sounds as if he was a convert to Judaism:
"Thus says Cyrus king of Persia: All the kingdoms of the earth the Lord God of heaven has given me. And He has commanded me to build Him a house at Jerusalem, which is in Judah. Who is among you of all His people? May his God be with him, and let him go up to Jerusalem . . . and build the house of the Lord God of Israel (He is God), which is in Jerusalem. And whoever is left in any place where he dwells, let the men of his place help him with silver and gold, with goods and livestock, besides the freewill offerings for the house of God which is in Jerusalem"[117]. Cyrus was an enthusiastic fundraiser for Israel! Many articles of gold and silver of Solomon's temple were returned by Cyrus. There were large numbers of the tribe of Benjamin and the priestly class of the tribe of Levi in Babylon with the tribe of Judah. Many thousands returned to Jerusalem and the rebuilding of the temple took place[118]. The Babylonian Gemara likely went to Israel too, but it may not have been fully developed at this return.

Just as today there are many opponents of the return of the Jews to their homeland, there was fierce opposition then. These non-Jews succeeded in getting King Artaxerxes to cause a stoppage of the rebuilding until the reign of Darius, King of Persia. The Jews cited Cyrus' decree and Darius then issued a further decree: "Let it be done diligently". So the temple was completed and dedicated[119]. The issue of the taking of multiple wives from among the idolatrous pagans came up subsequently and under Ezra's influence intermarriage with unconverted idolaters was discontinued. Israel had a major penchant for idols[120]. We need the spirit of Zerubbabel and Ezra in Israel today. THE TEMPLE MUST BE REBUILT. The spirit of Isaiah, Haggai, and Zechariah are sadly missing in modern Israel.

4. The Return from the Worldwide Diaspora:

The Roman conquest and destruction of Israel in AD 70 resulted in a great slaughter and diaspora of the remnant to the ends of the earth. Over the centuries their resilience was seen in that almost in every city in every country there were enclaves of Jews, some very small but nonetheless strong. These enclaves were often hotbeds of reformation. It is amazing that destruction and persecution resulted in remnants of Jews who turned to their God and preserved the Torah by obedience to it. They were like "gold tried in the fire" where the dross was consumed away. Their perseverance and persistence were exceptional. They gave God more attention in an environment of persecution and exile than they had done in a comfortable living in the Promised Land. God was helping them and all the time wanting to bring them back. He wanted them back in the Promised Land to be a beacon to the world and he had a promise to keep, his promise to Abraham: "I will make your children as numerous as the stars of the firmament", and "in you shall all the nations of the earth be blessed". God smiled at the little groups of Jews scattered all over the earth and looked forward to the time that he would reunite them in the Land of their fathers, a land that they had possessed and lost. And so these groups of his people were prosperous beyond measure. They caused envy and jealousy. Some of them were wayward and left the worship of the true God. No one can accuse them of being a closed society. They lost a lot of their number to intermarriage and conversion to other religions. In exile some became godless. Because of their giftedness and hard work they became prominent and rich and philanthropic. They were good citizens despite being accused of exclusiveness. But assimilation was also devouring them. Some were exclusive in the worship of the true God, but it was an open and 'welcoming exclusiveness'. And despite being unable to return to their land they prospered often as 'little Israels' wherever they were prominent in numbers. They built synagogues all over the world and were a witness to the worship of the true God. They were always longing to return home to Israel, and many of them did. But there was also a extremism that set in and some rabbis became inbred with attention to the Talmud and loss of the Tanak as the true Torah. Others succumbed to secular assimilation.

The Israelites were harassed by many of the surrounding nations in their history. The prophets of Israel always pointed to their waywardness and the worship of idols as the causes of these upheavals. The message the prophets preached was that God was trying to reform them with such punishments.

The return of the diasporic Jews to their land over the last two thousand years is as follows:

1. Voluntary return: where through much hardship many managed to get back to the land of Israel.
2. State Ordered expulsion of Jews caused many of them to return: by England in 1290; by France in 1391; by Austria in 1421; and by Spain in 1492.
3. Zionism active between 1897-1948: Palestine was a part of the Ottoman Empire from the 16th to the 20th Century. By 1917 Zionism had given them a significant boost in numbers. The power of Zionism was remarkable.
4. The Aftermath of World War I: In 1917 Britain formulated The Balfour Declaration, which stated that Palestine was favoured as a home for the Jewish people. When World War I ended in 1918 the League of Nations assigned Britain a mandate for Palestine. As a result Jews entered Palestine but were restricted severely by the British. This continued till the onset of World War II. The return of the Jews incited the Arab Uprising of 1936-1939. Because of this Britain's Peel Commission recommended a two-state solution. But then World War II broke out.
5. World War II and its aftermath: The dynamics in Zionism affected the events during this period. Weizmann was active in Britain and Ben-Gurion was active in Palestine. Both made trips to the US during the War. Both leaders were preoccupied with the rescue of European Jews from Hitler and not very concerned at this time with statehood in Palestine. President Roosevelt's Evian Conference produced no protection. Both Zionist leaders were thwarted by Britain and the US. Weizmann continued to be very Anglophilic, even to the extent of envisioning a future state of Israel as a Dominion within

the British Commonwealth. Ben-Gurion faced the problems of the non-cooperative British in Palestine who were not implementing the Balfour Declaration. Despite the favourable attitude of Churchill the gates to Palestine for European Jews were kept shut by the British. Some 'illegal' entry continued. The British were ruthless in turning immigrant ships away. The Biltmore Conference in New York highlighted the problems, which then created a shift to Revisionisn within Zionism. But the major powers took no notice, being occupied with the conduct of the war. The US was protectionist at the time and it took Pearl Harbour to bring the Americans into the war. The catastrophe of the holocaust awakened American Jews who became much more active in support of Zionism and Jewish statehood in Palestine.

After the holocaust of the Jews by Adolf Hitler the United States of America supported a United Nations agreement to allow 100,000 Jews to immigrate to Palestine. But Britain refused to implement it. The Jewish Uprising of 1945-1948 resulted. The United Nations General Assembly passed a motion to create a two state settlement and ordered the British out. As the last British forces were leaving Palestine in 1948 David Ben-Gurion unilaterally declared the creation of the State of Israel. The tide was taken at the flood. The US and Russia recognised the State of Israel.

As of 2011 within the pre-1967 borders of Israel the Jewish population was 5,837,400 while the Israeli Arabs numbered 1,587,000[121]. The entire population of the West Bank in 2007 was 2,461,267, which included 267,000 Jews. The population of Gaza in 2007 was 1,551,859, the majority being Arab[122]. Population figures can be controversial.

The Golan Heights and the southern part of Syria including Damascus were taken from the Amorites and was a part of Solomon's kingdom. The Golan Heights were retained again from Syria in the 1967 Six Day War. The Yom Kippur War of 1973 witnessed another battle over the Golan Heights. The IDF was almost at the gates of Damascus in 1974, when the US brokered a ceasefire agreement between Israel and Syria. The exact current Arab population in the Golan Heights is not known, but is estimated to be small. There are 20,000 Israelis living in the Golan Heights as of 2007[123]. This number may have increased considerably since.

Today Israel is well established in The Promised Land and must diligently adhere to the resolve to fulfil the Abrahamic Covenant. They had slowly returned and occupied "in between space" in Palestine over the 2000 years of the diaspora[124]. But their numbers swelled after 1948. The resilience of Israel is unsurpassed by any other nation.

NOTES

[104] Exodus chapters 5-11: The ten plagues, the last being the slaying of the Egyptian firstborn by the Angel of Death

[105] Exodus chapter 12: ". . . On the 10th day of this first month every man shall take for himself a lamb . . . a lamb for a household . . . a lamb without blemish, a male of the first year . . . kill it at twilight . . . take of the blood and put it on the two doorposts and of the lintel of the house where they eat it . . . roasted in the fire, with unleavened bread and bitter herbs . . . And thus you shall eat it with a belt on your waist, your sandals on your feet, and your staff in your hand. So you shall eat in haste. It is the Lord's Passover. For I will pass through the land . . . and will strike all the firstborn . . . . And when I see the blood I will pass over you . . . . Therefore you shall observe this day throughout your generations as An everlasting ordinance . . . ."

[106] Exodus 14, 15 Pharaoh's pursuing armies drowned in the Red Sea

[107] Exodus 13:21; 14:19 Pillar of Fire and Pillar of Cloud

[108] Exodus chapter 16 Manna from heaven

[109] Exodus chapter 17 Water from the rock

[110] Exodus 32:1 "Now when the people saw that Moses delayed coming down from the mountain, the people gathered together to Aaron, and said to him: Come, make us gods that shall go before us . . . ."

[111] Exodus 32:7-14,32: "Yet now if you will forgive their sin—but if not I pray, blot me out of your book which you have written".

[112] 2Kings chapters 16 & 17.

[113] 2Kings 17:24

[114] 2kings 23:37

[115] Isaiah 44:28 "Who says of Cyrus 'He is My shepherd, and he shall perform all my sayings to Jerusalem you shall be built', and to the Temple 'Your foundation shall be laid".

[116] Jeremiah 25:11
Jeremiah 29:10-14

[117]   Ezra 1: 1-4

[118]   Ezra 1:5-11

[119]   Ezra chapter 6

[120]   Ezra chapter 10

[121]   See the 'Jewish Virtual Library' 2011.

[122]   The World Factbook and CIA population figures. Also see Wikipedia Population of Israel.

[123]   unrwa West Bank and Gaza Strip population census of 2007

[124]   Eichmann in Jerusalem—a Report on the Banality of Evil, by Hannah Arendt, page 263: "No State of Israel would ever have come into being if the Jewish people had not created and maintained its own specific in-between space throughout the long centuries of dispersion, that is prior to the seizure of its old territory". She is making this point in discussing the questioned jurisdiction of the Israeli court that tried Eichmann. It is a very valid description of Israel's survival during the darkest period of its history.

CHAPTER 13
JEWISH COMPREHENSION OF THE ABRAHAMIC COVENANT

The Tanak defines the Abrahamic Covenant. No extraneous opinion should be necessary. What shall we do with plurality of interpretations? The Tanak should interpret itself contextually and conceptually. If an opinion does not harmonize with all of the Tanak, that opinion should be discarded. The Tanak does not contradict itself. The question must be asked: is Messiah as defined by Moses in harmony with all other definitions of the Messiah, and do the descriptions of Messiah harmonize with all the other descriptions in the Tanak? Examination of the major religious groups in modern Israel and their understanding and alignment with the Abrahamic Covenant is enlightening. Thomas Friedman has much to offer in the understanding of this matter[125].

1. **The Secular Non-Observant Jews:** Living in Israel is the basic hallmark of their being Jewish. They possess the LAND for no particular reason other than that it was pioneered and is theirs because they retain it by conquest. They have nothing to say about the Abrahamic Covenant, and do not discuss TORAH or MESSIAH. They draw their security purely from the Israeli Army, a strong economy, and competent leaders. They are in the majority estimated at 50% of the Jewish population.

2. **The Religious Zionists** (modern Orthodox Jews) and the Abrahamic Covenant: Religious Zionism is highly pluralistic. They can be moderate and traditional basing their orientation in Messianic terms. The settling of the Land is a crucial step in bringing the Messiah. They support the secular state but their greater emphasis is on the synagogue. In summary, the Religious Zionists understand the Abrahamic Covenant in principle and correctly orient LAND, TORAH, and plans for the MESSIAH.

They have little if any definition of the Messiah and his role derived from the Tanak. They need to move to a unity of belief and action and seek alignment with all other religious Jews. The Religious Zionists constitute 30% of the Israeli population.

3. **The Messianic Zionists** and the Abrahamic Covenant: Again there is pluralism of beliefs in this group. Messianism is the dominant feature[126]. But some have moved to the impractical point where they reject all nationalistic ideas and actions[127]. This latter group could hardly qualify for a proper understanding of the Abrahamic Covenant where LAND, TORAH AND MESSIAH are intertwined. They seem to deny that there are explicit references to Messiah in the Tanak and rely on the Talmud. The Gush Emunim are much closer to the Abrahamic Covenant. They correctly understand the LAND deal in the Covenant and have acted with their settlements to prevent the ceding of Judea and Samaria (The West Bank). The LAND aspect is perceived as a necessary instrument for bringing the Messiah. They believe that if Abraham were alive today he would not cede a square inch of the Land conquered by Israel in the Six Day War. The Gush Emunim need a definition of function of the Messianic mission as portrayed in the Tanak. The Messianic Zionists constitute 5% of the population.

4. **The Haredim** (the ultra-Orthodox Jews) and the Abrahamic Covenant: They are correctly oriented as 'Observant Jews' taking the Torah 'seriously'. There are Hasidic and Lithuanian-Yeshiva streams or subsets. Written Torah (Tanak and Talmud) and Oral Torah (authoritative writings and pronouncements by influential scholars and rabbis) have usurped the sole place of Tanak. Together the Written and Oral Torah constitute Halacha, their guide for every detail of life. Some are very extreme, getting tied up in the minutiae. They totally despise secularism and make no plans to consolidate and defend the borders. They incorrectly treat the rebirth of Israel as only a religious event, and do not see the need for the IDF. It is true that every return from captivity has been of great religious significance, especially in the restoration of Jerusalem and the rebuilding of the Temple. It is lamentable that after 45 years since the 1967 borders were established the rebuilding of the Temple still has not taken place. Their aim of bringing back the religious fervour that existed in "yeshivas and rabbinic dynasties in the Jewish towns and ghettos of Eastern Europe . . . ." is extremely commendable[128]. But their extremism, which embraces slavishness to the Talmud is divisive. Their lack of desire and emotion for defending Israel by

not enlisting in the Armed Forces is grossly wrong. Supporting the defence of the security of Israel by the Armed Forces is vital. It is deplorable that they do not rise to defend Israel. In this they lack the understanding that the Abrahamic Covenant involves an intertwining of LAND, TORAH and MESSIAH. If there is no LAND and no Jerusalem, where will the Messiah reign? The Haredim correctly label the 50% secular Jewish segment as 'empty'. Thomas Friedman quotes the Haredim as saying: "Behold these empty secular Jews! In another generation they will realize that the Jews' return to their land is not a political act but a spiritual one. Forty years from now they will all be like us". This call by the Haredim is laudable. Here is an absolutely important call for reformation, a clarion call to secular Jews to forsake their idolatry and return to the worship of the one true God. But there is no virtue in the Haredim's non-support of the armed defence of Israel, which is absolutely necessary for the survival of Israel. Israel would not exist today if they had lost the Six Day War. And Israel is always only one lost war away from ceasing to exist. Despite their high degree of religious practice the Haredim do not clearly comprehend the role of the Messiah as outlined in the Tanak. They minimize the importance of LAND. They major in the expanded and "confused" Torah because of their dedication to the Talmud. They have no clear emphasis of MESSIAH despite believing the Messiah when he comes will usher in the glorious kingdom. The Haredim constitute 15% of the Israeli population.

5. **The Messianic Jews** and the Abrahamic Covenant: Messianic Judaism is composed of Jews practicing a religious Jewish lifestyle who believe that Yeshua of Nazareth is the Messiah of Israel[129]. The Tanak is used to provide the foundation of their faith and reason for their acceptance of Yeshua as the Messiah. Messianic Judaism is firmly based on the Abrahamic Covenant. They believe that the Abrahamic Covenant was renewed by Yeshua in fulfilment of Jeremiah 31:31-34 as a New Covenant with Abraham's descendants. Yeshua's death atoned for the sins of the Jews and the whole world. His resurrection and ascension to the right hand of God is their hope for the future. They look for his return to earth to rule from Jerusalem. Messianic Jews embrace the B'rit Hadasha for its information of the Gospels and Pauline writings[130]. If Christianity is defined as faith in the God of Israel and Jesus as the Messiah and Saviour of the world, Christians and Messianic Jews share core beliefs. Messianic Jews practice circumcision, Kosher and other rabbinic teachings that do not contradict the Tanak. They reject the idea that 'Rabbinic Judaism' is superior to the

Tanak. Messianic Jews do not carry the denominational baggage that Christians do. Messianic Jews embrace gentiles who believe the same as they do as per the Abrahamic Covenant, which promised to bless all the nations of the world through Abraham. Messianic Judaism therefore believes in LAND, TORAH, and based on their interpretation of the Tanak they embrace Yeshua of Nazareth as the MESSIAH. Messianic Judaism does not look for a 'yet to come' Messiah but believes he has already come and that he is coming again. They consider themselves a complete package. Yeshua is divine and human. Some believe that the incarnation and conception of Yeshua was not from earthly sperm and ovum but an implant from God, described as 'That Holy Thing'. Mary's was simply a surrogate womb. Yeshua lived a perfect life. Messianic Jews see their origin commencing with the Jewish disciples of Yeshua. The Passover and the Day of Atonement are observed as powerful celebrations of the efficacy of the Messiah. They are Sabbath keepers. There are reportedly 30,000 Messianic Jews living in Israel and about 500,000 worldwide. These do not include movements like 'Jews for Jesus', which are Christian in orientation.

6.   Friedman adds more groups. He applauds the religious orientation of **Reformist and Conservative Jews**, whose modern movements appear to have been spawned in the US. Some did exist in central and western Europe and were very active in Zionism. They do not take the Torah seriously despite paying homage to it. Their observance is lax. They have no expressed deep understanding of the Messiah based on the Tanak. The Abrahamic Covenant is not part of their motivation. Their Jewishness is very American and with the freedom and wealth in America they have not truly experienced the spirit of the 'European Yeshivas'. The majority see no mission to be relocated in Israel. They are happy in diaspora but take pleasure in Israel's accomplishments. They understand that their support for Israel is vital.

There are multiple other religious units probably best enumerated under Israeli political parties. These political parties are seen by some as a complicating issue, most having arisen from religious motivations. Thomas Friedman colourfully described the situation in Israel: "Nothing better dramatized the radically different Jewish trends that have grown in the Israeli hothouse in the last 40 years than the November 1988 national election campaign, which involved 27 different parties competing for 120 Knesset seats"[131]. The main three parties tentatively classified as 'secular' are Kadima, Likud and Labour.

The following is the list of 14 political parties who have Knesset seats[132]:

PARTY	LEADER	SEATS
Kadima	Tzipi Livni	28
Likud	Benjamin Netanyahu	27
Yisrael Beiteinu	Avigdar Lieberman	15
Labour Party	Eitan Cabel	8
Shas	Eli Yishai	11
Independence	Ehud Barak	5
United Torah Judaism	Yakov Litzman	5
United Arab List-Ta'al	Ibrahim Sarsur	4
National Union	Ya'akov Katz	4
Hadash	Mohammad Barakeh	4
New Movement-Meretz	Haim Oron	3
The Jewish Home	Daniel Hershkowitz	3
Balad	Jamal Zahalka	3

There are 27 other parties active today without Knesset representation. Since 1948, 92 other parties have existed with sometime representation in the Knesset. Some of these parties have merged with current parties. The religious penetration of politics is to be expected in Israel because they are a people with a connection with Abraham who had a mission from God, which is now their mission. It cannot be any other way in Israel. To consider Israel as a purely secular state is not possible. Israel's God-given mission must guide the state. But what disunity this pluralism has brought! What power is available by greater unity! The Talmud, which arose from "The Jewish Home in Exile"[133], provides many lessons and much discussion, but it is not at the sacred level of the Tanak, which should be the guiding light. The Tanak alone is Israel's Torah.

Recently a group called Humanistic Jews has been identified in America[134]. They have some roots in Zionism and their beginnings were the product of the Enlightenment. It is not clear whether this group is entirely atheistic. The group is seeking an identity without God and the Abrahamic Covenant. But they want to celebrate the high holidays. This is impossible and their enthusiasm is hollow. The good deeds people do are always laudable. There does not need to be a religious motivation for these good deeds. Humanity can shine by good deeds as God's creatures without their acknowledgement of God. But history cannot be ignored and in the case of Israel as a nation there is no 'religious' godless history. God is always imposing his plans in Jewish history. The Tanak contains that unmistakably.

Look again at the map of the Middle East. The tiny Judaistic state of Israel is miniscule when compared with the sea of Arabic and non Arabic Muslims surrounding it. If God had been made the centre of the Jewish cause by Palestinian and diasporic Jews, the Middle East should be immersed in Judaism. There is no proselytising zeal noted. It was the reason that Abraham was given the Promised Land. It was to propagate Torah and Messiah. Israel can still fulfil the Abrahamic Covenant but not through humanism. Secular Jews ignore or neglect their religious duties of worship. Humanistic Jews appear to deny God's existence. They declare they are "independent of supernatural authority". They are idolaters of their own machinations and want to remove the very foundation of the state of Israel.

To summarize, only religious Jews have any significant comprehension of the Abrahamic Covenant. They have some understanding of Land, Torah and Messiah. Some of the extreme right wing do not see the necessity of defending land and this is deplorable. They are more absorbed in the minutiae of a confused 'Torah'. But even more deplorable is the majority of Israelis who only have land in their comprehension and see only a secular state. Equally reprehensible is the majority of American Jewry who see a 'land for peace' solution but whose religious life is superficial and increasingly secular as they become more 'Americanized'. The number of synagogues in the US and their crowding for Passover and Yom Kippur services are no guarantee to their understanding of the Abrahamic Covenant. There is insufficient realization by them of the intricacies of Israel's security and the fact that Israel is only one lost war away from another slaughter and diaspora. American Jews live a secure but numbed life because they are under the safety of the 'greatest country' in the current world. Only God knows whether Israel will enter another two thousand years of diaspora after another lost war. Israel cannot risk that happening. Prevention is better than cure.

NOTES

[125] 'Beirut to Jerusalem' by Thomas Friedman: Chapter 12

[126] See 'My Jewish Learning' by Daniel Septimus

[127] 'Messianism, Zionism, and the State of Israel', by Chaim Waxman. Modern Judaism, Vol. 7, No. 2, May 1987

[128] See 'Beirut to Jerusalem' by Thomas Friedman page 287
See also 'Overturning the Haredi Draft Exemption is a Mistake' by Donniel Hartman who comments on the recent Supreme Court cancelling of the exemption. Published in Ha'aretz March 5th 2012

[129] See 'Congregation Shema Yisrael'
See also 'The Association of Messianic Congregations'

[130] innvista The Orthodox Jewish B'rit Hadasha, AFI International Publishers (1997) Tyndale House, Cambridge, UK

[131] 'Beirut to Jerusalem' by Thomas Friedman page 288.

[132] Party Registrar, Israel Ministry of Justice, cited by Wikipedia

[133] See Dr. Gerhard Falk, Professor of Sociology, Buffalo State University of New York.
See also Judaism 101: 'Torah' by Shirley Rich

[134] See 'Society for Humanistic Judaism' Humanistic High Holiday Celebrations

CHAPTER 14
THE PRIME MINISTERS
OF ISRAEL

Modern Israel was born as a democracy. In this chapter the prime ministers of Israel are sketched so as to emphasize their contributions and the significance of those contributions to the security of Israel. This is measured in their dedication to and preservation of the Abrahamic Covenant with God. These parameters are very simple. What did they do to guard the LAND, protect and magnify the TORAH, identify the MESSIAH and advance the Messiah's mission? Those were the factors promised to Abraham. The fulfilment of those parameters would result in the Children of Abraham becoming as the stars of the firmament and enabling the happiness of all nations.

The Prime Ministers are the leaders of modern Israel. They mostly were pioneers who came from the diaspora. They came out of dreadful persecution and deprivation. They were visionaries and brave souls. They had to fight local and international powers. But they considered the time was right and God was stirring and calling them out of two thousand years of extreme hardship and landlessness. They were responding to the deepest yearnings of the heart and mind, which were to return to their God-given homeland. They were naturally preoccupied with obtaining the LAND. For them the fight to regain the LAND was the toughest of the three elements of the Abrahamic Covenant. TORAH and MESSIANIC realisation are internal matters with universal importance that were still to come. Obtaining the LAND had to be their primary concern and they have had fantastic success. Nonetheless TORAH and MESSIANIC realisation are of massive significance. So it is of great concern that TORAH and MESSIAH are such confused and divisive issues. The ardent hope of Israel after the LAND is secured should be to embrace the true TORAH and MESSIAH. The future must provide similar visionaries and leaders as these great Prime Ministers who have given attention to securing Israel. Leaders of

TORAH and MESSIANIC hope must soon appear and wrest Israel from succumbing to the modern idolatry of indifference or on the other hand to the extremism of religious minutiae. Israel must focus on the worship of the one true God. He is a jealous God and is much more motivated than they have ever been to be in their embrace. They are the 'apple of his eye' and through them the benefits of deity are to flow to all mankind.

These Prime Ministers sketched are the life-blood of modern Israel. Religious Israelis consider that God personally culled them out of the diaspora after 2000 years of suffering. But there is more to achieve regarding Torah and Messianic expectation. People like Herzl, Weizmann, Nordau, Herbert Samuel, Brandeis and Jabotinsky laid the foundation and engineered the return. But David Ben-Gurion deserves the greatest credit for his initial massive effort in the founding of the modern State of Israel.

These are the briefest sketches of the talented and dedicated lives of Israel's prime ministers since 1948. There is danger of not doing them justice in the assessment of their contributions. Underestimation of their achievements is so easy with the superficial assessment. Trends in Israel were influenced by their attitudes and insights. There is a gross lack of appreciation and adoration in Israel for these prime ministers.

DAVID BEN-GURION: 1948-1954, 1956-1963 [135]

He was born in Plonsk, Poland in 1886 as David Green. He founded a Jewish Youth Group named 'Ezra'. He moved to Warsaw and joined the Poalei Zion Party and then emigrated to Palestine in 1906 at the age of twenty years. His life was motivated by his belief in the future of Israel. He became involved with Marxist-Zionist-Socialist politics. He changed his name to David Ben-Gurion in 1910. He studied Turkish in Salonika and law in Istanbul between 1911 and 1914 and then returned to Palestine. He was deported in 1915 by the Ottoman authorities and went to the US. From there he went to Britain, joined the Jewish Legion of the British Army and returned to Palestine. He formed two Israeli armed groups to consolidate and protect the Israeli community on the land. He encouraged Jewish immigration to Palestine. He joined and then led the left wing Mapai Party (Hebrew for Workers' Party) and unilaterally declared the creation of the State of Israel on the departure of the British Mandate in 1948. He became the first prime minister and Weizmann was installed as the first president of the State of Israel. These were massive accomplishments.

What had Ben-Gurion achieved? He had at this point a foothold in Palestine, which he called Israel and now had to defend that foothold in the ensuing Arab-Israeli War or War of Independence. At the end of that war the 1949 Armistice Agreement drew the boundaries of Israel. Two lines separated the territories occupied by Israel and the Arab Palestinians. The Blue Line separated Israel from Lebanon. The Green Line separated Israel from Gaza, which was under Egyptian rule. It also separated Israel from the West Bank, which included East Jerusalem, which contained the Old City. The West Bank was under Jordanian rule. In the north the Green Line separated it from Syria, which retained the Golan Heights. King Abdullah I of Jordan tried to make further final arrangements with Israel for his permanent annexation of the West Bank. King Abdullah I was assassinated by a Palestinian for these overtures.

At the subsequent Israeli election the Mapai Party won the most seats but not a majority. The runner-up party was the Mapam. So Ben-Gurion formed an alliance with several other parties to form government. Even at its beginning the political landscape of modern Israel was a mosaic. He formed an alliance with the United Religious Front Party, the Oriental Communities Party, the Sephardim, and the Democratic List of Nazareth to consolidate himself as Israel's Prime Minister. He formed the Israeli Defence Force, established a relationship with France's De Gaulle and sought reparations from West Germany's Konrad Adenaeur. Ben-Gurion retired to his Kibbutz in the Negev at the end of 1953 during which time Sharet, his foreign minister, became Prime Minister. But then he returned and was re-elected in 1955. He was involved with the British and French in the 1956 Sinai debacle and in securing the Straits of Tiran waterway to international shipping.

In June 1963 he resigned and was replaced by Levi Eshkol. He then left the Mapai Party and formed the Rafi Party, which won 10 seats in the Knesset in the ensuing election. But the new Rafi Party decided to join with Mapai and the Achdut Ha'avoda Party to form the Israeli Labour Party. Ben-Gurion then formed the Hamamlachtit Party, which won 4 seats in the 1969 election. He retired in 1970 and died in 1973. Ben-Gurion was a visionary and a strong leader. He saw his destiny as Jewish and he did not let anything obscure his desire to establish the State of Israel and the return of the diaspora to the homeland. His involvement in armed politics showed his resolve. His religious views however did not lead to any strength in the religious life of Israel or the magnification of the TORAH. But he understood the Abrahamic Covenant.

His effort was great in establishing a secular state, securing The LAND. He was the founding father of the modern State of Israel. In 1949 he settled for land he could get but in his wisdom he let the arrangements have a temporary flavour. The surrounding Arab nations and the Arab Palestinians at that point continued the goal of utterly destroying Israel. The United Nations Resolution 194 and the Lausanne Conference did not change anything. After 2000 years Israel was at last a nation.

MOSHE SHARET 1954-1955 [136]

He was born in the Ukraine and came to Israel at age 12 years. He attended the first Hebrew high school to be established in Israel in Tel Aviv, the Herzliya Gymnasium. He was fluent in Arabic and Turkish and took Ottoman citizenship. He was an interpreter in the Ottoman Army in World War I. He then studied law in Istanbul and economics in the London School of Economics in England. He returned to join the Mapai Party and became active with Ben-Gurion in similar politics in Palestine before the founding of modern Israel. He was Ben-Gurion's assistant in the Jewish Agency. He supported the United Nations partition plan and was one of the signatories of the Unilateral Declaration of the State of Israel in 1948. He was the first foreign minister of the new country. As prime minister for a short time he presented a weak front and Ben-Gurion easily returned subsequently to take control. He did nothing mentionable to improve Israel's spirituality. But that was not his specialty.

LEVI ESHKOL 1963-1969 [137]

Levi Eshkol was born in 1895 in the Ukraine and moved to Israel in 1914. He joined the Mapai Party. He fought in the British Army as a member of the Jewish Legion. He initiated the founding of several Kibbutzim. He helped to form the Israeli Labour Party. On being threatened by the Arab States he formed a national unity government in coalition with Menachem Begin's Herut Party. The year before the Six Day War saw an intense enmity between him and Ben-Gurion. He forged a solid relationship with the United States. He quietly strengthened the IDF in cooperation with Chief of the IDF Rabin during the time leading up to the Six Day War. His significant act was the choice of the charismatic and astute Moshe Dayan as the Defence Minister. In some quarters Eshkol is viewed as a hesitant prime minister who was more concerned with what the United States thought of him. But he did initiate the pre-emptive strike that won the 1967 Six Day War. Israelis consider this a demonstration of the mighty hand of God in confounding their enemies. He was concerned with the establishment and strengthening of the secular state. But the current borders of Israel, carved out in 1967 was his reclamation of the LAND, closer to the blueprint, and are the current borders of the State of Israel. He made a significant speech to the Knesset:

> "... The Arabic-speaking States extend over an area of eleven and a half million square kilometres, and generally speaking are thinly populated. The four Arab States which have borders with us alone extend over an area of one million two hundred thousand square kilometres, and Israel has only a sixtieth part of the area in its possession, in other words, slightly more than 1.5 percent—twenty one thousand square kilometres. In this situation, there is neither sense nor justice in territorial changes to Israel's disadvantage, and there exists neither power nor possibility, juridical or practical, to carry them out. And this without saying a word on the fundamental and natural historic rights of the Jewish people to its Land, to its only Homeland, from which it was expelled by brute force".

This was a realistic evaluation. Following the occupation of the Sinai after the 1967 Six Day War, Nasser initiated the War of Attrition to try to get it back. That war came to an end in Golda Meir's tenure and she retained the Sinai for Israel.

GOLDA MEIR 1969-1974 [138]
Golda was born in the Ukraine in 1898. She migrated to the US with her family in 1916. As a youth she embraced socialist Zionism. She married Meyerson and they both went to live on a Kibbutz in Jezreel in 1921. Subsequently they settled in Jerusalem. She returned to the US to represent the Moetzet HaPoalet between 1932-1934. In 1938 she attended Franklin D Roosevelt's Evian Conference on the Jewish Refugees fleeing Nazi persecution. In 1946 she became head of the Political Department of the Jewish Agency. In early 1948 she paid a short visit to the US during which she raised $50 million in aid of the Jews in Palestine. This was a massive amount for that time. On 14th May 1948 she was one of the 24 signatories to the Unilateral Declaration of Independence. Carrying the first Israel-issued passport she was appointed as Israel's first ambassador to the Soviet Union. But she returned in 1949 and

was elected to the Knesset and served first as Minister of Labour and then as Foreign Minister. When Levi Eshkol died in 1969 she became Prime Minister. Soon after she organized the coalition of the Mapai, Rafi, and Ahdut Ha'Avoda parties to form the new Israeli Labour Party. She ended the War of Attrition with Egypt on the initiation of the US. That war was designed by Egypt to reclaim the Sinai but it did not succeed. Following the Munich Olympic massacre of the Israeli Team by the Black September and Popular Front for the Liberation of Palestine, she ordered the Mossad to hunt them down and assassinate them.

The Yom Kipper War occurred on her watch and Israel was somewhat unprepared for it. The Yom Kipper War was a setback at first in its early days, but then the Israeli Defence Forces pursued the Egyptians almost to Cairo, and the Syrians to a short distance from Damascus. Following a decisive victory she won the next election but resigned as Prime Minister. She was sick. Four years later she died of lymphatic cancer. Yitzhak Rabin succeeded her.

YITZHAK RABIN 1974-1976, 1992-1995 [139]

Rabin was born in Jerusalem in 1922. He graduated from an agricultural college with distinction. He then joined the 'Palmach', the elite military unit of the Haganah. During Israel's War of Independence he led the Harel Brigade. He next served with the Israeli Defence Forces (IDF), progressing to Chief of Staff. He commanded the IDF during the 1967 Six Day War. After the war he served as Ambassador to the United States. He returned to Israel in 1973 and was elected to the Knesset as a member of the Labour Party. He became Minister for Labour in Golda Meir's government. In 1974 at her resignation he became Prime Minister. He then took significant steps to improve the economy. He solved social problems and reinforced the IDF. He initiated measures to make peace with Egypt and Syria, which led to the Camp David Accords of 1978. His party lost the election in 1977 and he was active in opposition. In the National Unity Government which tenured from 1984-1990 he served as Minister of Defence. In the June 1992 election he led the Labour Party to victory and again became Prime Minister. In addition he took the portfolios of Religious Affairs, Social Affairs and Labour.

He wrote three books: A biographical sketch titled 'Service Notebook' in 1979; a book on Lebanon titled 'Peace for Galilee' in 1983; and his autobiography titled 'The Nobel Lectures' in 1995, having been awarded the Nobel Peace Prize for his efforts in the Oslo Accords.

Rabin took a leading role in the Oslo Accords. He adopted strong measures against offending Palestinians during the first Intifada. On September 9th 1993 Rabin received a letter from Yasser Arafat renouncing violence and officially recognizing Israel. On that same day he replied officially recognizing the Palestine Liberation Organization. Rabin signed the Israeli-Jordan Peace Treaty in 1994. Rabin's consent to the Oslo Accords earned him a Nobel Peace Prize, but created much opposition from Israelis and American Jewry. Rabin was assassinated by a rightwing Orthodox Jew, Yigal Amir, on November 12th 1995.

In assessing Rabin's tenures as Prime Minister he is viewed as a man of compromise. His planned achievement of peace by acquiescing land in the Oslo Accords was not popular in Israel. Outside Israel he was hailed for it. He held the Portfolio for Religious Affairs but was viewed as the most a-religious Prime Minister of Israel to his time. A motion of non-confidence was brought to the Knesset in 1977 over a national breach of the Sabbath on an Israeli Air Force Base when delivery of four F15 jets from the US occurred. This and other factors led to his dissolving his government and holding a new election. Compromising TORAH (Sabbath breaking) and ceding LAND are generally anathema in Israel.

MENACHEM BEGIN 1977-1983 [140]
Begin was born in Poland in 1913. At the age of sixteen he joined the Zionist Movement. He graduated with a law degree from Warsaw University in 1935. In 1932 he became the head of the Organization Department of Betar for Poland, and then for Czechoslovakia. He was arrested and imprisoned for demonstrating outside the British Legation in Warsaw over British policy in Palestine. He organized and facilitated 'illegal' immigration to Palestine. He was arrested by Russian authorities and sent to a concentration camp in Siberia but was subsequently released under the terms of the Stalin-Sikorski Agreement. On return to Poland he joined the Polish Army and was sent to the Middle East ending up in Palestine. Once there he took command of the clandestine National Military Organization called the 'Etzel' directing its operations against the British. The British Administration in Palestine offered

a reward of 10,000 English Pounds for his capture but he evaded them by living in disguise in Tel Aviv.

After the Unilateral Declaration of the State of Israel in 1948 he founded the Herut Movement and in the first elections held he was elected to the Knesset. From 1967-1970 he served as Minister without Portfolio in the National Unity Government. His activity in the Likud Party while in opposition culminated in the landslide victory of 1977 when he became Prime Minister. This victory signalled a fundamental restructuring of Israeli society in which the founding socialist Ashkenazi elite were being replaced by a coalition representing the marginalized Mizrahi, and Jewish religious communities who were more religious than the eastern European Jewish immigrants. Begin promoted a socially conservative and economically liberal agenda. He was very astute in comprehending the ramifications of his decisions.

The Peace Treaty he achieved with Anwar Sadat in 1979 leading to the return of the Sinai to Egypt won him the Nobel Peace Prize.

He authorized the bombing of the Osirak nuclear plant in Iraq. He also sent the IDF into Lebanon to knock out the harassment the Arab Palestinians there were inflicting on Israel. This resulted in the IDF being mired in Lebanon, and the Israeli economy suffered greatly. He resigned in 1983.

His involvement with the formation of Israel was intense. In the early days of struggle he served two prison sentences for his clandestine activities in restoring Land. As Prime Minister he relinquished power when he perceived his efforts were waning. His leadership in Israel was exemplary.

YITZHAK SHAMIR 1983-1984, 1986-1992 [141]
He was born in Ruzhany, Belarus in 1915. He was sent to Hebrew high school in Poland. He joined Betar, the Revisionist Zionist youth movement there. He started studying Law at Warsaw University but left to emigrate to Palestine in 1935. He joined the Irgun Zvai Leumi, an underground Jewish Militia and was captured and imprisoned by the British for these activities. He escaped in 1942 but was recaptured and interned in a camp in North Africa. In 1948 he was allowed back after the Unilateral Declaration of the State of Israel. He became active again in the Lehi, the militant faction of the Irgun Zvai Leumi. Lehi was disbanded after the killing of the United Nations representative, Count Folke

Bernadotte. He was active in the War of Independence. He joined Mossad and served from 1955-1965. He joined the Herut Party in 1969 but was elected to the Knesset as a Likud Member in 1973. He became Foreign Minister in Menachem Begin's Government in 1980 and succeeded him as Prime Minister when Begin resigned. He neglected the economy and lost the next election in 1984 when a National Unity Government was formed. As prearranged he served as Prime Minister in that government from 1986-1988. He was re-elected in the 1988 election and remained Prime Minister till 1992.

The First Gulf War occurred during his tenure when Iraqi Scud Missiles rained on Israel, but the United States prevented him from retaliating. He brought the Ethiopian Jews to Israel. He initially opposed the Madrid Peace talks but then reluctantly joined them and as a result lost the next election to Yitzhak Rabin in 1992. Benjamin Netanyahu succeeded Shamir as Likud leader in 1993.

His autobiography titled 'Summing Up' was published in 1994.

SHIMON PERES 1984-1986 [142]
He was born in Poland in 1923. His family migrated to Israel in 1932. His education in Tel Aviv preceded his several years on Kibbutz Geva. Later he founded Kibbutz Alumot. He describes his early youth as an ardent Haredi. He once smashed the family radio when he apprehended his parents listening to it on the Sabbath. In 1946 he joined the Haganah, which was the predecessor of the Israeli Defence Forces and was responsible for personnel recruitment and arms purchases. He became Deputy Director-General of the Ministry of Defence in 1952, and Director-General from 1953-1959. He was elected to the Knesset as a member of Mapai in 1959 and was Deputy Minister of Defence from 1959-1965. In 1965 he left Mapai with Ben-Gurion to form the Rafi Party. In 1968 he brought the Rafi Party back to Mapai in order to form the Israel Labour Party. In the Labour Party he became Minister for Immigrant Absorption in 1969 and then served as Minister of Transport and Communications from 1970-1974. He served as Minister of Defence from 1974-1977. In 1977 he was elected to the Chairmanship of the Labour Alignment.

In 1984 he became Prime Minister in the National Unity Government serving till 1986 and then as its Deputy Prime Minister and Minister of Foreign Affairs.

During his term as Prime Minister he implemented an important economic stabilization plan and withdrew Israeli troops from Lebanon.

In the National Unity Government of 1988-1990 he served as Deputy Prime Minister and Minister of Finance. From 1990-1992 he was Leader of the Opposition in the Knesset. When the Labour Government regained power in July 1992 he became Minister of Foreign Affairs.

He is currently the President of Israel and is well regarded internationally.

He has authored several books: The Next Step (1965); David's Sling (1970); And Now Tomorrow (1978); From These Men (1979); Entebbe Diary (1991); The Middle East (1993); and Battling For Peace (1995).

He was awarded the Nobel Peace Prize with Yitzhak Rabin for his efforts in the Oslo Accords.

Assessing his tenure he is attributed with capitulation in the proposal to cede LAND. His ardour as a Haredi changed into a great desire to attain peace by ceding land. His religious enthusiasm faded into neglect of the TORAH.

BENJAMIN NETANYAHU 1996-1999, 2009-Present [143]

Netanyahu was born in Tel Aviv in 1949 and grew up in Jerusalem. He attended high school in the United States since his father was doing research there. On returning to Israel he enlisted in the Israel Defence Forces and rose to the rank of captain during the Yom Kippur War. He then resumed study in the US obtaining BSc (architecture) and MSc (business administration) degrees in the Massachusetts Institute of Technology besides doing courses in political science at MIT and Harvard University.

Subsequently he worked in the private sector in the US but also became active against international terrorism. US Secretary of State George Schultz credited Netanyahu with influencing American Foreign Policy against Terrorism. In 1982 he became deputy ambassador in the Israeli Embassy in Washington DC. He served as Israeli Ambassador to the United Nations between 1984-1988. He returned to Israel and was elected to the Knesset in 1988 from the Likud Party. He was an active participant in the Madrid Peace Talks. He became Chairman of Likud in 1993 and Prime Minister in 1996. During his tenure he implemented a policy against terrorism, liberalised foreign currency regulations, privatised government owned companies, reduced budget deficit and brought in billions of dollars of foreign investment. He refused to cede land for peace in the negotiations with the Arab Palestinians under Clinton's auspices. He left politics after defeat by Ehud Barak in the 1999 election but returned in 2002 as Minister of Foreign Affairs and in 2003 as Minister of Finance in the Ariel Sharon Government. In this capacity he was responsible for the significant growth of the Israeli economy.

He formed government again as Prime Minister after the 2009 election and currently continues in office. He is in a great tussle at present to maintain the post 1967 borders. His current dilemma will be taken up again in a later chapter.

EHUD BARAK 1999-2001 [144]
Barak was born in 1942 on a kibbutz founded by his father, an immigrant who came from Lithuania in 1932. He joined the IDF in 1959 commanding battles in the Six Day and Yom Kippur Wars. Eventually he rose to Chief of General Staff of the IDF. He was awarded many decorations for his valour. His education along the way was a BSc in physics and mathematics from the Hebrew University and a MSc in economics from Stanford University. He was appointed Minister of Internal Affairs in the Yitzhak Rabin Government in 1995 and went on to serve as Minister of Foreign Affairs for 1995 and 1996. He was elected to the Knesset in 1996 becoming leader of the Labour Party. He became Prime Minister in 1999. He was responsible for Israel's withdrawal in 2000 from the 22-year occupation of Southern Lebanon. Skirmishes with Hezbollah followed resulting in the kidnapping and killing of three Israeli soldiers. His tenure as Prime Minister was not considered as successful. He lost the leadership of the Labour Party and left politics.

However he returned on several occasions to contest the leadership and eventually regained it in 2007. He became Minister of Defence in Olmert's cabinet in 2007. The war with Hezbollah occurred in 2006 and the Winograd Commission was appointed to assess that war which it assessed as poorly conducted. Elections and the Netanyahu Coalition Government followed in which Barak continues as Defence Minister.

ARIEL SHARON 2001-2006 [145]

Sharon was born in Kfar Malal in central Israel in 1928. He joined Haganah at the age of 14 years in 1942 and fought in the 1948 War of Independence. Later he obtained a law degree from the Hebrew University of Jerusalem. He commanded divisions in the IDF in the 1956 Sinai Campaign, the 1967 Six Day War, and the Yom Kippur War. He was elected to the Knesset in December 1973 but resigned after a year to become security adviser to Prime Minister Yitzhak Rabin. He was re-elected to the Knesset in 1977 for the Shlomzin Party but then joined the Herut Party and became Minister of Agriculture in Menachem Begin's government. In 1981 he was appointed Minister of Defence but resigned in 1983. He was blamed for The Sabra and Shatila Palestinian Refugee Camp Massacres by the Lebanese Phalangists, which occurred on his watch. He remained as Minister without Portfolio and then as Minister of Industry and Trade 1984-1990. In this capacity he concluded the Free Trade Agreement with the US. He was Minister for Construction, Housing, and Immigrant Absorption 1990-1992. He was Minister for National Infrastructure in the Netanyahu Government and fostered joint ventures with Jordan, Egypt, the Arab Palestinians and the Bedouins. In 1998 he became Foreign Minister. He became Chairman of Likud in 1999 when Netanyahu resigned.

On September 28th, 2000 he visited the Temple Mount, where the al-Aqsa Mosque is located. He did this with the permission of Israel's Minister of Internal Security, Shlomo Ben-Ami and Palestinian Security Chief Jabril Rajoub. He was there for 34 minutes during tourist visitation hours. The Palestinians used Sharon's visit as an excuse for the commencement of the al-Aqsa Intifada. The US Mitchell Report after an independent investigation of the matter in 2001 cleared the Sharon visit as being causative.

On February 6th 2001 Sharon was elected Prime Minister, which coincided with George W. Bush's election. He adopted the Bush 'Road Map for Peace' but it failed. To counter violence against Israel he built the wall. He then unilaterally dismantled all Jewish settlements in the Gaza Strip and removed Israeli troops from inside Gaza as well. This unilateral withdrawal has been termed 'Sharon's Folly'. It strengthened Hamas. The Likud Party split because of the Gaza disengagement so Sharon resigned and formed the Kadima Party on November 21st 2006.

He suffered a massive stroke and Ehud Olmert took over, called a new election, which he won and became Prime Minister.

EHUD OLMERT 2006-2008 [146]

Olmert was born in 1945 in Binyamina, Palestine. His parents had come to Israel from China where they had fled from persecution in the Ukraine and Russia. As a youth he joined the Betar Organization. He graduated from the Hebrew University in Jerusalem with degrees in psychology, philosophy, and law. He then joined the IDF but was injured and later completed his service as a journalist, notably in the headquarters of Ariel Sharon during the Yom Kippur War. He was elected to the Knesset in 1973 and served as Minister without Portfolio and Minister of Health 1990-1992 in the Shamir Government. He was Mayor of Jerusalem 1993-2003 paying attention to education, and road and rail infrastructure and transportation. In 2003 he was again elected to the Knesset and served as Minister of Industry, Trade and Labour, and then Minister of Communications and Minister of Finance. He originally opposed any change of the post 1967 borders but agreed with the Sharon unilateral pullout of the Gaza. When Sharon left Likud to form Kadima, Olmert went with him.

He replaced Sharon following his massive stroke and became Prime Minister after the 2006 election.

As Prime Minister he declared he would make "painful concessions" to achieve peace with the Arab Palestinians. So had Sharon. He used the Annapolis Conference of November 27th 2007 to articulate his acceptance of a two-state solution in the presence of the United Nations, the US, the European Union and the PLO. Hamas and their backer Iran vehemently opposed the tenets of the Annapolis Conference. They vowed annihilation of Israel. Annapolis was opposed as well by Arab Palestinians in the West Bank and by American Jewry and the religious right in Israel. There was opposition in Israel to any division of Jerusalem. Hamas in Gaza began raining rockets into Israel and Israel responded by invading Gaza. There was destruction and a loss of life. Both sides responded to a US requested ceasefire. Olmert resigned subsequently and new elections brought Netanyahu to power.

✦ ✦ ✦ ✦ ✦

To summarize: The reactions of the Israeli population to the various decisions of the Prime Ministers concerning LAND, TORAH and the MESSIANIC hope are important. Most of their decision-making concerned LAND. Ben-Gurion ended his tenure with the massive achievement of the State of Israel. He thought that his new state would have the borders as described by UN resolution 194. Instead the Green Line was better territorially. There was no change during Sharet's tenure. Ashkol's Six Day War in 1967 gave Israel Gaza, the West Bank, the Golan Heights and the Sinai. Golda Meir retained the Sinai in the War of Attrition. It was viewed as useful to secure a Peace Treaty with Egypt. Giving it away was not popular with the Israeli population, but Rabin's Camp David Accords made the Sadat gestures very popular. Rabin's involvement with the Oslo Accords was unpopular with Israelis and eventually cost him his life, although it won him and Peres the Nobel Peace Prize. Begin's embrace of the Mizrahi and other religious communities marginalized by the Ashkenazi elite was notable. Shamir lost an election over his cooperation with the Madrid Peace Talks indicating again that giving away land was not popular. In his first tenure as Prime Minister Netanyahu became involved with the Madrid Peace Talks as well but he left office before anything eventuated from it. Barak was a great general but not a great Prime Minister. Management of his skirmishes with the Hezbollah and the loss of the lives of the three Israeli soldiers made him unpopular.

Sharon made a great and memorable visit to the Temple Mount. This magnified the Temple Mount as the holiest site of the Jews and emphasized anew its ownership by Israel. The religious communities in Israel rejoiced over it although it allegedly 'started' the al-Aqsa Intifada. But his dismantling of Jewish settlements in Gaza and making a unilateral withdrawal of the IDF from Gaza were not popular. His adoption of the 'Road Map' for peace would have had him compromise the 1967 borders. Olmert's involvement with the Annapolis Conference would have destroyed his reputation in Israel as he promised to make significant concessions. But the war with Hamas was a major problem and distraction for Israel. Events led to his resignation.

The entire Prime Ministerial history of modern Israel has been completely preoccupied by LAND. The only significant religious event was the Temple Mount visit by Ariel Sharon. This was the only link with TORAH as it was the site of Solomon's Temple. It also linked with the promise of the MESSIAH with Abraham's symbolic offering up of Isaac on Mount Moriah, the Temple Mount.

There is still a major preoccupation of Israel's energies with LAND. Netanyahu's current government wrestles with it. Israel remains bombarded by the UN, US, EU, and the Arab world for another two state settlement.

NOTES

[135] bio.TRUESTORY David Ben-Gurion (David Green) Biography
See also 'David Ben-Gurion' by Michael Bar Zohar in Encyclopedia Brittanica.
He retired to Bible study at Sde-Boqer Kibbutz in the Negev.

[136] See Israel's Ministry of Foreign Affairs—Moshe Sharett Zionism and Israel—Biographies: Biography of Moshe Sharett

[137] AzureONLINE Azure No. 44 Spring 5771/2011 'Levi Eshkol, Forgotten Hero' by Michael B. Oren Israel Ministry of Foreign Affairs: Israel's Story in Maps
See Zionism and Israel-Biographies: Biography-Levi Eshkol
See also Jewish Virtual Library: 'The Israeli Peace Plan of Levi Eshkol
See also '1967' by Tom Segev, 2008 by Abacus

[138] See Encyclopedia of World Biography—'Golda Meir-Biography'
Jewish Virtual Library—Golda Meir
About.com.Judaism: 'Golda Meir' by Lisa Katz

[139] Jewish Virtual Library—Yitzhak Rabin
Ibid: A Flawed Portrait of Yitzhak Rabin by D. Kurzman
Israel Ministry of Foreign Affairs—Yitzhak Rabin
Famous People—'Yitzhak Rabin'
See also the Official Website of the Nobel Prize

[140] See Encyclopedia Brittanica eb.com 'Menachem Begin'
Nobelprize.org—Menachem Begin-Biography
Menachem Begin Heritage Centre
See 'The Iron Wall' by Avi Shlaim
See also Wikipedia: 'Menachem Begin'

141   Answers.com: Yitzhak Shamir
       'Israel: Land of Tradition and Conflict' by Bernard Reich Encyclopedia.com:
       Yitzhak Shamir
       Shamir Autobiography: 'Summing Up'
       See Wikipedia 'Yitzak Shamir'

142   Academy of Achievement: Shimon Peres Biography
       Nobelprize.org: The Nobel Peace Prize 1994
       Wikipedia: Shimon Peres

143   biography.com: Benjamin Netanyahu Biography
       See 'A Durable Peace: Israel and its place among Nations 1992 by Ben Net
       International Terrorism: Challenge and Response-editor, 1979
       Wikipedia: Benjamin Netanyahu
       See Website of Citizens for Netanyahu

144   Academy of Achievement: Ehud Barak
       Wikipedia: Ehud Barak

145   Life Story/A Biography: Ariel Sharon
       Infoplease: Ariel Sharon—Soldier/Prime Minister of Israel
       MidEastWeb: Biography-Ariel Sharon, Prime Minister of Israel
       See also Jewish Virtual Library

146   About.com Judaism: Ehud Olmert
       Political Biography: Ehud Olmert, The State of Israel
       See Danielpipes.org: Middle East Quarterly December 1997 Interview With
       Ehud Olmert

PART III
PALESTINIAN ARAB HISTORY

As Christians and professed Spiritual Jews Seventh-day Adventists have shown a zeal for proselytising that is enormous. My Jewish aunt Ellen Sophia La Faber was descended from French Jews who had come to India for trade and commerce. They settled there for generations, mixing with the Nasrani Sabbath-keeping Indian Christians who traced their Christianity to St. Thomas, the disciple of Jesus. Obviously they had strayed from their Jewish heritage when they embraced Nasrani Syrian Christianity. Ellen's grandparents had settled in Sri Lanka and were quite wealthy. But she was looking for more than prosperity. The desire for excitement and mission in her life drove her to embrace Seventh-day Adventism and its tenacious proselytising fervour. Despite identifying herself as a physical Jew she became a 'Spiritual Jew'. She saw no contradiction. She embraced the very admirable 'refined' SDA value system that every human is highly prized by God. (It took SDAs awhile to arrive at this viewpoint having previously expressed 'amalgamation' ideas and the 'heathen shall be as they had not been' in God's reckoning). This is no ordinary philosophical stance. The value of a human has an extremely rich and strong foundation. Current Israeli opinion is that it was worthwhile that over a thousand prisoners were given in exchange for Gilad Shalit. The story of Abraham raising an army just to rescue his renegade nephew Lot is cited. Lot it seemed was not worth the trouble, since he had compromised himself by living in wicked Sodom. Shalit had made no such compromise. But underneath all the finite examples of humanity going to the rescue was God's sacrifice of his son to redeem mankind. This idea puts an infinite price deity is willing to pay for one human. God's promise of Messiah is a promise that deity wants to rescue all mankind. The sacrifice of Isaac by Abraham was the ultimate and shocking demonstration of the price God is willing to pay. Ellen Sophia La Faber's proselytising zeal knew no bounds. She poured her wealth into the fledgling SDA Church in Sri Lanka. She found this more exciting than the lack of proselytising in the Judaism she abandoned. The reason that I describe this is that there is lacking in the combined Jewish psyche a desire to proselytise. It should be stronger than the desire to aliya. Religious Jews hold the conviction that their belief system is the correct one. I am guilty of this stance as well. But there is no compulsion that drives Jews to proselytise. Their attitude is: "I have something good and if you like it you are welcome to check it out". Their attitude should be: "I have something good and I am here to convince you to share this compelling and satisfying happiness with me". As a religious entity and as a nation Israel has failed to do this. The Abrahamic Covenant demands that all nations find blessedness in what Jews have to offer. The road back to the Edenic perfect state is through Torah and Messiah. But Israel feels no compulsion to share it.

The majority of the Christian world takes proselytising very seriously. Their reason is that they have salvific efficacy to offer. There is a perception that all non-Christians need conversion. There is a perception among SDAs that Israel has failed miserably at its God-given mission of propagating Torah and Messiah. If Israel had not failed, perhaps the whole of the Middle East would have been converted to Judaism.

Throughout Christendom there is widespread sympathy for the current plight of the Jews who are seen as threatened again by annihilation by elements of extreme Islamic Jihad. Overt demonstration of this sympathy from the Southern US Protestant Movement is noted. Guilt also lingers in the conscience of the Christian world that they showed little sympathy during the Nazi Holocaust and could have done much more to prevent it. I believe this to be true. Despite this widespread sympathy for Jews and the desire to preserve them as a nation, there is also widespread sympathy for the plight of the Arab Palestinians who have been displaced. Christians generally feel very strongly that the Jews have a right to be there ahead of the Arab Palestinians. Israel is viewed as having the 'Super Story'. But some kind of accommodation of the Arab Palestinians is desired so as to address their plight. This may be akin to the anxiety existing in some of the minds of secular American Jews. Christians are also very aware of the extremism of Islamic Jihad and their own vulnerability to Islamic terrorism. The killing of Coptic Christians in Egypt has not helped the Moslem world. Nonetheless Christian humanitarianism is more awake now than during the Nazi Holocaust. An appeal is being made for Israel to show more pragmatism. But this should not be at the risk of the security of Israel.

The Jewish loss of their homeland as a nation occurred in AD 70. A remnant of the poor Jews remained in Canaan; those who could not leave persevered. Those who escaped wandered to the far corners of the earth. Persecution and loss of their homeland brought out the best in them and they remembered their God. Many slowly trickled back. The Arabs came after about AD 670 and coexisted with those Jews. Life went on happily between the two communities. Neither community made an attempt to form a national identity. And then with the rise of Zionism and World Wars I & II, and their aftermath, a great influx of Jews occurred into Palestine. Instead of accommodating Israel the Arab Palestinians and the surrounding Arab States decided to crush the rise of a Jewish State. Wars have taken place ever since with Israel in the ascendancy. The plight of the Arab Palestinians deserves sympathy but their leaders have not been helpful in coming to a settlement with Israelis who are now firmly ensconced in their own ancestral homeland. It is true the Arab Palestinians have been there for centuries, but the Jews have been there for four thousand years. It is hoped that a settlement will soon be reached. Part III is an attempt to describe the Arab Palestinian presence and the difficult demands being made by their leaders and extremist factions. The friction is more than palpable.

CHAPTER 15

THE STRUGGLE BETWEEN THE
JEWS AND
THE ARABS IN PALESTINE

A summary of the history of Israel is important as a preamble. It is necessary as an establishment of the historic existence and claim Israel has to Palestine, which predates the Arab claims. After the 'David—Solomon' zenith in their nationhood a downhill course followed. The idolatrous heathen tribes in Canaan had been despatched in the time of King David. They were killed in battle or driven out of the land. Solomon's peaceful reign ended about 931 BC. Israel was divided into the north kingdom known as Israel, and Judah as the south kingdom. Some of the heathen tribes slowly returned with their idols and the Israelites fell into idolatry. After 722 BC with the Assyrian and Babylonian invasions and captivities the number of Israelites in Canaan decreased. When the Persian Empire followed after 538 BC some Israelites in captivity were allowed to return to Canaan and the rebuilding of Jerusalem and the Second Temple occurred. But a strong Jewish state resembling the David-Solomon glory did not materialise[147]. During this time several judges and prophets guided Israel[148].

The Hellenistic or Greek period followed when in 333 BC Alexander the Great conquered the land of Israel. Hellenization was bad for Israel and there were many influential Jews who repudiated their birthright and subjected themselves to Greek influence and lifestyle. This was very evident after the death of Alexander the Great. During the reign of Antiochus Epiphanes of the Seleucid Period the priesthood and Temple services were desecrated. The Maccabean Revolt occurred at this time bringing significant reformation to Israel[149].

The Hellenistic period was followed by the Roman Period when Pompey annexed the land of Israel in 63 BC[150]. During this time much corruption prevailed in Judaism. Commercialism dominated the Temple services. In 70 AD Roman Emperor Titus destroyed Jerusalem and Herod's Temple and the diaspora of the Jews occurred. Rome disabled Israel for the first 500 of the 2000 years of the diaspora. The Roman power faded by the 4th Century AD.

The Byzantine Empire commenced about 325 AD and lasted for about a thousand years. Canaan or Palestine as it began to be called, came under the influence of Christianity. "Churches were built on Christian holy sites in Jerusalem, Bethlehem and Galilee, and monasteries were established in many parts of the country. The Jews were deprived of their former relative autonomy, as well as of their right to hold public positions, and were forbidden to enter Jerusalem except on one day of the year (Tisha b'Av—ninth of Av) to mourn the destruction of the Temple"[151].

During the Byzantine period, and starting about 636 AD Egyptian and Syrian forays occurred into Palestine. The prophet Mohammed, an Arab, was born in 571 AD in Makkah province, which is in present day Saudi Arabia. He founded the Islamic religion and by 630 AD it became a religio-political power when he and his henchmen conquered Mecca and forced the Meccans to adopt Islam. About this time Arabization commenced across the Middle East spreading Islam[152]. Arabization is discussed further in the chapter titled Arabization and The Arab Spring. The Dome of the Rock and the al Aqsa mosque were built between 690 and 705 AD. The Moslems believe that Mohammed ascended to heaven from this spot. But the site is Israel's most sacred in that Israel's three temples were located here upon Mount Moriah where Abraham offered Isaac sealing forever the Abrahamic Covenant. The foundation of the Temple with its western wall survives. The Covenant of Omar, which gives an account of Arab activity in Palestine at the time is considered a retrospective document spuriously dated 638 AD. Caliph Omar I is said to have entered Jerusalem on that date. He is said to have protected Jews and allowed them to live in Jerusalem despite being forbidden to do so by Christians. There is no evidence of his having set up an Arab country in Palestine after a slaughter of Jews. The activity of the Umayyad dynasty centred in Damascus in Syria and Palestine was considered an extension of Syria. The Umayyad influence lasted till about 750 AD. The Abbasid caliphs followed, centred in Baghdad. During this time an influx of Arabs occurred into Palestine and Jerusalem. This extended into the Ottoman conquest and rule. Despite this period of Arabization tenacious Jews who had survived in Palestine persevered and maintained their religion.

Between 1095 and 1291 AD the Crusaders invaded with the aim of displacing the Moslems[153]. The Crusaders also suppressed the Jews living in Palestine.

The Byzantine Empire fell in 1453 AD. Constantinople fell to the Ottoman Turks and the Ottoman Empire was established. The Turks are not Arabs but they adopted Islam. The invasion of Palestine by the Turks followed. During the period of the Ottoman Empire the Arabs trickled into Palestine but they did not conquer Palestine and did not establish an Arab state in Palestine[154]. These Arabs considered Palestine as an extension of Syria. Palestine became a integral part of the Ottoman Empire. When Zionism awakened it had to deal with the Turkish Sultan in the matter of increasing Jewish immigration to Palestine. There was no Arab state that controlled Palestine, nor any Syrian state machinery involving the Arab Palestinians. Herzl had urged Wilhelm II, Emperor of Germany to provide a German protectorate to the increasing Jewish immigrant settlements being established in Palestine so he could speed up migration there. The Turkish Sultan's blessing was paramount. The Emperor visited the Sultan in Constantinople and then went to Jerusalem. Herzl followed his footsteps and received an audience from him in Jerusalem. But the Emperor disappointed him. Later Herzl met three times with the Sultan but nothing substantial was achieved. This is evidence that Zionists had not to deal with Arab Palestinians who, though present in Palestine, had no jurisdiction there. All political and practical Zionist contacts to further Jewish immigration to Palestine were with the Turks till the onset of World War I and subsequently with the British after the enactment of the Balfour Declaration.

The first fourteen years in the 20th Century saw an increasing Zionist influence in Palestine and an awakening of Arab Palestinian resistance to Jewish immigration. The Zionists were hoping to establish good relations with the Arab Palestinians and some even imagined that a bi-national state would eventuate. But at no time did the Arab Palestinians show any cooperation. The socialist Zionists hoped to collaborate with the Arabs as part of a worldwide socialist revolution. But soon there would be a parting of the ways. It was wishful thinking on the part of Zionists and some Arabs that a happy coexistence would eventuate in any form of Arab-Jewish collaboration. Both sides now started advocating and establishing rights to nationhood in Palestine. By 1914 the total population of Palestine was 700,000 of which the number of Jews had arisen from 23,000 in 1882 to 85,000 according to Walter Laqueur. The good relationship that existed between the Jews and the Arabs in Palestine deteriorated with the rise and progress of Zionism. After World War I and the Balfour Declaration the friction increased as the Arab Palestinians realised that sooner or later there would be a Jewish state in Palestine. The 1920-21 and the 1929 riots occurred which placed the Jews and the Arab Palestinians in significant direct armed conflict. The Hashomer developed into the Haganah as the British could not be relied upon to protect the Jews in Palestine. Trouble kept brewing till the outbreak of the 1936 conflict between them. This lasted till the outbreak of World War II in 1939.

Stateless Jews who were scattered around the Middle East by the AD 70 diaspora struggled to survive Arabization. They were highly motivated to return to Palestine. By 1918 the Ottomans were driven from Europe and their power in Palestine was weakened. The return of the Jews to Palestine commencing with the antecedent expulsion of Jews from Europe and with the Zionist movement increased their numbers. Under the protection of the Balfour Declaration, Jews migrated to Palestine. They were coming home to their land. They were destined to fulfil the Abrahamic Covenant. This was a huge undertaking as the immigrants had to be self reliant to eke out a living from the soil. Only the most determined and hardy were able to do the pioneering. Many who came got discouraged and went on to America or returned to their origins in the diaspora. The dedicated perseverance and industry of the Jewish socialist workers underwrote the success of those who stayed on. Jewish immigration slowed down with the British tightening entry with their modifications of the Balfour Declaration. The rise of the Nazi Party, World War II, and the holocaust then occurred which would significantly affect the course of events.

The weakened British Mandate preceded the Jewish uprising, which occurred during the years 1945-1948 culminating in the unilateral declaration of the Jewish State in 1948. Most of the Jews in the Arabized Middle East returned to Israel after 1948. The UN apportioned area, which constituted the new Jewish State, was unilaterally modified by Israel after the United Nations voted on a two-state solution. The declaration created borders called Green and Blue Lines. The War of Independence followed between the Israelis and the Arabs. Israel was ascendant and the war ended in 1949 at which time an armistice was drawn up between Israel and their opponents Egypt, Jordan, Lebanon and

Syria. Gaza and the West Bank (Judea and Samaria) were to be under Arab jurisdiction. At this settlement the boundaries were redrawn in excess of the Green Line and Israel now held more of the area west of the Jordan River, a net gain from the Green Line Border. During the War of Independence some Arab Palestinians lost their lives but many left voluntarily in anticipation of the war or fled in fear creating a refugee problem in Egypt, Lebanon, Syria and Jordan. Displaced Arab Palestinians also migrated into Gaza and the West Bank. This conflict created Palestinian refugee camps. However a large number of Palestinians also remained in Israel as Israeli citizens.

In summary, by 1949 several groups of Arab Palestinians were identified:
1. Arabs still residing in Israel as Israeli citizens.
2. Arabs in Gaza and the West Bank who had been domiciled there for a long time.
3. Arabs in refugee status in Gaza and the West Bank.
4. Arabs in refugee camps in Lebanon, Syria, and Jordan.

The Arab Palestinians who were displaced to Lebanon, Jordan, and Syria, were not welcomed by their fellow Arab hosts. There was no concerted effort to integrate them. The camps were perpetuated. With the rise of the Palestinian Fatah Movement there were hostilities between these refugee Arab Palestinians and their Arab hosts. This was obvious when Egypt had control of the Gaza strip and Jordan had governance of the West Bank. The Palestinians in camps in Jordan were able to participate somewhat in Jordanian life. Arab Palestinians in Lebanon destabilized that country, which was already in an upheaval with its own fractured religio-political status. The hostility between Israel and the Arab nations of Egypt, Lebanon, Syria, Jordan, and the Palestinian entities of the West Bank and Gaza escalated. The Arab Front continued to vow annihilation of Israel. This animosity increased and culminated in the 1967 Six Day War in which Israel soundly defeated her enemies listed above. The borders changed again with the annexation of East Jerusalem and the Golan Heights, and the occupation of the West Bank and Gaza by Israel. Egypt no longer governed Gaza and Jordan no longer administered the West Bank. This change in the borders brought another million Arabs under Israel's jurisdiction. The Sinai also was now in Israeli hands.

1967 WAS A WATERSHED YEAR. Following the 1967 Six Day War, Israel began settlements in the 'occupied territories'. Israelis consider it their land.

By 2007 about 267,000 Israelis had settled in the West Bank and 200,000 in the annexed part of East Jerusalem. About 15,000 Israelis settled in the Golan Heights. From 1968-1970 Egypt and Israel fought the War of Attrition over the control of the Sinai. In 1970 both sides signed the ceasefire accepting United Nations Resolution 242[155]. This made two affirmations and called for a decrease in belligerence and affirmed the right of all parties to live in peace and exercise free use of the international waterways in the area. There was also an obligation to continue to seek a permanent peace. In 1970 the PLO was driven out of Jordan for destabilizing that country. The PLO moved to Lebanon.

The Yom Kippur War started in October 1973 in which Egypt tried to regain the Sinai Peninsula and Syria aided by its ally Iraq, tried to regain the Golan Heights. The Soviet Union supplied Egypt and Syria with massive military aid. Despite the superiority of Egyptian and Syrian numbers and firepower Israel tactically beat back the enemies. The Israeli Army was within a few kilometres of Cairo and Damascus when the US was able to broker a ceasefire. Following cessation of hostilities Egypt and Israel arrived at a peace treaty when Anwar Sadat unreservedly recognized Israel's statehood and right to exist. He would pay for this with his life. The countries exchanged ambassadors. Israel withdrew from the Sinai finally by 1982. This was achieved following the Camp David Accord in 1979. Israel kept the Golan Heights.

In 1982 Israel invaded Lebanon claiming that the Palestinian Liberation Organization was constantly harassing and bombing Israel from Lebanon. This Israeli invasion of Lebanon resulted in further destabilization of that country but succeeded in driving the PLO leadership to Tunis. This weakened the Palestinian presence in Lebanon. Israel finally withdrew unilaterally from Lebanese territory.

In 1987 the First Intifada occurred quite spontaneously. This Intifada hurt the Arab Palestinians economically more than it did the Jews and therefore was not successful in the long run. The Israeli economy had become dependent on Arab Palestinian labour, but this symbiosis had made the Arab Palestinians more dependent on Israel for their livelihood. There was no doubt that both parties benefited greatly from the symbiosis. In 1988 the PLO recognized Israel's 1949 borders and its right to exist. This was seen as the Arab acceptance that 78 percent of Palestine west of the Jordan was now Israeli territory.

Chairman Arafat and Prime Minister Rabin signed the Oslo Accords in 1993. This was the first face-to-face agreement between the Israelis and Arab Palestinians since 1948. This was viewed by the world as Israel's commitment to a Arab Palestinian State and the Arab Palestinian commitment to full recognition of Israel's right to exist as a nation. The Arab League had been established in 1945 and constituted an alliance of Arab States who were in solidarity with the Arab Palestinians. The Arab League was now faced with the recognition of Israel's statehood and right to exist. The Oslo Accords empowered transfer of administrative powers in Gaza and the West Bank to the Palestinian Liberation Organization in exchange for the recognition of Israel. These administrative powers were to be in education, health, social welfare, direct taxation and tourism. Election of a Arab Palestinian Council by Gaza and the West Bank was planned to occur within nine months. Negotiations on the final status of the territories were to commence in two years and a final settlement to be reached in five years. The responsibility for security, defence and foreign affairs would remain with Israel as the occupying power. The Oslo Accords were silent on the East Jerusalem annexation, the Jewish Settlements and the Golan Heights retention by Israel.

Yitzhak Rabin was awarded the Nobel Peace prize for his part in the Oslo Accords. Yigal Amir assassinated Rabin on November 4th 1995 for the concessions he had allowed. By 1996 it was clear that the Oslo Accords had failed to progress. The Israeli population appears convinced that Israel's security as a nation would not have been served by the success of the Accords.

Events since 1996 can be summarised. These events were all permutations and combinations of various ideas to reach a two-state settlement (except for the Elon Plan). They were as follows:

Camp David Summit of 2000
This emphasized the right of return of all Arab Palestinian refugees, East Jerusalem, including the Temple Mount to be part of the new Arab Palestinian State, the return to the pre 1967 borders[156]. This plan was not accepted by Israelis.

The Elon Peace Plan of 2002
Its logic was based on the cessation of Arab Palestinian violence, the cooption of Jordan to provide citizenship to all Arab Palestinians, and

resettlement of Arab Palestinian refugees to Jordan and other Arab states. This plan went nowhere[157].

The Road Map for Peace of 2003

President George W. Bush and the US State Department drew up the Road Map For Peace. It included the cessation of all Arab Palestinian violence against Israel, cessation of all Israeli settlement activity in Gaza and the West Bank, the holding of democratic Arab Palestinian elections and a subsequent international conference to determine final borders of a two-state settlement. There was no progress with it[158].

The Geneva Accord of 2003

This consisted of a plan for almost a complete withdrawal of Israel to pre-1967 borders but allowing a 1:1 land swap for territory retained, the division of Jerusalem, compensation for refugees and the new Arab Palestinian State to be a non-militarised state. It was not carried out[159].

The Sharm el Sheikh Summit of 2005

The motivation for this appears to have been the second or al Aqsa Intifada, which started in 2000. This devastated the economic wellbeing of both the Israelis and Arab Palestinians. Arafat had died. Ariel Sharon, Mahmoud Abbas, Hosni Mubarak of Egypt and King Abdullah of Jordan met together and pledged reaffirmation of the Road Map for Peace. Abbas made a declaration explicitly ending all violence (the Intifada) between the Arab Palestinians and the Israelis[160].

Hezbollah

On July 12th 2006 Hezbollah attacked Israel and started the war causing Israel's second foray into Lebanon. Israel's air strikes on Lebanese infrastructure and naval blockade of its ports proved tactically superior. An estimated 1,200 people lost their lives, mostly Lebanese. The United Nations brokered a ceasefire on 8th September 2006[161].

Hamas (The Islamic Resistance Movement)

Hamas was formed in 1987 following the first Intifada. Hamas was composed of militants inspired by the Muslim Brotherhood and dedicated to Islamic fundamentalism. Its declared aim is to annihilate Israel and establish an Islamic fundamentalist state in all of Palestine. It draws ideological and financial support from fundamentalist Iran and also from Saudi Arabia. Hamas won the elections in Gaza decisively in 2007 and broke with Abbas and his Fatah party, which was dominant in the West Bank. The US, Canada and the EEC labelled Hamas a terrorist organization and suspended financial aid to Gaza. Hamas increased its guerrilla attacks on Israel to an intolerable point. As a 'political party' it could not legitimise such activity. Israel cracked down on it with an invasion of this area under its jurisdiction. The Franco-Italian-Spanish Peace Plan was advanced to stop the resulting bloodshed. This war with Gaza ended with a no-win situation for Hamas and a continuing land and sea siege of Gaza by Israel. In times as recent as May 2011 there is a plan afoot to reunite Hamas and Fatah. They have signed a unity pact but its details are unclear except for the aim of presenting a plan for declaration of an independent Arab Palestinian state at the United Nations[162].

The Peace of Jerusalem of 2010

This is perhaps the most significant development in Israel: The Yom Yerusheyaem (Jerusalem Day) was celebrated on 12th May 2010 and marked the 43rd anniversary of the unification of Jerusalem after the 1967 Six Day War. It is significant because it was a prayer of thanksgiving and a prayer for peace. It is significant because it is a spiritual awakening in Israel that is dedicated to the security of Jerusalem and Israel. The 12th May 2011 is the 44th anniversary and Jerusalem and Israel are still intact since the Six Day War, which gave Israel a resounding victory over those who would destroy it[163].

Obama's Plans for the Middle East are as yet to be detailed although he appears to be committed to a two state settlement. He is preoccupied by worldwide terrorism stemming from al Qaeda and Islamic Jihad and two wars started by his predecessor. The Arab Spring may be muffled or successful and will call for some readjustments. The Iranian nuclear threat is a problem. Obama is dealing with a destabilized Pakistan, which is significantly subsidized by the US. In the meantime the economic clout of the US has weakened considerably. Israel's current security depends on the support of the US. In an interview with the British Broadcasting Corporation President Obama re-emphasized that changes to the post 1967 Six Day War borders could only be negotiated with land swaps between the two parties. He also stated that the US would not cooperate with an attempt to create a new Palestinian State by declaration at the United Nations. He declared that any future Palestinian State would have to be negotiated with Israel[164].

The title of this chapter is THE STRUGGLE BETWEEN THE JEWS AND THE ARABS IN PALESTINE. In summary: The Arabs arrived in a land severely depleted of its people who had been driven out. The Jews had been slaughtered and expelled by the Romans. The remnants had been scattered throughout the length and breath of the world. They suffered abuse and slaughter in the host countries but survived as a people because of their diasporic dedication to God and his promise to Abraham. They are now back but do not have all the land that David and Solomon owned in the glory days of empire. But they have the land west of the Jordan and appear resolved to keep it. The Arabs took Canaan without routing Israelis. The Israelis have some of it back after dispossessing them. Israelis strongly feel that they have repossessed what is rightfully their homeland. The dispossessed Arab Palestinians need reparation.

The Arabs have much other land. Consider the Arab States in the world today with large tracts of land and oil riches giving them wealth untold. These Arab states have sometimes held other countries to ransom because of the dependence on oil in the modern world. The Arab Palestinians outside Israel are considered displaced. The Arab Palestinians outside the confines of the 1967 borders appear destined to stay where they are. Forty-four years have now elapsed and most of them are born in the Arab countries where they are situated. The Arab Palestinians now within the confines of the 1967 borders have the choice of living as Israel's citizens where they are. Those in Gaza, and the West Bank (Judea and Samaria) have an uncertain future. But it is true that all Arab Palestinians living in the confines of the 1967 borders of Israel have more freedom than in the undemocratic Arab States where Islamic fundamentalism is rife, women are denied basic human rights, homosexuals are killed, and the masses are impoverished. They do not risk violence from Israel by living in Israel as long as they do not act violently toward Israel. They are guaranteed peace if they live peacefully. There is less freedom for them currently in Gaza and the West Bank. This is purportedly because of their constant avowal of violence towards Israel, and the suicide bombings perpetrated on Israeli soil. They are policed by the IDF. Israel contains and restricts their freedom as a matter of self-protection. This situation can be changed for the better when those threats are renounced so they could live at peace with the utmost freedom.

Recent suggestions that Israel will evolve into a purely secular state poses a great threat to the validity of the Abrahamic Covenant and will lead to Israel's demise according to the predictions of the Tanak. The novel idea that it is possible to transform Israel from a "Jewish State" to a "State of the Jews" as being more palatable to the Arab Palestinians is absurd considering the avowal of Arabs to wipe out every last Jew. As well, the Abrahamic Covenant that emphasizes the Jewishness of the mission contained in it, is incompatible with Israel being a "State of the Jews". If the 'Jewishness' of the Jew and the state of Israel is lost, a 're-diaspora' or reversal of Zionism must take place and then Israel must be declared null and void in the world. The idea of a "State of the Jews" as opposed to a "Jewish State" has no meaning for Jews or Israel in any logical sense[165].

Both World Jewry and the world in general are faced with the realization that the Jews are the only extant indigenous people of and in Palestine and now they are back in possession of part of it. Turkey appears to be seeking to intimidate Israel but cannot resurrect the Ottoman Empire. Erdogan will not be successful in the long run using Islamic fundamentalist rhetoric to forge secularism and democracy in the Arab Spring. His only tie with these Arab countries is religion but since he is a 'moderate' Moslem he will find it extremely difficult to placate the Muslim Brotherhood who has welcomed him as a hero. Erdogan possibly aspires to be the 'champion' of the Arab Spring.

It is obvious that the struggle between the Jews and the Arab Palestinians can only be settled by negotiation. The sooner they start to negotiate seriously the sooner the struggle will be over.

NOTES

[147]   2Chronicles 36:22-23, Ezra chapters 1 & 2.
[148]   See books of Ezra and Nehemiah.
        With regard to Caliph Omar see MidEast Web: Israel and Palestine: A Brief History—Part I
        See also Macrohistory and World Report: Islamic Empire and Disintegration

[149]   Judeo-Christian Studies: The Festivals of Hanukkah and Christmas
        See also Wikipedia: The Maccabees.

[150] The Middle East (Edukit): Ancient Israel and the History of "Palestine" 1273
BCE to 1948. Source Joan Peter's 'From Time Immemorial' Harper and Rowe
Publishers
'History of the Jewish People—The Second Temple Era' by Mesorah
Publications.

> *Comment*
>
> It is interesting to note a statement made at the Paris Peace
> Conference in February 1919: "The only Arab domination since
> the Conquest in 635 AD hardly lasted, as such, 22 years . . . ," said
> the Muslim chairman of the Syrian delegation. "Yes, the existence
> of a separate Palestinian identity serves only tactical purposes.
> The founding of a Palestinian state is a new tool in the continuing
> battle against Israel . . ." Quoted in the Dutch daily Trouw, March
> 1977. The idea that the Arabs conquered Palestine in 635 AD is
> spurious.

[151] Byzantine Rule (313-636) Jewish Virtual Library (A Division of the
American-Israeli Cooperative Enterprise)
Stand for Israel: History of Israel—The Byzantine Empire

[152] MidEast Web: Islam and the Arabs: A Concise History

[153] Jewish Virtual Library: 'The Crusader Period'.

[154] See 'The Case for Israel' by Alan Dershowitz, page 33: ". . . there had never been
a Palestinian state in this area. A Jewish homeland would not be carved out of
a pre-existing Palestinian state. Instead, a decision had to be made about how
to allocate a 45,000 square mile area of land that had been captured from the
Ottoman Empire and was populated by Arabs, Jews and others'.
See also 'The State of the Middle East: An Atlas of Conflict and Resolution'
(updated second edition) by Dan Smith for an excellent depiction of the
historical and geographical progression of Palestine from Ottoman times to
the present. Sadly he has not given attention to developments from Biblical
times. He declares that his book is for those ". . . who are interested and
concerned by the region's conflicts and its prospects for peace. Facts without
context—especially today's facts without the context of history—do not really
aid the process of understanding issues as complex and deep as those in this
region". Although he mentions that the Middle East is the origin of three great
religions: Judaism, Christianity and Islam, he disobeys his own dictum of

attention to context by failing to recognize the Abrahamic Covenant, which is the beginning of the oldest religion of the three, and from which Christianity sees a continuation and Islam builds an alternative.

155   See 'A History of Zionism' by Walter Laqueur, Schocken Books, New York, for details of Herzl's diplomatic efforts with the German Emperor and the Sultan of the Turkish Ottomon Empire. Pages 104-112.
See also Jewish Virtual Library: The Meaning of Resolution 242
Ibid: The Declaration of Principle
See also United Nations Security Council Resolution 242, 22nd November 1967. The two affirmations were drawn up without Israel's input and with no consideration for Israel's security in view of the war footing of the surrounding Arab states of Egypt, Lebanon, Syria, Jordan and Iraq. All their armed forces had again been directed against Israel with the hope of destroying Israel. The two principles of the first affirmation:
1.   Withdrawal of Israeli armed forces from territories occupied in the recent conflict.
2.   Termination of all claims or states of belligerency and respect for and acknowledgement of the sovereignty, territorial integrity and political independence of every state in the area and their right to live in peace within secure and recognized boundaries free from threats or acts of force. It is clear that Israel could not comply with the first and the Arabs would not comply with the second. The goal of Arabization of all Palestine has not been set aside.

156   See 'The State of the Middle East, An Atlas of Conflict and Resolution' by Dan Smith pages 56-61
Israel Ministry of Foreign Affairs—History of Israel: The Middle East Peace Summit at Camp David—July 2000

157   Arutz Sheva Israel National News.com: The Elon Peace Plan—Both Sides of the Jordan
158   Council on Foreign Relations—Foreign Affairs Website: 'Middle East: The Road Map to Peace', Sharon Otterman, February 7, 2005
159   The Geneva Accord   Information Clearing House, Draft of Permanent Status Agreement
160   Peres in Sharm el Sheik: Saudi Plan can bring Peace to the Middle East HAARETZ.com (Tammuz 4, 5771) by Yoav Stern, The Associated Press

[161]   2006 Lebanon War—From Wikipedia

[162]   Hamas (Islamic Resistance Movement)—FAS Intelligence Resource Program

[163]   The Peace of Jerusalem of 2010 CHARISMA—News—Online: Millions to Pray for Peace in Jerusalem

[164]   Deutsche Welle—WORLD.DE—Diplomat, 21.05.2011 Israeli PM firmly rejects Mideast Peace Plan

[165]   See 'The Moral Lives of Israelis: Reinventing the Dream State' by David Berlin
        In referring to the pioneers who established the state of Israel, Berlin's statement: "I realized that there was no clause in their pioneering spirit that required them to nurture those children—the nation they had conceived" shows an ignorance of or disregard for the existence of the Abrahamic Covenant and the conscious and unconscious inborn urge of Jews for aliya. Berlin's dying father's advice to "Look after my little country" appeals to all Jews.
        Diasporic Jews not yet assimilated are consciously or unconsciously deferring aliya. Jewishness is lost on assimilation. Undenied but as yet unfulfilled aliya preserves Jewishness and prevents assimilation.

CHAPTER 16
ARABIZATION AND THE ARAB SPRING

The Arab States include 21 countries with a population of 360 million. There were significant numbers of Jews living in these states but most of them have returned to Israel after its inception in 1948. Some left ownership of land and comforts of a prosperous existence in those countries[166]. There are Arab Christians throughout Arab lands but the majority of Arabs profess Islam. The Arab Christians live in harmony with the majority Moslems, but as with the Coptic Christians in Egypt there has been some persecution of Arab Christians by Arab Muslims[167].

It is of interest to enumerate the Arab states to get an idea of the territory the Arabs occupy in contrast to the miniscule amount of land within the 1967 borders of Israel.

ARAB COUNTRIES of the Middle East are:

Algeria, Bahrain, Comoros, Djibouti, Egypt, Iraq, Jordan, Kuwait, Lebanon, Libya, Mauritania, Morocco, Oman, Qatar, Saudi Arabia, Somalia, Sudan, Syria, Tunisia, United Arab Emirates, and Yemen.

Arabs originally lived in the Arabian Peninsula, but infiltrated to other countries spreading their religion and 'Arabizing' those countries. Arabization is defined as the successful colonization and ownership of countries they have overrun. Egypt is a prime example where this happened, at the expense of the Nubians and others. The Dakhleh Oasis Project gives ample archaeological evidence that "the Neolithic Revolution of the Nile Valley was home grown, with important, even decisive inputs from the Western Desert, and that it grew in complexity to become the OLD and NEW KINGDOMS" of the Pharaohs. The 'Masara' people and the 'Bashendi' people preceded, and perhaps laid the groundwork for the very advanced Pharaonic civilization that started about 5000 BC[168]. "The Edfu text is an inscription in the Temple of Horus at Edfu. It tells us that the origin of Egyptian civilization was taken from the south by a band of invaders led by King Horus"[169]. "Egypt had been a coherent political entity with a recorded history since about 3200 BC. One of the first civilizations to develop irrigated agriculture, literacy, urban life, and large-scale political structures arose in the Nile Valley . . . . Muslim Arab invaders conquered Egypt in 641 AD, and Egypt has been a part of the Muslim and Arab worlds ever since"[170]. Would the logic of this history, which gives the Arabs ownership of Egypt, establish conquering Israeli armies as the rightful owners of the post Six Day War of 1967 Israel? Most Israelis feel that it more than does legally and logically provide ownership. Many Israelis believe the Arabs should evacuate Egypt before Israel surrenders their homeland. The Arabs were not in Egypt before the Pharaohs and the Nubians but the Jews were in their homeland two thousand and seven hundred years before the Arabs arrived in Palestine.

The Arabs have a history as old as the Jews since they trace their origins to Abraham. They have long occupied the Arabian peninsula from where they have a history of maritime influence and have made several contributions to the foundation of modern civilization. They have successfully colonized and spread Islam in Eastern Europe, Western Asia and Northern Africa. The 'Arabization' of North Africa and elsewhere is not sufficiently understood by those who are sympathetic only to the Arab Palestinian cause. The Arabs occupy a large swathe of land outside the Arabian Peninsula. Palestine is one place where they did not establish an Arab state and instead considered themselves as part of Syria under the Ottoman Empire. 'Arabization' is now being reversed in Palestine. The Jews have conquered it in ancient times and again in modern times. Modern Arabization was noted when Saddam Hussein drove the Kurds out of Kirkuk.

The fragmentation of the Ottoman Empire resulted in Arab states in the Levant, which have been ruled by despotic families. These were helped by colonial powers like the British and the French. The Sykes-Picot Agreement of 1916 laid the foundations of these eventualities. Family fiefdoms developed, and in some cases dynasties with kings[171]. Many of these states have an abundance of oil, which benefits a few while the majority of the population is impoverished.

In more recent times the attempts at Arab unity starting with Nasser's United Arab Republic have repeatedly failed. The wars between them illustrate their entrenched disunity. Oil has been their biggest weapon but it also has failed to unite them.

The Arab Spring should be welcomed. Tunisia, Egypt, Libya, Syria, Jordan, Bahrain and Yemen are ripe for change. Democracy is overdue and it is fantastic that the 'Arab Spring' is happening. It will provide freedom from poverty by proper redistribution of wealth. It will provide the opportunity to be free from Islamic fundamentalism, with its archaic system of justice, denial of the education and freedom of women who should have the same rights as men. With a rise in freedom and economic stability they will become attractive and prosperous sites in which to live, in an Arabic milieu. It would be marvellous to see democracy right across the Arab Middle East and North Africa.

A review of Arab Palestinian attitudes is consistent with Arabization. As it rolled across the Levant and North Africa no consideration was given to the indigenous people of those countries. Egypt is an example where the Arabs totally subjugated the land and its people substituting their culture and religion. In Palestine they felt they had been there since at least 640 AD. They had established Mount Moriah as their own holy place with the al Aqsa Mosque and the legend of Mohammed's ascension to Heaven. They had lived in symbiosis with the Jewish remnants in Palestine. When the European Jews started arriving their consciousness and feeling of ownership of Palestine began to be aroused and gel. At the Balfour Declaration they did everything to persuade the British that they were in the game with hopes of another Arab country when they realised that they were no longer considered a part of Syria. As a result the British backtracked on the Declaration and in their Mandate, and their White Papers constituted their reaction to the claims of the Arabs. The British Mandate was shouldered with British determination to accommodate the Arabs in order to retain the loyalty of the Islamic Middle East. The creation of Transjordan and the continuous restrictive measures to prevent Jewish immigration catered to the Arabs. The prevention of Jewish settlers from going east of the Jordan River was a British imposed ethnic wall. The British closure of Palestine as an escape for European Jews is a monument to cruel calculated British inaction. The US also took a similar attitude at that time. The failure of the Evian Conference convened by President Roosevelt showed how the Jews had been cornered and doomed. The turning back of shiploads of

Jews escaping from Nazism, arriving at the shores of Palestine after the Evian Conference and during World War II resulted in many deaths of beleaguered Jews. Arab Palestinians have resolutely bargained for all of Palestine[172]. Chaim Weizmann constantly attempted to salvage a cordial relationship of the Jews with the British. He was an enduring Anglophile. The relationship improved after Churchill became Prime Minister because Churchill's attitude then favoured the formation of a Jewish state. But the assassination of Lord Moyne changed Britain's mood and further developments had to await the end of World War II[173]. British ideas for a second two state settlement before World War II were ill conceived and impractical. If the Jews had not won all of their skirmishes with the Arabs they would have no state. They have succeeded in the prevention of total Arabization of Palestine. Basic to this thinking is that the Jews belong in Palestine. Another annihilation will have to be invented to move them out. Hamas has vowed this to happen.

But Arabs today in the Middle East deserve their current desires for prosperity and democracy. They have long been tyrannized by greedy fiefdoms, mostly installed by the British and French colonial powers. The Arab Palestinians should be amicably accommodated by Israel. Arabs should drop their demands for all of Palestine and seek a realistic outcome. The Arab Spring is a boon and hopefully will be highly successful. In a recent interview of Christiane Amanpour by Piers Morgan on CNN there was a discussion of the Arab Spring. Amanpour is a very astute journalist and brilliant thinker who has a great understanding of what is transpiring in the Middle East. A Christian Iranian by birth who is married to a practising Jew her understanding is unbiased and enormous. In her opinion the Arab Spring is not an anti-Israeli movement, nor a Jihad inspired movement. She sees it as a grass roots movement of peoples who desire democracy so that they can have freedom from dictators and have control over their own lives, economic prosperity and happiness. Amanpour feels that the west should wholeheartedly support these aspirations of the Arab people. Prime Minister Netanyahu has himself endorsed the Arab Spring as a grass roots movement worthy of support. It would be a pity if the Arab Spring were to be hijacked by Islamic fundamentalism and Jihadic movements. It would be a great tragedy if a new cycle of religious dictatorship is installed in these aspiring countries.

When the aspirations of the Arab Spring become a reality the Middle East will become a land of freedom, peace and prosperity and poverty could be vanquished. Islam should banish its fundamentalist and violent extremism. It is in the main a peaceful religion and its moderate adherents are happy practicing their religion. Obama sees land swaps as a compromise in the formation of the two state settlement he envisions, if he insists on a two state settlement with pre-1967 borders. In his endorsement of the Arab Spring he is trying to tie the two state solution to it. He may be mistaken as the Arab Spring has nothing to do with Israel and the Arab Palestinians. Israel has a Palestinian Spring to offer the Arabs within its borders. All they have to do to prosper in the democratic country of Israel is to renounce violence against Israel and live in peace. Any Prime Minister of Israel who does not secure defensible borders for Israel in the compromises he makes will destroy Israel.

Tunisia has held its first democratic election. Egypt is in a state of flux trying to establish democracy. Libya is also in a similar place. The upheaval and bloodshed in Syria going on at present perpetrated by the Assad regime must abate. Syrians must be allowed democracy. The peoples of the Arab states are in the winter of their discontent and deserve to embrace a glorious springtime.

NOTES

[166] See Alan Dershowitz 'The Case for Israel' page 5: ". . . the 850,000 Sephardic Jews who had lived in Arab countries before 1948, most of whom ended up in Israel were either forced to leave, or left on their own, or experienced some combination of fear, opportunity, and religious destiny".

[167] 'Coptic Christian Persecution in Egypt' by Melissa Matters, Associated Content from Yahoo.
'Disappearing Christians of the Middle East' by Imad Boles, Middle East Quarterly, Winter 2001 pp23-29

[168] 'Before the Mummies: The Desert Origins of the Pharaohs' written by Graham Chandler, photographed by Michael Helsa. Saudi Aramco World, Vol 15, no. 5

[169] 'Who are the Nubians'? by Richard A Lobban Jr. 2003 Historical Dictionary of Ancient and Medieval Nubia 'From 7500 BC—Black Africa's Oldest Civilization', see Nubian Royal History

[170] Arab World Multi Media CD-ROM: Egypt

[171] See New World Encyclopedia: Emirate Abdullah became King Abdullah I.

[172] See Dan Smith 'The State of the Middle East—An Atlas of Conflict and Resolution'

See also 'A History of Zionism' by Walter Laqueur, Schocken Books, New York, Pages 511-545

[173] Google "The French Connection": Lord Moyne, British Minister of State. He was assassinated by two members of the Stern Gang who were later hanged for it.

CHAPTER 17
THE TRUTH ABOUT THE TWO STATE SOLUTION

Following the Roman sacking of Jerusalem in 70 AD the Jews were absent as a nation from their homeland of Canaan for 2000 years. Starting about 650 AD, facilitated by the Umayyads, Abbasids and the Ottomans, the Arabs trickled into this Jewish homeland now called Palestine. Residual Jews lived there already and their numbers slowly increased over the centuries by trickling back from the diaspora. So Jews and Arabs lived side by side, mainly in peace. In the early 20th Century under the agitation created by the Zionists the western world felt that the Jews had a right to be a nation in Palestine, previously their homeland. The Balfour Declaration enunciated this in 1917 as a World War I strategy. On December 11th 1917, British General Allenby entered Jerusalem ending Ottoman rule. World War I ended in 1918. Palestine came under British rule. At the Treaty of Versailles in June 1919, the League of Nations gave Britain a Mandate for Palestine. Britain spoke favourably with both Arab Palestinians and Jews implying recognition of nationhood to each. But they had difficulty delivering on the promises. They had already been plotting with the French and Russians on the future dismemberment of the Middle East. Britain backtracked on the Balfour Declaration and began watering it down. Winston Churchill who was colonial secretary at the time drew up a White Paper to facilitate his plans.

In the dismantling that followed the fall of the Ottoman Empire, the 'secret' Sykes-Picot Agreement between France, England and Russia in 1916 drew up borders between Lebanon, Syria, Iraq and Palestine, which were enacted after World War I[174]. The starting point in any settlement for a two state solution of Palestine should at least have been the 1920 territory, which the League of Nations gave as a mandate to Britain. In 1921 Winston Churchill, despite his pro-Israel rhetoric, made a unilateral decision to create the Arab Protectorate of the Hashemite Kingdom of Transjordan[175]. It was later granted independence in 1946 and in 1949 it became modern Jordan. Creation of this Hashemite Kingdom is viewed as A TWO STATE SETTLEMENT imposed by Britain. That was four fifths of the territory and integrally a part of Palestine. Britain forbade Jewish migration to that territory. Britain imposed ethnic restrictions in an attempt to keep the territory labelled Transjordan Arab in population.

At this time the chief British Zionist with influence was Chaim Weizmann. Herbert Samuel, a Jewish Englishman had a role in the formulation of the Balfour Declaration and was later the First High Commissioner in Palestine. Their ambitions for Jewish nationhood were muted at this time. Weizmann thought that the Arab Palestinians would be cooperative with the Jewish coexistence. And as an Anglophile he wanted to cooperate with Britain. He was blind "to the colonial officials' discrimination against the Jews". As a result the Zionist Revisionists led by Vladimir Jabotinsky became prominent. Jabotinsky was seeing the future as it was in reality. Jabotinsky saw the need for a military defence force after the bloodshed occurred at the 1920,21 riots, which clearly pitted the Arab Palestinians against the Jews. He saw that it would take money to organize and maintain a defence force. His vision of the future Jewish nation was territorially on both sides of the Jordan. He saw that Jewish immigration into Palestine needed to increase drastically to create a Jewish majority in order to declare nationhood. He also saw the gathering anti-Semitic storm in Central Europe, which eventually developed into the powerful Nazi Party in Germany. This made it necessary in his mind to hurry Jewish immigration to Palestine. He therefore opposed the acceptance by Weizmann of the British White Paper, which was watering down the Balfour Declaration, and slowing Jewish immigration. Laqueur cites Jabotinsky's thoughts as quoted in 'Sefer Betar', Tel Aviv, 1969, volume 1, page 32:
"The programme is not complicated. The aim of Zionism is a Jewish state. The territory—both sides of the Jordan. The system—mass colonization. The solution of the financial problem—a national loan. These four principles cannot be realised without international sanction. Hence the commandment of the hour—a new political campaign and the militarisation of Jewish youth in Eretz Israel and the diaspora".

Unfortunately Zohar was too late to prevent the big Churchillian unilateral give away of land to the Arab Palestinians in the formation of Jordan and the prevention of Jewish migration there. Originally all of Jordan was part of

Israel's Homeland. Israelis view it as a huge give away of land to the Arabs that should have been available to Jews as part of their heritage. This was Churchill's unilateral two state solution. Logically the just view is that dividing up Palestine has been in the immense favour of the Arab Palestinians, who already have the major share. Ambitious Jews today see Israel in terms of the Kingdom of David, which included Southern Syria and all of Jordan. Still others remember the area from the Euphrates to the Nile. Weizmann dominated Zionism at the time of the Churchillian giveaway. Laqueur quotes Weizmann: "Nothing is stated about the Jewish state . . . in the Balfour Declaration. The essence of Zionism is to create a number of important material foundations, upon which an autonomous, compact and productive community can be built". Weizmann was deluding himself trying to be pragmatic. Or else he felt Zionist ambitions were best muted at that time. The truth is that the British created a two-state solution in 1921, which favoured the Arab Palestinians, to the great disadvantage of the Jews. In the succeeding Zionist Congresses Jabotinsky continued to openly push his logical drive for a Jewish state, until a split occurred in 1931 when he realistically declared that the Balfour Declaration and the British Mandate had degenerated into anti Jewish causes. Britain was clearly impeding Jewish immigration into Palestine. Jabotinsky would triumph in 1933 in the Eighteenth Zionist Congress and the rise of Betar. There is no doubt that Jabotinsky was motivated by Britain's creation of the Kingdom of Jordan and the deterioration of the British Mandate in favour of the Arab Palestinians.

In 1937 the Peel Commission spelled out a further partition plan as another two-state solution. This is viewed as unfair and greatly favouring the Arabs. The British Plan for this was published in 1938. Alan Dershowitz discusses this in his book 'The Case for Israel'[176]. This second partitioning plan was completely impractical and untenable. It seemed to have part of Palestine (containing Jerusalem, Bethlehem and Ramallah) remaining under a British Mandate, presumably in perpetuity. In July 1938 President Roosevelt sponsored the Evian (France) Conference where delegates from thirty-two countries met to consider help for German Jews to escape the stringent measures of frank persecution Hitler had imposed. Britain refused to allow further immigration to Palestine. The Dominican delegate offered to take refugees, but not one other country represented offered to take German Jews. The Australian delegate said that they had no racial problems in Australia and were not anxious to import one!

Deuteronomy 34:1-6 records the story of the arrival of the children of Israel in the Promised Land: "And Moses went up from the plains of Moab unto the mountain of Nebo, to the top of Pisgah, that is over against Jericho. And the Lord showed him all the land of Gilead, unto Dan, and all Naphthali, and the land of Ephraim, and Manasseh, and all the land of Judah, unto the utmost sea, and the Negev, and the plain of the valley of Jericho, the city of palm trees, unto Zoar. And the Lord said unto him: This is the land which I swore unto Abraham, unto Isaac, and unto Jacob, saying I will give it unto thy seed . . . ." Standing on Pisgah's Peak, the top of Mount Nebo, now situated in Jordan, the panorama of Israel is awesome.

Retrospectively, a TWO STATE SETTLEMENT HAS ALREADY BEEN MADE. MOST ANALYSTS DO NOT REALISE THIS. What Israel has today is a shrivelled part of the Kingdom of David. Israelis consider they had no alternative but to swallow that first huge give away of land imposed unilaterally but historically possessed by them. They had no part in that decision. The Arab Palestinians who had come to live in Palestine did not want the Jews anywhere and vowed to destroy them. It was obvious that there was not going to be a peaceful coexistence. As early as the Balfour Declaration there was an assumption that the Jews would have their own country. The Arabs however were entrenched in the idea of retaining all of Palestine. In 1949, when the Green and Blue lines were drawn, the Arab Palestinians had possession of the West Bank and Gaza. But it was not enough and was rejected by Arafat. Zionism and the Holocaust greatly increased the influx of diasporic Jews. They came to Palestine to stay. After World War II the United Nations enlarged on the idea of what would be a second two-state solution. The United States supported Jewish return to Palestine while Britain became hesitant in view of the duplicate promises made to the Arabs and so restricted Jewish entry into Palestine. At the Unilateral Declaration of the State of Israel in 1948, Israel was forced to countenance the 'Churchill-imposed' TWO STATE SOLUTION. They had no alternative at the time. Israelis consider there is an alternative now. Most are not willing to let the Arabs have another two state solution.

Today, it appears that the majority of the Israeli population has settled for the post Six Day War 1967 borders. But it is not compatible with the number and aspirations of Arab Palestinians living in the West Bank and Gaza. Israelis may consider Judea, Samaria, and Gaza as an integral part of Israel, but that wish complicates Israel's future. They wish that Arabs who live there would migrate to Arab countries where they might feel more at home than in an Israeli state. Israelis consider Egypt, Jordan, Syria and Lebanon as viable lands for these Arabs to live in, especially Jordan, which is the state created by the ORIGINAL 'Churchillian' TWO STATE SOLUTION where there is lots of land for them.

It is alleged that Ben-Gurion had implicitly accepted another two-state solution. At the 38th Memorial Ceremony for David Ben-Gurion held at Kibbutz Sde Boker, south of Beersheba, the compromising Shimon Peres stated: "Ben-Gurion was the first to support the two-state solution"[177]. Was Peres misunderstanding him? Peres did not quote authentic recorded or written words of Ben Gurion. The evidence is that Ben-Gurion had no alternative to accepting that imposed opinion of the day, which was supported by the British Mandate, Americans and the United Nations. In a letter to Chaim Weizmann dated October 1946 he had stated: "we should be ready for an enlightened compromise even if it gives us less in practice than we have a right to in theory, but only as long as what is granted to us is really in our hands". Ben-Gurion was very glad to have a foothold. Ben-Gurion agreed with the Green Line and the Blue Line borders, which materialized after the War of Independence and not exactly what the UN had in mind[178]. There is no evidence that Ben-Gurion accepted the Green and Blue Lines as Israel's permanent and eternal borders. In that speech Peres was putting words into Ben-Gurion's mouth in his own attempt to compromise.

International pressure, Arab belligerence, Arab Palestinian violence, and the repeated wars of aggression initiated by the Arab League have worn down the resilience of the Prime Ministers after Ben-Gurion. But none of them after 1967 initiated a concrete offer to return to the pre 1967 war borders. Sharon and Olmert under pressure were "ready to make painful concessions"[179]. But Sharon and Olmert did not define these "painful concessions".

Some influential Jews view the management of a couple of million Arab Palestinians living in their midst an impossible task. This is likely a valid view. Thomas Friedman, Walter Laqueur and Alan Dershowitz appear to be in that group. To focus on very recent times, the only high-level attempt in Israel to embrace the second two-state solution comes from the Knesset. Kadima Party Opposition Members of the Knesset: Tzipi Livni, Avishey Braverman, and Yoel Hasson, among other members of the Knesset listed by OneVoice, have formed a caucus to launch the first ever 'two state solution' arising from the Knesset[180]. Is this conciliatory stance a stalling tactic or a capitulation? This resolve will need to be tested at the next Knesset election to survive as a viable attempt to have another two state solution. It would appear that any party that proposes this will lose at the polls. But the alternative to a second two state settlement does have huge consequences for Israel.

International efforts since 1949 for a 'second' two state settlement are many. The extremists of the Arab world (Hamas and Hezbollah and their allies) are still publicly intent to wipe Israel off the globe. But the more temperate Arab elements want to go back to the pre-1967 borders. They want legitimisation of a Palestinian state.

The initiatives to a second two-state settlement may be summarised as follows:

The Balfour Declaration	(1917)
The Paris Peace Conference	(1919)
The Faisal Weizmann Agreement	(1919)
The Lausanne Conference	(1949)
The Armistice Agreements	(1949)
The Camp David Accords	(1978)
The Israel-Egypt Peace Treaty	(1979)
The Oslo Accords	(1993)
The Israel-Jordan Peace Treaty	(1994)
The Camp David Summit	(2000)
The Taba Summit	(2001)
The Road Map for Peace	(2002)
The Arab Peace Initiative (Beirut Summit)	(2002)
The Geneva Conference	(2003)
The Annapolis Conference	(2007)
The Riyadh Summit	(2007)
The Sharm el-Sheikh Conference	(2010)

There is no point in considering each of the above separately and assessing their success or reasons for failure. They are significant only to illustrate how far each Israeli Prime Minister was willing to compromise and how big were the demands and refusals of the Arab Palestinians and their friends. The essential fact is that none of these conferences and pledges was successful in establishing another two state solution and fixing all the other problems involved. Each effort was a repetitive enumeration of the requirements of each side and one is left to conjecture whether any of them would have brought a solution. The conferences and the pledges made had dreadful results for some of the main people involved, eg. King Abdullah I, Yitzhak Rabin and Anwar Sadat who paid for their compromises with their lives. And when wars were fought, suicide bombers exploded, and intifadas occurred there was a dreadful loss of military and civilian lives, not to mention the people who were maimed, displaced and orphaned. Israelis find it difficult to consent to ANOTHER TWO STATE SOLUTION. They see Churchill's Transjordan creation as enough.

Some of the main issues considered at these discussions are:

+ Mutual recognition of the PLO and Israel. (The PLO is not an acceptable name to most Israelis as it implies a desire to "liberate Palestine" and therefore an implication to destroy Israel). The Palestinian Authority is more acceptable
+ Return to the pre-1967 borders
+ Acceptance of international interference and peace keepers
+ The status of Arab Palestinians in Egypt, Syria, Lebanon, and Jordan
+ Return of Arab Palestinians to Israel
+ Return of Arab Palestinians in Egypt, Syria, Lebanon, and Jordan to the West Bank and Gaza
+ The Jewish Settlements and their fate
+ Security and Defence
+ The transfer of powers
+ Reparations
+ Jerusalem
+ Hamas and Hezbollah and the constant threat of war

There has been no continuing agreement on any of the above listed problems. There appears to be mutual recognition at least for the purpose of talking to each other. This recognition is restricted to Fatah only. In the more recent discussions the estrangement of Hamas and Fatah has been a problem. Their qualitative and competitive policies remain unclear. Hamas' continuing vow to annihilate Israel has been a great barrier to any further rapprochement. Hamas demands are not ethereal fundamentalist wish lists. They are real. Iran is implicitly involved with Hamas. Recently Hamas and Fatah have made some reconciliation, but details are lacking.

In his book 'The Case for Israel' Alan Dershowitz, a dedicated defender of Israel, strongly favours another two state solution. His preface to the paperback edition of his book summarises his thoughts. He cannot see Israel retaining all the land in the post 1967 borders. He appears to favour that most of the West Bank and Gaza should be shed by Israel to form that Arab Palestinian state. He feels that a one state outcome (Israel within the post 1967 borders), which has long been labelled a "bi-national state""is a transparent fraud calculated to end Israel's existence. The one state that would emerge would be a Palestinian Muslim state"[181]. It could be deduced that he fears the sheer numbers of Arab Palestinians that the 'one state' would include, and their prolific birth rate, would soon overwhelm the Israelis. This would be the outcome in a democracy. An alternative proposition is stated in the chapter in this book called 'The Palestinian Spring'. In this vision of the future, many Palestinians would emigrate to Arab states. This is unlikely. Those who remain would do so because they can coexist without Islamic nation status, but as loyal citizens of the state of Israel. The success of this plan assumes that the vast majority would emigrate. The existence of six and a half million Jews in the US without the necessity of having a bi-national arrangement with the US is a significant example. Can Arab Palestinians live similarly in an Israeli state? (Admittedly, numbers are disparate and the comparison quite dubious).

In summary, Winston Churchill made a unilateral division of Palestine in separating out an Arab Transjordan. A second two state solution is not a glorious option for Israel nor is it a guarantee of Israel's future security. Israelis feel they need LAND no less than the post Six Day War 1967 borders. Israel's own government, military establishment, and allies, committed to preserving it, understand this verity. A recent poll in the European Community as to the greatest threat to world peace has listed Israel as being that threat[182]. What does that mean? In the face of worldwide terrorism this poll is saying that it is because of Israel's existence. So the question arises: shall Israel be wiped out to bring peace to the world? Israel will not accept this kind of logic. Israel is the strongest democratic bastion of the western world against Arab terrorism and is poised to defend itself. The Hashemite Kingdom of Jordan is a two state settlement imposed unilaterally by Britain. Israel finds it difficult to tolerate the imposition of a second two state settlement, but is also faced with accommodating a very large Arab population, and a compromised future.

Today Israel is beset with a barrage from many sides to relinquish more LAND. Israelis point out that there will never be a truly 'just' settlement between Israel and the Arab Palestinians until Israel reclaims all its land. To them, giving away more land is not going to be a 'just' settlement. Reclamation of all its original land will not happen any time soon unless the Palestinians and Arabs repeat the 1967 experience and Israel gains all of Jordan and southern Syria within its jurisdiction. Having to be satisfied with the post 1967 borders is not considered a 'just' settlement. It is today's pragmatic settlement. An Israeli Prime Minister finds it difficult to relinquish any of this land. That is understandable. In the event of another war, which Israel could theoretically lose, there will be no land left, no Nation of Israel to talk about. Israel is on the precipice of a "lost war" to face another annihilation and diaspora. Israelis feel that Judea and Samaria and Gaza belong in Israel. The Arab Palestinians living in that land could find a home in southern Syria and in Jordan in the spirit of the first 'Churchillian' two state settlement, thereby still 'sharing land with Israel'. Israelis point again to the area of the Kingdom of King David and declare they are indeed in a situation where they are generously sharing the land.

Thomas Friedman's solution by implementing another two state settlement is worth discussing[183]. Friedman is a very intelligent and pragmatic person who is advocating peace in Palestine at all costs. It should be mentioned that these ideas of his were stated around or before 1990. Arafat was still a significant player and Hamas had not won the election in Gaza, and Israel had not yet unilaterally withdrawn from Gaza, further empowering Hamas. What were these ideas? The problem Friedman envisions is well stated when he says: "Do we want to be the kind of people, or see the kind of Israel, that is sure to develop from us having to hold under occupation 1.7 million Palestinians in the West Bank and Gaza Strip for the rest of our lives . . . . ?"[184]. He is convinced that in the future the Arab birth rate will turn Israel into an Arab state. He feels Israelis will get more prosperous and more westernised in the future and will have small families, and he is right. See his hypothetical Israeli leader's (Prime Minister) speech who is a "bastard for peace"[185], and his second hypothetical Prime Minister's speech[186]. Friedman suggested two possible courses of action, both based on unilateral withdrawal of Israel from the West Bank and Gaza[187]:

> "*A tribal solution to a communal war*". He models this after Israel's withdrawal from Lebanon.

> And "*. . . a diplomatic solution*". He models this after Anwar Sadat's peace made with Israel.

Friedman emotionally appeals to the "moderates" on both sides for the success of his plans. From what has occurred since he put forward these ideas Israelis see the futility of such actions as has unfolded. Hamas has virtual control of Gaza after Ariel Sharon unilaterally pulled down the 'Israeli settlements' and withdrew the IDF from Gaza[188]. This has been labelled Sharon's Folly. Land for Peace did not bring Israel peace in this instance. The blockade of Gaza continues because of the extreme hostility of Hamas that still vows to wipe Israel off the map and continues to rain rockets on Israel. And this is happening despite a unilateral withdrawal, so that no greater security has been achieved by it. And with the Egyptian 'Arab Spring' and the demise of Anwar Sadat and his successor Hosni Mubarak from power, Egypt has opened the border to Gaza. Israel now fears an influx of arms from Iran and elsewhere into Gaza to strengthen Hamas resolve. And there is evidence that Libyan 'Arab Spring' rebels' arms are being smuggled into Gaza. This proves that Israel cannot control another state within the post 1967 borders without continued hostilities.

Friedman does not express a deep spiritual knowledge of the Abrahamic Covenant. His sympathies appear to be with the Reformist and Conservative Jewish movements, whose recent developments are born in the USA. They are so secularly oriented that their religious depth is assessed as shallow. Secularism goes hand in hand with shallowness of religious conviction. Presumably the Abrahamic Covenant is what he calls the "Super-Story". His idea of retaliation for an attack from the West Bank after a unilateral withdrawal of Israel is to "Throw you [the Palestinians] over the Jordan River. Have no doubt about it"[189]. Over the Jordan River is the country of Jordan of course. And how will that be accomplished when Israel is at peace with Jordan, without all out war and accusations of ethnic cleansing and genocide? The Palestinians will never accept a state with only a police force of their own while surrounded by the Israeli Army. After the unilateral withdrawal from Gaza Hamas increased its rain of rockets on Israel. Shall Israel throw the Gazans over the Egyptian border into Egypt?

The treaty between Israel and Egypt forged by Sadat and Begin needs further examination. Sadat got the Sinai back with recognition of Israel's right to exist. What Israel received in this "land for peace deal" was entirely symbolic, despite an enemy becoming dormant. This dormancy is not guaranteed whereas the land has been relinquished and leverage lost. The two countries exchanged ambassadors and began cooperating in the usual peaceful activities that occurs between two neighbours not at war. Egypt was no longer fighting a war and its economic stability was enhanced. Jewish tourists in hordes spent their money in Egypt. Sadat paid for it with his life, and Mubarak maintained the peaceful relationship. But look now at what the Arab Spring in Egypt has done. Mubarak is being prosecuted for corruption and murder. The relationship is destabilized and Israel cannot relax its vigilance to prevent Iranian arms being shipped through the open border between Egypt and Gaza. Land for peace is not shaping up as the lasting solution to Israel's security problem. Will Israel ever be able to prevent Iranian violence being perpetrated through Gaza if she were to relax the blockade of Gaza? The answer is obvious to all Israelis.

The Arabs in Palestine already have a two state solution. The current logic is that they can settle in the land already assigned by that 'two state' solution: Jordan and Syria whose southern territory includes what was part of David's kingdom. Israel is helping Jordanian farmers with drip irrigation. Israel can help all her neighbours with technical know-how. Much can be achieved by cooperation.

The Abrahamic Covenant needs the validation of a stable and strong Israeli state.

NOTES

[174] 'What is the Sykes-Picot Agreement' by Reannan Raine, eHow Contributor
Encyclopedia Britannica—Sykes-Picot Agreement
Also see WWI Document Archives> Official Papers>Sykes-Picot Agreement
See also The Balfour Declaration by Jonathan Schneer

175 'From Amir of Transjordan to First Hashemite King of Jordan' by Neil Gunn
Middle Eastern History by suite 101
'Transjordan' by Wikipedia (Exercising the British Mandate for Palestine
granted by the League of Nations Winston Churchill, Britain's Colonial
Secretary unilaterally created the Hashemite Kingdom of Transjordan. Jews
were forbidden to settle there. Transjordan was part of David's kingdom)
See also 'The Case for Israel' by Alan Dershowitz, chapter 4—'Was the Balfour
Declaration Binding International Law"?
See also The Balfour Declaration by Jonathan Schneer

176 Ibid pages 45-52
177 See 'A History of Zionism' by Walter Laqueur, Schocken Books, New York,
pages 508,509
See also English News.cn

178 Quoted in Eban, 'Tragedy and Triumph', page 288, cited by Walter Laqueur in 'A
History of Zionism' page 581, Schocken Books, New York
See 'The 1949 Armistice Borders'. See Wikipedia (Israel)

179 See Israeli Opinion 'Painful Consequences' Ynetnews
See Wikipedia-Olmert
See also 'The Case for Israel' by Alan Dershowitz page 177 re Sharon's "painful
concessions".

180 One Voice Israel—Knesset Two State Solution 17th January 2011.
See also: 'Knesset's Two State Solution Caucus Launches Amid Political
Shakeup', CNW news.

181 Alan Dershowitz 'The Case For Israel' see Preface to the Paperback Edition.
He openly states: "The premise of this book is that a two state solution . . . is
both inevitable and desirable . . . . There are really only four possible alternatives
to a Jewish and a Palestinian state living side by side in peace". To summarize
the four: 1. Wipe Israel off the map (the Hamas plan). 2. Keep the post 1967
borders and expel or subjugate the Palestinians who become marooned. 3. Israel
and a Palestinian state as a federation. 4. A single binational state. See pages 3,4.
'The Palestinian Spring' I offer is perhaps a modification of plan 2.

[182] The Jewish Federations of North America (Jewish Life)—European Poll: Israel Biggest Threat to World Peace (European Commission poll) Reported by the Simon Wiesenthal Centre

[183] Beirut to Jerusalem by Thomas Friedman chapter 18

[184] Ibid: Page 517

[185] Ibid: Pages 517-520

[186] Ibid: Pages 525-528

[187] Ibid: Pages 516-528

[188] Israel's Unilateral Disengagement Plan—Passed in Knesset June 6, 2004 and enacted August 2005.
See "Ariel Sharon's Folly" Daniel Pipe's Blog (Lion's Den), and "The Forcible Removal of Israelis from Gaza" by Daniel Pipe.

[189] Beirut to Jerusalem by Thomas Friedman Page 520

CHAPTER 18
WHAT EVERY JEW SHOULD KNOW ABOUT HAMAS

Hamas was founded in 1988 with the establishment and declaration of the Hamas Covenant[190]. It is a branch of the Muslim Brotherhood, which was the brainchild of Hassan al-Banna and founded in Egypt in 1928. Its original aim was to have the Quran define every aspect of a Moslem's life. But with the passage of time achievement of its political aims became underpinned by violence. When it tried to overthrow the secular Egyptian Government Hassan al-Banna was killed and it was outlawed in Egypt. Its advocates in Syria met the same fate when it tried to overthrow the Syrian Government. The Muslim Brotherhood's extreme and more powerful faction has been openly advocating Jihad since 1971. With the arrival of the Arab Spring it is gaining more power in these two countries[191].

The Hamas Covenant of 1988 consists of 36 articles[192]. It can be summarized in its relevance to Jews as follows:

Preamble: Israel will exist until Islam obliterates it.

Article 6	The goal of Hamas is to raise the banner of Allah over every inch of Palestine.
Article 7	The Day of Judgment will not come till the Muslims kill the Jews.
Article 11	Palestine is consecrated for future Moslem generations until Judgment Day—No one can renounce or abandon any part of Palestine.

Article 13	Palestine is an Islamic land and its liberation is the individual duty of the Arab wherever he may be. There is no solution except by Jihad. Peace initiatives and international conferences are a waste of time.
Article 15	Jihad is the individual duty of every Moslem in the face of the Jews' usurpation.
Article 22	The Jewish Conspiracy in the world should be recognized for its evils.
Article 32	Egypt's Peace Treaty with Israel is high treason.
Article 33	Worldwide Islamic masses will work to liberate Palestine.

Hamas has been funded from its inception mainly by Saudi Arabia and Iran[193]. Hamas was at first a radical minority movement. Arafat died in 2004 and his successor Mahmoud Abbas of the Fatah dominated representation of Gaza and the West Bank. Prime Minister Ariel Sharon carried out his unilateral withdrawal from Gaza during 2005. Israeli settlements were demolished, and withdrawal of the IDF posts in Gaza was complete by September 12, 2005[194]. Abbas permitted Hamas to field candidates in the January 2006 elections that occurred in Gaza and the West Bank. Hamas won a majority of seats in the Gaza elections and took control of Gaza unilaterally away from Abbas. There was total break between Hamas and Fatah, the former behaving like Gaza was its own separate state. Subsequently Hamas became more belligerent and continued to rain rockets on Israel. This resulted in 2008 in Israel's retaliatory invasion of Gaza and the killing of 709 Hamas militants, with the loss of 15 Israeli soldier's lives. Israel then imposed a blockade of Gaza[195].

Secret talks between Hamas and Fatah have taken place in Cairo over a period of several months. These culminated in the public signing of an agreement between Hamas and Fatah on 4th May 2011, ending their 4-year split[196]. But the details have not been released although it is being surmised that a Palestinian Unity Government will be formed after new elections, purported to have taken place in September 2011. Abbas applied for a unilateral declaration of a new Palestinian State at the United Nations at its Fall Session. President Obama has indicated already that he does not support such a declaration, which he states will be meaningless without Israel's input. Meanwhile there has been a "Arab Spring" of sorts in Gaza City and Ramallah. This has been quietly suppressed. Palestinian popular mobilization was praised rhetorically and accepted all the time it happened in areas under Israeli control, but not in areas ruled by Hamas and the Palestinian Authority[197]. They tolerate no dissent in Gaza or the West Bank.

During their four years of estrangement, Fatah had detained several Hamas operatives in the West Bank, and Hamas had detained Fatah operatives in Gaza. A month after the agreement being signed, Human Rights activists had not noted any signs of release of these detainees[198]. In the meantime Hamas has opened its own office in a 'embassy style' in Cairo, and the border between Gaza and Egypt has been opened.

It is noted that Hamas in Gaza and Hezbollah in Lebanon, both classified as terrorist Jihad organizations by Britain, the US and Canada, have sought legitimacy by entering into the democratic process. Both Hamas and Hezbollah are motivated by the express aim of wiping Israel off the map. Despite her desire to have a second two state settlement Tzipi Livni believes: "With more accountability such groups would be tempted to abandon their military approach in favour of a purely political platform. But this analysis ignores the possibility that some radical groups sought participation in the democratic process, not to forsake their violent agenda but to advance it"[199]. Livni did support Sharon's unilateral withdrawal from Gaza but she does believe that Hamas is a menace to Israel.

Hamas and other terrorist groups have been sending an increasing number of rockets into Israel since 2001. There was a significant increase of rocket and mortar fire in 2008. Finally Israel decided to invade Gaza when the Gaza-Egyptian border was breached and Russian and Iranian arms were smuggled into Gaza. During the 22 days of the Gaza invasion by Israel 511 rockets and 205 mortar shells landed in Israel from Gaza[200].

Thomas Friedman has given significant insight into the situation, which motivated Yitzhak Rabin. His ideation came into being before 'Sharon's Folly', that is before Sharon unilaterally withdrew the IDF from inside Gaza after dismantling every Jewish settlement there. Sharon's unilateral move out of Gaza, a quasi 'Land for Peace', is assessed as not having worked. Further land for peace agreements are considered doomed to fail. Israel is forced to encircle the new Hamas' Gaza by land and sea to prevent it becoming the theatre for the organization of a Hamas war effort to "kill every last Jew". Friedman quotes

Yitzhak Rabin. They were discussing Hamas' and the Islamic Resistance Movement's false belief that "the land of Palestine has been an Islamic inheritance throughout their generations and until the Resurrection"[201]. Apparently Rabin said to Friedman: "It is not unlimited and the main threat at the present and in [the long] run is the ugly wave of Islamic fundamentalism, which I call Khomeinism without Khomeini, whether it is Algeria or Sudan. About 90% of the terrorist capability from the Palestinians vis-à-vis Israel comes from these fundamentalists. They are also the infrastructure of worldwide terrorism against Jewish and Israeli targets. They are the threat to the moderate Arab regimes, which have made peace or are ready to make peace. In the long run the source of inspiration and assistance to these groups comes from Iran, with its conventional and non-conventional armaments. Seven or ten or fifteen years from now, Iran is the major threat". Rabin's next sentence showed his resolve: "To cope with it let's make peace. Let's have regional development, bring up the standard of living of the people in the Arab countries, and in this way answer the main threat"[202]. The idea is very noble, and Israel should have a policy to help all downtrodden people. But Hamas has different ideas and does not want peace without the POSSESSION OF ALL OF PALESTINE. Rabin's hope for peace with the Arab Palestinians on the basis of their economic prosperity alone will not be realised. His dream to overcome Iran by improving Arab Palestinian lifestyle and prosperity in such a demure setting is considered a pipedream. Israel does not see its security realised through such a plan alone.

Can Israel talk peace to Hamas? The Israeli answer is an emphatic negative. Can Israel talk to Fatah, in glove with Hamas? Again it finds it difficult to trust them. There is some sympathy for the Arab Palestinians emanating from American Jews, some of it as a response to what is surmised as Israeli intransigence. Palestinian poverty and living conditions do invoke sympathy. But there is so much Israel can do to benefit them if they renounce violence and recognize that Israel is in the land ahead of them and are going to stay. The strong sentiment is that you cannot occupy my home when I have been driven from it by a third party (the Romans) and on my return declare it was never mine, but yours from eternity. The rank and file Arab Palestinians do not understand this and need to learn history. The siege of Gaza by land and sea is to prevent the flow of arms into Gaza and this siege will be maintained as long as Hamas is there, vowing Israeli liquidation. This is a strong conviction in Israel despite many who feel the need to make peace with the Arab Palestinians.

NOTES

[190] Avalon Project, Lillian Goldman Law Library, Yale Law School

[191] See The Jewish Virtual Library: The Muslim Brotherhood and the Arab Spring

[192] Avalon Project, Yale Law School

[193] Israel Ministry of Foreign Affairs: 'The Financial Sources of Hamas'. July 2003.
See also Front Page Magazine.com: 'Funding Hamas', January 2006

[194] See 'Ariel Sharon's Folly' by Daniel Pipe

[195] Gaza War 2008-2009 HistoryGuy.com
See also 'Israel's Gaza Invasion A Go' by Stirling Newberry, and Gaza War, Wikipedia.

[196] See World/Home: 'Significant Progress Reported in Secret Talks Between Rival Hamas and Fatah Factions'

[197] 'Fatah and Hamas Announce Outline of Deal' reported by Etwan Bronner and Isabel Kirshner, April 27, 2011.
See also 'The Alternative Information Centre, Italiano Costellano' June 3rd 2011.

[198] See People's Daily On Line by Emad Drimly and Abu Ramadan, June 2nd 2011

[199] MK Tzipi Livni (Kadima) quoted in Wikipedia.

[200] "Israel Vows War on Hamas" December 30th 2008
See also War with Hamas-winter 2008-2009, Wikipedia, and Palestinian Rocket Attacks of Israel, Wikipedia

[201] The Hamas Covenant

[202] Beirut to Jerusalem by Thomas Friedman page 548

PART IV
CONFLICT AND RESOLUTION

In this final section, which constitutes the recent or modern history of the Jews, there is a discussion of Zionism. Zionism is not a modern development in worldwide diasporic Jewry. It has existed throughout the history of the Israelites since Abraham. Recent Zionism is the starting point for the conflict now current in Canaan or Palestine. The conflict between Arab Palestinians and Jews has been active since several years before Herzl but became an active force to be reckoned with, since Herzl and Weizmann gave the Jews in diaspora the push needed to challenge for a place in the sun. The modern expression of Zionism ended with the unilateral declaration of the Jewish state in 1948. Anti-Semitism then came into focus, since Zionism had achieved its goal. As a result of the creation of the modern nation of Israel the conflict with the Arabs took on a continuing war footing. Jewish immigration to Israel swelled. 1967 saddled the young state with a very large population of Arab Palestinians. The whole question of sharing the land is now the focus. The modern situation is discussed in terms of Arabization, the colonial developments after World War I, the Balfour Declaration, and the other actions of the British, Americans and the United Nations. All this has received serious consideration ad infinitum. But it is now important to reconsider it in the recent setting. The threat to Israel from Islamic extremism continues.

Over the years since 1948 the internal conflict in Israel has come into focus. It is the religious—secular conflict. Two conflicts now involve the Jews. Both are very daunting and their resolution imperative. The conflict within Jewry needs to be resolved by reformation. The conflict with the Arab Palestinians must be resolved by negotiation. Both conflicts are intertwined with the Abrahamic Covenant.

The study of eschatology in the Tanak is fascinating and challenging. A J Jacobs recognizes this and I stand to be educated by his thoughts. Premature interpretations can be unbalanced and undesirable. The Tanak must talk to us. The eschatology of the Tanak is in the Abrahamic Covenant. Messiah must be defined, recognized and embraced. Then shall all nations rejoice and be blessed in the blessedness of Israel. Part IV addresses the conflict with the Arabs and offers a possible resolution in the chapter titled the 'Palestinian Spring'. If this cannot eventuate, then the further division of the land between them will have to be achieved. Israel must ensure that its security is not compromised in this outcome. That is essential to the Abrahamic Covenant. The Palestinian Arabs must eliminate their threat and desire to annihilate the Jews because the Abrahamic Covenant will not disappear from the earth. Israel must strongly present this verity to the world.

Israel's aspirations need clear definition. The practice of Judaism needs clarity, simplicity and motivation. The important role of the US in Israel's welfare and security is extremely vital. Faithfulness to the Abrahamic Covenant is the governing factor. Dedication to it must take place and will solve both Israel's conflicts.

CHAPTER 19
ZIONISM

The conflict leading to the realization of the modern state of Israel starts with Modern Zionism. A description of Zionism is essential to discussing the current situation in Israel. The commencement of Modern Zionism came about in Europe with the prominence and writings of Theodor Herzl, which are dated in the 1890s. The publication of his book Der Judenstaat occurred in 1896. Chaim Weizmann based in Britain also made a massive contribution. The very exhaustive book on Zionism, Walter Laqueur's 'A History of Zionism', was published in 1972. As Laqueur himself cites in his book there are two other notable books on Zionism written by Nahum Sokolow and Adolf Bohm. The latter titled Zionistische Bewegung is considered more complete[203]. Laqueur lived in Israel for 10 years and writes with authority. There was a second printing of his book in 1989 and it contained a second Preface. Both his Prefaces are very revealing. The book is more than an account of Modern Zionism and contains a lot of history of the whole period occupying his interest. He summarizes in the Conclusion Chapter what he titles Thirteen Theses on Zionism. He talks of Classical Zionism, Secular Zionism, Religious Zionism, Political Zionism and Anti-Semitic Zionism. His Thirteen Theses are a masterful description of the many facets of Zionism.

But Laqueur's core definition of Zionism misses the mark as he thinks only in terms of the European experience and as an attempt of the Jews to solve their own 'Jewish Question'. Definition of the Jewish question has as many facets as Zionism. But Jews generally understand it as the condition of being a homeless, landless people. Certainly they lived in homes, no matter how rich or poor and destitute, in foreign lands. But the Jews who were not willing to be assimilated continued to be homeless, landless strangers. It was a problem that caused the realisation that they were motivated by a past history. And because of Moses the patriarch this was recorded in the Torah, which consisted of the Pentateuch and the rest of the Tanak. It took the Jews back, not just to Abraham but empirically to Adam. That is the core definition of the 'Jewish Question'. It is assumed that Laqueur and most secular writers call this 'THE MYTH'. This 'myth' is variously described as 'nostalgia', 'mystical longings', 'psychological necessity', 'variant dreams', 'homesickness', etc. Analysis of this shows it to be not a simple homesickness, since all of them outside Palestine had never had a home in Palestine. So the feeling of homesickness was constituted by 'the myth'. To the Jews who had the slightest religious bent, 'the myth' was their whole tangible history. 'The myth' on further analysis is the call of Abraham to fulfil a mission, which was God's plan to settle his chosen people in the Land of Israel for the restoration of a perfect world, by a coming Messiah. Laqueur refers to people like Disraeli, George Eliot, Karl Marx, Engels, Pinsker and Moses Hess as 'The Forerunners', who had variant dreams of a Jewish homeland. But he missed the fact that the divine time was ripe. Hess recognized it. Laqueur quotes Hess' words of divinely inspired self-realization:

"After twenty years of estrangement I have returned to my people. Once again I am sharing in its festivals of joy and days of sorrow, in its hopes and memories. I am taking part in the spiritual and intellectual struggles of our day, both within the House of Israel and between our people and the gentile world .... A sentiment, which I believed I had suppressed beyond recall is alive once again. It is the thoughts of my nationality, which is inseparably connected with my ancestral heritage, with the Holy Land and Eternal City, the birthplace of the belief in the divine unity of life and of the hope for the ultimate brotherhood of all men"[204].

Here is Hess' recognition of the Abrahamic Covenant in terms of Land, Torah and Messianic fulfilment. It is all in his confession of his return to Judaism. Moses Hess was standing with Adam and Abraham at the Gates of Eden and longingly peering in. Laqueur accuses Hess' conversion back to Judaism as half-baked or lukewarm, but it seems obvious that both Moses Hess and Moses Mendelssohn were seeking a middle ground similar to the religion of Moses the Patriarch's Judaism and not the extremes of ultra-Orthodox and Hassidic Judaism, nor of bland secularism. It is obvious that Laqueur recoiled from extremism as well. Laqueur's objection is that he finds a Jewish nation state to be incompatible with extreme ultra-Orthodox Judaism and he is right. A return to the middle ground is needed, and that middle ground is the basic Abrahamic Covenant around which the whole Tanak revolves.

Zionism is best defined as the deep feelings of desire, longing, and yearning for aliya that always engulfs the Jew in diaspora. At their best the Jews are a very deeply religious and god-fearing people who enjoy their dialogue with God. Torah talks to them. They genuinely missed their Homeland during their captivities and diasporas and longed to be back and in communion with their God. 'The Myth' kept them alive. Laqueur dabbled in this characteristic when he wrote that the nationalistic ingredients of classical Zionism "are rooted in national myths and in religious fundamentalism; they are based on divine promise . . . . This Zionism is an instrument in the hands of the Almighty which prepares the people of Israel for their Redemption.". This is a fantastic and realistic admission. He admits a lack of sympathy for this sentiment and resigns it as ". . . metahistorical issues best left to prophets and charlatans". And that is Jewish history, an account of prophets and charlatans. The charlatans were the ones who twisted their history for personal gain as did the Scribes and Pharisees in the period just prior to AD 70. He is more forthcoming when he admits: "Jewish religion, Zion as a symbol, the nostalgia for the homeland and other mystical factors played a role in the development of Zionism . . . . For the Jewish masses in Eastern Europe Zionism was the dream of redemption from their misery"[205]. Theodor Herzl was a visionary who came closer to describing this deep religious feeling: "We have returned home. Zionism is the return of Judaism even before their return to the Jewish land"[206]. He was exercising faith. And again Herzl's early writings reflected the longing for the ancient Homeland[207]. Here is the great, powerful and compelling motivation that energized the machinations of European Zionism, which put the wheels in motion. Here is the burning desire that consumed the emotion of Theodor Herzl, Max Nordau, Chaim Weizmann and Vladimir Jabotinsky. The young men that formed the clubs called 'Lovers of Zion', originally in Russia and then in Britain and France were imbued with Zion. Consider the Russian 'Lovers of Zion' movement, actually a spontaneous multi-site expression of the longing for aliya in the hearts of young Russian Jews. The core group called itself Bilu, (Bet Yaakov lechu ve nelcha), which is a quotation from Isaiah 2:5: "O house of Jacob, come ye, and let us go". The original core group of high school and university students acted on their beliefs. Of a hundred of them who set out to the Holy land, only sixteen survived the journey. The Lovers of Zion movement caught fire in Western Europe and more groups arrived in Palestine. It is fair to say that these young people were responsible for the establishment of the original agricultural kibbutzim[208].

Zionism has a much more ancient history than Laqueur allows. Every captivity or foreign sojourn in Israel's history has invoked yearning for Zion. When Joseph was in Egypt he suffered immense pangs of homesickness. During his glory years as Prime Minister of Egypt he anticipated return to the yet unclaimed Promised Land. He understood the Abrahamic Covenant well, and this was prior to the chains of Hebrew slavery. When Jacob died in Egypt Joseph had his body embalmed and they carried his body on a special trip to Hebron where he was buried in the Cave of Machpelah, which Abraham had bought. And when Joseph died he was embalmed, placed in a coffin and years later at the Exodus they carried his bones back to the Promised Land where they were also interred in the Cave of Machpelah[209]. And during the miserable years of slavery "the children of Israel sighed by reason of the bondage, and they cried, and their cry came up unto God by reason of the bondage. And God heard their groaning, and God remembered his covenant with Abraham, and with Isaac and with Jacob, and God looked upon the children of Israel, and God knew their plight"[210]. This was dynamic Zionism in powerful motion. God inspired Moses and Joshua to lead them back to the Promised Land. With Laqueur's own immersion in Judaism was this a possible parallel that he was seeing in European Zionism? And was he ignoring it?

Psalm 137 captures the great Zionist movement in Babylon. "By the rivers of Babylon, there we sat down, yea, we wept, when we remembered Zion. We hung our harps on the willows in the midst thereof. For there they that carried us away captive required of us a song; and they that wasted us required of us mirth, saying, sing us one of the songs of Zion. How shall we sing the Lord's song in a foreign land? If I forget thee O Jerusalem, Let my right hand forget her cunning. If I do not remember thee, let my tongue cleave to the roof of my mouth, if I prefer not Jerusalem above my chief joy"[211]. Ezra, Nehemiah, Zerubbabel, and others took the leadership and returned to rebuild the temple and Jerusalem. The religious zeal and fervour of diasporic Jews, which motivated Zionism cannot be denied. The Torah was speaking to them.

Colossal organizational work was built on this motivation. Even Jews who expressed no religious emotion were caught up in organizing emigration to the Holy Land. Walter Laqueur deserves great credit for his research and recording of it. This was Zionism at work. Homeless Zionism concentrated on the Land aspect of the Abrahamic Covenant by motivating aliya. Torah and Messiah would have to wait for attention later. But their time is now. The hard work that went into Zionism by all its inspired leaders is monumental. Zionism cannot be called racism. Its detractors labelled it racism. Zionism represented the intense energy that it took to bring the Jews back to nationhood in their land, a fulfilment of the Abrahamic Covenant. Hirsch Kalischer, Theodor Herzl, Chaim Weizmann, Max Nordau, Vladimir Jabotinsky, David Ben-Gurion, and many others expended their lives on reclaiming the Homeland.

Enumerating the gains in the progress of Zionism is of value:

(i) Achievement of the Balfour Declaration and the establishment of the Jewish Agency were largely due to the inspiration of Theodor Herzl and Chaim Weizmann's efforts. The British Mandate followed World War I.

(ii) President Truman's commission of the Earl Harrison Refugee Report resulted in the request he made for Britain to allow another 100,000 European Jewish refugees into Palestine, much to the chagrin of the Attlee Government, which did not comply. This caused further action.

(iii) Formation of the Anglo-American Committee resulted, which sought to enforce the order for the 100,000 Jewish visas to be granted and also requested rescinding of Britain's White Paper, which aimed to reverse the Balfour Declaration. Britain continued to resist.

(iv) Palmach, Hagana and Irgun created sufficient trouble in Palestine to increase the pressure on Britain.

(v) Discussion in the House of Commons in Britain on 18th February 1947 resulted in the decision to refer the matter to the UN. The Secretary General of the UN called for a special session of the General Assembly.

(vi) Russian support for the partition of Palestine and the establishment of a Jewish state was a big surprise to the Zionist Movement.

(vii) UNSCOP (UN Special Committee On Palestine) was formed for a study of the matter and its majority report favoured a Jewish state in Palestine. It appeared to assume that an Arab Palestinian state would also result, in some sort of association with the Jewish state.

(viii) The UN General Assembly on 29th November 1947 voted in favour 33 to 13, of partitioning Palestine, outlining the territory to be occupied. The Arab nations voted against the resolution and there was no effort to form an Arab Palestinian state simultaneously. Britain abstained in the UN vote.

(ix) Britain then announced it would leave Palestine on 16th May 1948, giving up its mandate.

(x) On 14th May 1948 a Unilateral Declaration of the State of Israel occurred. The US and Russia immediately recognized the new State of Israel. Various other members of the UN followed with recognition. Arab hostilities escalated and the War of Independence began.

Laqueur's Thirteen Theses capture the different facets of Zionism extremely well and are worth repeating here. They are summarised briefly with some added comments:

1. "Zionism is a response to anti-Semitism". It is under this heading that Laqueur discusses the religious motivation behind Zionism. Perhaps this segment should have been titled Zionism is a response to the yearning for aliya. He also lists the triggers of other movements such as the 'ancien regime' prior to the French Revolution and tsarism prior to the 1917 Russian Revolution.

2. "Anti-Semitism in its most rabid and murderous form . . . . came to power in Central Europe, where the relatively small Jewish communities had progressed far on the road to assimilation and where the Jewish question was no longer a major socio-economic problem". Hatred has rarely been as intense.

3. "Zionism has always regarded assimilation as its main enemy . . . . It has decried life in the diaspora as physically unsafe and morally degrading . . . . Zionism has preached the more or less inevitable 'ingathering of the exiles'". Laqueur counts persecution, anti-Semitism, and the Nazi Holocaust as being indirect 'blessings', which prevented greater assimilation than did take place.

4. ". . . Zionists had their historical opportunity only after the First World War". Here, Laqueur clearly expresses the inevitable clash with the Arab Palestinians who were occupying Israel's Homeland at their mandated return. There were Jews already living there but the sheer increase in Jewish influx posed a problem to the Arab Palestinians.

5. ". . . Zionism from the very beginning was a movement in a hurry . . . . Both the Balfour Declaration and the UN resolution of November 1947 came at the last possible moment". The Zionists took them at the flood.

6. "Zionism had neither money, nor military power, nor even much political nuisance value. It could only rely on moral persuasion . . . ." It is certainly true that the Balfour Declaration was the monumental achievement of Chaim Weizmann. But Jabotinsky saw a more practical set of circumstances needing attention.

7. "The United Nation's decision of November 1947 was in all probability the last opportunity for the Zionist Movement to achieve a breakthrough". Again the Zionists took it at the flood.

8. "Herzl proclaimed that a Jewish state was a world necessity . . . . That it was an immediate necessity was preached by Jabotinsky . . . . [But] it took the Advent of Nazism, the holocaust and total Arab rejection of the national home to convert the Zionist Movement to the belief in statehood". Jewish anti-Zionists also played a part in motivating the determination of the Zionists, which led to the success of Zionism.

9. "The Arab-Jewish conflict was inevitable . . . . Zionism, the transplantation of hundreds of thousands of Jews, was bound to effect a radical change in Palestine, as a result of which the Palestinian Arabs were bound to suffer . . . . The effect of Zionism on the Arabs should not be belittled . . . . Had the Arabs accepted the Peel Plan in 1937, the Jewish state would have been restricted to the coastal plain between Tel Aviv and Haifa. Had they not rejected the UN partition of 1947, most of Palestine would still have been in their hands". They have been rejecting all accommodations since because they want all of Palestine. "Arab intransigence was the natural reaction of a people unwilling to share its country with another . . . . But despite all concessions in the cultural or economic field, the Arabs would still have opposed immigration with an eye to the inevitable consequences of mass immigration". Was it any more 'illegal' for the Jews to move back to the Holy Land than for the Arabs to have come and settled there in the time of Israel's weakness?

10. ". . . Zionism was an aggressive movement, Jewish immigration was an invasion . . . . Throughout history nation states have . . . . developed from invasion, colonisation, violence and armed struggle . . . . Zionism has been challenged on the level of abstract justice: it has been argued that the Jews had no right to a state of their own . . . because it was bound to affect the fate of another people . . . . Hence the fact that the territorial changes in Eastern Europe have been accepted as irreversible, while those in the Middle East continue to be challenged by many . . . . If a

case can be made for a just distribution of property among individuals the same applies (again on the level of abstract justice) to peoples and nations . . . .".

11. ". . . Zionism has been rejected from various angles". Arab opposition, ultraOrthodox Jewish opposition, the extreme Left, that the Jews had been away from their homeland too long for them to warrant nationhood, that Jews should have accepted assimilation", etc. These ideas were advanced to prevent the realization of Jewish nationhood. But these reasons do not hold water.

12. "The establishment of a [Jewish] national home in one of the world's main danger zones . . . meant that the future of the state would inevitably remain uncertain for a long time to come". But there is strength to be drawn from the Abrahamic Covenant and God's ultimate plan, which Torah bears out.

13. "The basic aim of Zionism was twofold: to regain Jewish self-respect and dignity in the eyes of Jews; and to rebuild a Jewish national home . . . . The establishment of the Jewish state has been the greatest turning point in two thousand years of Jewish history and has had a profound effect on Jewish life all over the world"[212]. These achievements must be preserved to fulfil the Abrahamic Covenant.

Having briefly outlined Laqueur's admirably stated theses of Zionism ('the myth' and the triggers) his closing words in the book are disappointing and discouraging. They belittle the great future of Israel in respect to the potential influence it has on the world, which is embodied in the Abrahamic Covenant. Laqueur dismisses this as ". . . the more fanciful claims (Zion as a new spiritual lodestar, a model for the redemption of mankind, a centre of humanity) . . .". He particularly dismisses Messianic hope with these words. Zionism helped to achieve nationhood for Jews by its sheer belief in divine destiny. But now he wants to forsake the longing that Israel has had for a continued communication and fellowship with God. He does not see Israel's idolatrous past, the multiple national disasters and captivities, the turmoils of the previous Zionist movements, and joyous returns to the Homeland. He gives no weight to the fact that Israel's history has repeated itself in the past and can repeat itself again in the future. Israel can either advance to a future in relation to its glorious past or start another downward path into idolatry and punishment. The eschatology of the Torah does not seem to have any relevance to Laqueur. He sees a dismal secular future ahead as he goes it alone. He says: "The state created by Zionism thus faces an uphill struggle in its endeavour to make its neighbours recognize its right of existence. While this struggle continues, the existence of the state and its independence is no more assured than that of other small countries whose geopolitical location exposes them to the expansive designs of a superpower". He cannot see the grand designs of the Superpower Jehovah who made the Covenant with Abraham, to bring blessedness to the whole world. Laqueur wrote his second preface for the 1988 re-publication of his book. I wonder whether he is still of the same mind in 2011? Laqueur was interviewed in 1993 by David Keymer when he published his book 'Thursday's Child Has Far to Go: A Memoir of the Journeying Years". David Keymer concluded: "Laqueur ... is unwilling to spend time on searching his soul ...."[213]. Perhaps he should, so we can benefit from the rich, perhaps bitter experience he likely has to offer concerning his spiritual status. The Abrahamic Covenant cannot wait for prophets or charlatans. Both prophets and charlatans have to be dealt with now, to achieve the God-given mission.

Zionism had its detractors. Anti-Zionists did much to disrupt it. There were two kinds of anti-Zionists: Gentiles and Jews. The Jewish Anti-Zionists were the more formidable for the Zionists to battle and overcome. This battle was no less than a civil war within Jewry. Jewish anti-Zionists have played a disastrous part in every return to Israel's homeland after captivity. They were against Moses in Egypt. They were totally successful in the Assyrian Captivity for which there was no return. They held up and thwarted the return from the Babylonian Captivity. And now they became active again. They were comfortable in the diaspora and had 'Do not disturb' signs on their doors instead of the blood of the Passover Lamb. Their feet wore no sandals. There were several factions. Those in Central and Western Europe were the most formidable. Those in Britain and America were also difficult to combat. They could be collectively labelled 'Liberals' who had decided assimilation had much prosperity to offer whereas a return to primitive Messianic Judaism was obsolete. Laquere has given a comprehensive assessment of this situation. Some quotes from him are appropriate: "If the American and British liberals were above all concerned with the political implications of Zionism, the Germans took it more seriously, trying to analyse and refute its philosophical roots. Felix Goldmann, an anti-Zionist rabbi, regarded Jewish nationalism as a child of the general chauvinist movement which had poisoned recent history but which would be swept away in the new era of universalism"[214]. "The Zionists in Germany and the US complained that their supporters were being systematically discriminated against, that Jewish communities were refusing to employ Zionists as rabbis, teachers, or even librarians .... There was no place for those who denied German consciousness, who felt themselves merely guests in their native country. These declarations caused great indignation among Zionists". The Zionists retaliated: "If German, French and British Jews nevertheless chose to stay in their respective countries, it was because they longed for the fleshpots [of Egypt] rather than the Messiah"[215]. For those who preferred not to be pioneers in an 'inhospitable Homeland' a case may be argued in the name of personal freedom that they were perfectly entitled to stay in the diaspora where they could practice primitive Judaism and remain true to the Messianic hope. In 1887 an American Jewish Rabbi Convention in Pittsburgh declared: "We consider ourselves no longer a nation but a religious community. And therefore expect neither a return to Palestine . . . nor the restoration of . . . the Jewish state"[216]. The Central Conference of American Rabbis in 1920 declared: ". . . Israel was not a nation, Palestine not the homeland of the Jewish people—the whole world was its home"[217]. For them the assimilation wolf would be waiting at the door. But then today in Israel the wolves of secularism and extremism are already feasting.

NOTES

[203]   'A History of Zionism' by Walter Laqueur, Schocken Books, New York, page XX

[204]   Ibid pages 40-86. Note Walter Laqueur's comments on Hess' book 'Rome and Jerusalem'

[205]   Ibid page XV and page 590

[206]   Ibid page 104.

[207]   Ibid page XIX

[208]   Ibid page 75,76. See also The Jewish Virtual Library, The Kibbutz.

[209]   Genesis: chapter 50.

[210]   Exodus 2:23-25

[211]   Psalm 137

[212]   'A History of Zionism' by Walter Laqueur, Schocken Books, New York, pages 54, 55 See also Ibid pages 589-599

[213]   See Books—Category Walter Laqueur—'Thursday's Child Has Far to Go' See also World Security Network for Dieter Farwick's Interview of Walter Laqueur February 20

[214] 'History of Zionism' by Walter Laqueur, Schocken Books, New York, pages 394, 395

[215] Ibid pages 396 and 397

[216] Ibid page 402

[217] Ibid page 403

CHAPTER 20
JEWISH IMMIGRATION TO ISRAEL SINCE 1948

1 948 brought the turning point in the diaspora of the Jews inflicted by the Romans in AD 70. Return to Israel had already long begun in dribs and drabs. Now it was happening in torrents. The Nazi extermination of 6 million Jews marked a urgency for relocation of the remaining Jews to Israel.

Immigration to Israel from other countries 1948-2008[218]:

1. North America   **134,000**
    (*USA 120,000; Canada 9,500; Mexico 4,500*)
2. South and Central America   **104,180**
3. Australia and New Zealand   **7,500**
4. Africa   **525,600**
    (*including Morocco 270,000*)
5. Asia   **398,100**
    (including Iraq 130,000)
6. Europe   **1,905,800**
    East Europe 1,733,500
    (Including Russia & FSU republics 1,112,000; Poland 173,000)
    West & Central Europe 172,800 (Including France 85,000; UK 32,500;
    Germany 21,000)

                                        Total 3,075,180

The Jewish population in Israel according to census 2008 was 5.66 million. The Jewish Population in the United States census 2009 was 6.544 million.

The question may be asked: Why have not more American Jews migrated to Israel? Do the 6.544 million American Jews constitute another Jewish state? It does not. Then is the US another 'Homeland'? The US today is indeed a land of freedom and a home for all ethnic people on its soil. The Jews do feel genuinely at home in the US. The correct conclusion possibly is that the US is home to the Jews there, but the US is not their 'Homeland'. Assimilation threatens all diasporic Jews. But then Americanization and secularisation threatens Israelis also, which is assimilation of a different stripe.

When Moses led the Israelites out of slavery he left some behind in Egypt. They were the idolaters and the ones who had intermarried with Egyptians. It was an easier task for Moses because escape from slavery was a great motivating factor. Had Moses arrived during the immediate post Joseph prosperity in Goshen he would have had a more daunting task. Suppose he had. He probably could have succeeded in leading out perhaps a small fraction of the prosperous Israelites in Goshen. But most had such a good life that they would not have left Egypt to pioneer in a Promised Land, yet to be conquered. Is there a comparison with American Jewry? The conclusion is that God allowed the Israelites to be enslaved to help their removal from Egypt. But it entailed a lot of suffering.

It was easier for Jews from Poland, Austria, Hungary, The Balkans, the Baltic States and the Soviet Union, etc where pogroms were rife, to move to Israel. There is a parallel situation between the slaves leaving Egypt and the persecuted Jews leaving Central and Eastern Europe. The idolatrous and hostile tribes already living in Canaan had to be displaced by Joshua's Army. Similarly, in 1948 the returning Jews were walking into a small embryonic insecure nation surrounded by the Arab Palestinians and their adjoining Arab supporters who threatened to annihilate them. As Thomas Friedman so aptly puts it: "The more important role played by Israel in the mind of most American Jews was as a bomb shelter, a haven against persecution, and a source of Jewish power and real estate that could protect Jews if another Hitler were to appear on the scene. But even though they saw Israel as a haven, most American Jews thought of it as a haven for other Jews, refugee Jews, displaced Jews—not for themselves"[219].

It is difficult to obtain up to date reliable figures about yerida with respect to Israelis leaving for the US and Canada. Thomas Friedman states: "By 1988, an estimated 300,000 to 400,000 of the roughly 4.2 million Israelis had moved to the United States on a permanent or semi-permanent basis—with an estimated 100,000 in California alone. These figures must be compared with the fact that only about 50,000 of the 6 million American Jews have moved to Israel since the Jewish state was founded in 1948—some of them having moved back since . . . ."[220]. These figures, dated 1988, smack a little of being inaccurate in comparison to those quoted at the beginning of this chapter, and especially when Friedman states there is a unspecified margin of 'estimation error' in 100,000 found in California. Also the US Jewish population in 2009 according to the US census was 6.544 million[221]. However Friedman rightly points out a major reluctance of American Jews to aliya and a desire for some Israelis to migrate to the US.

American Jews have a history of significant prosperity and freedom from persecution since World War II. They have pursued and realised the 'American Dream', perhaps more than any other ethnic group. They have entered into American culture and political life, which have obscured their ethnicity and religion. The majority are non-observant Jews although inordinate numbers may be seen to observe Passover and Yom Kippur. As a political entity in their adopted country they wield considerable influence. They are prominent in the business world, in science and technology and in the fields of law and medicine. It is difficult to allege a palpable anti-Semitism in the United States. So why should American Jews want to move to the 'big risk' of living in Israel? Even if Moses appeared today and tried to move them to The Promised Land he would be out of luck. They are already in the 'Promised Land' of their choice—America. Since they are non-observant in the main, American Jews have no concerted visible or audible internal conviction in their hearts for the Abrahamic Covenant to be fulfilled. LAND, TORAH, and the MESSIAH are not big in American Jewish thoughts, as long as Israel is secure. American Jews enjoy Israel by proxy. They outlay money for this. But they are not willing to aliya in significant numbers.

American Jews serve a very important purpose. Their political clout and their money are very important to the security of Israel. Their fund raising is enormous. Their donations to Israel are sustaining. Their influence on the American President is a boon to Israel. Can Israel complain? Would another 6.544 million American Jews counted in 2009 fit into Israel were they to aliya? It is possible but not likely to happen. The Gush Emunim are accused of wishing aliya of American Jewry through Apocalypse Now! It could happen especially if America is going downhill on the economic pathway. But it can be argued that it is in God's plan to run a parallel Jewish 'Nation' in America that has no connection with the Abrahamic Covenant in order to sustain the Israeli Nation that does? The answer to that argument is not easy. Can you be a true Jew by proxy and can you buy into the Abrahamic Covenant, and by proxy participate in what is happening in Judea, Samaria and Gaza? Are American Jews playing the part of Esther and Mordecai in the King of Persia's palace? Are they "called to the (Persian/American) Kingdom for such a time as this"?[222]. Will they save Israel by financially helping Israel to man the battlements and by lobbying for US assistance and protection? There is truth to the statement that America has no closer friend than Israel. Could Israel one day be another Hawaii? Not according to the eschatology in the Abrahamic Covenant.

Israel is not yet ready to go it alone. It needs the 3 billion dollars a year from the US Government (whether it is for Israel's benefit or whether it is America's "strategic asset" is arguable. Both nations are needy). Israel needs the influence the American Jews have over the electoral process, both in Congressional and in Presidential elections. It needs the massive influx of cash from the United Jewish Appeal. But Israel is prospering also on its own steam as well. One therefore cannot pass judgement that American Jews by refusing to aliya are not doing their duty by Israel. And who can question with justification whether they are motivated or not by the Abrahamic Covenant? Very religious American Jews are very committed to LAND, TORAH AND MESSIAH despite not proclaiming it too loudly. Their definition of Torah and Messiah may be confused, and when there is no unity there is no strength of action.

There is no need to set up and feed an enmity between North American Jews and Israelis because of the former's refusal to aliya or the latter's ambitions for yerida. American Jews can learn from Israel and Israelis can learn tremendously from America. Look at the great bilateral thinking of Benjamin Netanyahu. He understands what is going on in both places. He has lived in both places. So has Thomas Friedman to whose many insights this book is indebted.

1967 was certainly a vital year for Israel. American Jews are welcome to be awed by it. Israelis are proud of it. It is a watershed for the recognition of Israeli power over its foes. However, complacency and resting on past laurels is not a good idea. Israel is only one lost war away from annihilation and it would be disastrous for that to take place. Imagine Syrian and Iranian tanks manning control of the streets of Jerusalem and their planes patrolling Israeli skies, while Hamas arranges Judenrein in Israel. The current negotiating table between Israel and the Arab Palestinians has to be managed very carefully. It is very important for the US to pay attention to the nuclear threat of Iran for its own and Israel's security. Negotiators will have a very difficult task in planning a Arab Palestinian state composed of the West Bank and Gaza. This will be difficult if Hamas still resolves to secure all of Palestine at any cost.

Eastern European Jews have been predominant in the formation of modern Israel. Sephardic Jews and the Sabra perhaps have had a lesser part. As a nation the Israelis are still forming an identity[223]. Americanism and western European influences are invading. The Middle Eastern influence and culture are still strong in Israeli thinking, especially since a relationship with the surrounding Arab nations and the dialogue with the Arabs within its own borders must be accommodated. As well the tensions created within Israel by its culturally cosmopolitan Jewish characteristics play a role. Israel's religious mosaic is hugely affecting the formation of the new identity. The conflict with the Arab Palestinians and its resolution will have a significant influence in shaping the outcome of that identity. It is to their advantage to cooperate but that will not be easy.

NOTES

[218] See Council of Immigrant Association in Israel

[219] Beirut to Jerusalem by Thomas Friedman page 454

[220] Ibid page 464

[221] Wikipedia—American Jews (estimated at 1.7% of the population)

[222] Esther chapter 4:13,14 "Then Mordecai commanded to answer Esther: Think not with thyself that thou shalt escape in the king's house, more than all the Jews. For if thou altogether holdest thy peace at this time, then shall there relief and deliverance arise to the Jews from another place, and thou and thy father's house shall be destroyed. And who knoweth whether thou art come to the kingdom for such a time as this?".

[223] Israel: In Search of Identity, by Nissim Rejwan.

CHAPTER 21
JEWISHNESS

A definition of 'Jewishness' is almost impossible. It must be given some definition to argue the title of this book. This can be done with reference to: the cultures from which aliya Jews have come; from the political stances of American Jews; with regard to the 'American Dream'; and in the mosaic of Jewish religious convictions. To achieve unity of definition taking all these factors into consideration is almost impossible. There is only one foundation on which to base the assumption of declaring who is the 'true Jew'. Is Judaism that foundation? And what is understood by the word Judaism? The Judaism of Moses was not a philosophy but a conversation with the God of Israel.

It is worth looking at some definitions of Jewishness already out there. Some are entertaining. Others are serious descriptions of who are or who are not true Jews. There is significant debate in Jewish circles already. Some of the opinions are:

- Blacks are the true Jews because quotes from the Tanak are found referring to the visage of a true Jew as black[224]
- True Jews are against dispossessing the Arabs[225]
- Zionists are not true Jews[226]
- American Jews are not true Jews[227]
- Hasidic Jews are true Jews[228]
- Conservative Jews are the true ones[229]
- The Orthodox Jews are the true Jews[230]
- The Reconstructionists are the real Jews[231]
- The Reform Jews are genuine Jews[232]
- The Karaites Jews are the true Jews. This version is appealing in one sense: They reject the Talmud as being the infallible source of laws by which to live. They prefer living by the Tanak. Interpretation of the Tanak is not considered literal but rather contextual. The Talmud can

be a guide for discussion, but the divine source for instruction and final direction is the Tanak[233]

+ Jews who admit to being sinners are the true Jews. This group is also appealing. This belief is based on the quotes from Deuteronomy 6:25, Jeremiah 6:16 and Zephanaiah 2:1-3: "If my people which are called by my name shall humble themselves and pray, and seek my face, and turn from their wicked ways, then I will hear from heaven, and will forgive their sin and will heal their LAND" (emphasis mine). All Jews would agree with this definition. Any Jew who prays at the Wailing Wall admits that. But more than repentance is needed, although it is the first step in building a nation that is founded on the Abrahamic Covenant. Abraham's first step was cleansing his father's house from idols. Repentance from our idolatry is imperative. But then dedication to Land, Torah and Messiah must follow.

+ Haredi Jews are the true Jews[234]

There is a tussle going on in Israel as to which religious Jews are the legitimate Jews.

Thomas Friedman sincerely cites this religious battle for legitimacy. It is a battle for power more than a battle for legitimacy or true Jew definition. He cites the experience of Rabbi Levi Weiman-Kelman. Kelman was an American-trained rabbi from the Conservative stream of Judaism who moved to Israel. He had difficulty in finding a synagogue where he could use his talents. He decided to start his own and rented a hall and attracted a congregation of about 150 Conservative minded Jews who were not attending anywhere else. Friedman claims that 90% of synagogue affiliated American Jews are either Reform or Conservative congregations, which in the 1980s were almost non-existent in Israel. So Rabbi Kelman was filling a void. Friedman points out: "The Orthodox stream of Judaism is the only form of observance supported by Israel's national rabbinical council, known as the Chief Rabbinate"[235]. It happens that the members of the Chief Rabbinate are on the government payroll and they oversee all matters of religious practice involving the state. "The Orthodox and ultra-Orthodox Israeli rabbinical establishment believe that Conservative and Reform rabbis do not operate in accordance with the totality of the Jewish law or Halacha . . . . (and) since the Orthodox have a monopoly on religious authority in Israel, they do not want to see their power and funding diluted by having to share it with the Reform and Conservative movements"[236]. The outcome appears to have been that the Rabbinate used political and brute-force physical interference to break up Kelman's congregation. There is much animosity between the Orthodox Jews and the Reform and Conservative factions. The Reform Jews are extremely jealous of the inside line the Orthodox leaders have with Israel's Prime Ministers.

Jews must get their act together in order to survive. The house divided against itself will fall. What Thomas Friedman then argues in his book is absolutely and tragically frightening—it describes an internal religious war among Jews that will destroy them.

Friedman says:

"In America, Jewish life is organized around the synagogue, yet most American Jews in this day and age join a synagogue not for religious or ritual reasons but for communal solidarity. The synagogue is the island clung to by American Jews in order to avoid assimilation in a sea of Gentiles . . . . the actual religious content of the synagogue's service is secondary for most people . . . . In Israel, by contrast, the vast majority are non-observant Jews. They don't need to join a synagogue in order to avoid assimilation or feel part of a community, because there are other outlets for that which do not take synagogue or ritual forms. They avoid assimilation simply by paying taxes to a Jewish state, speaking Hebrew, and sending their children to state schools, which observe the Jewish holidays as national holidays. That is why a majority of Israelis neither belong to synagogues nor even know what to do once they get inside one"[237]

This situation or condition of both American and Israeli Jews is appalling. Thomas Friedman is well qualified to write on these matters. He is both American and Jewish and has lived for significant periods in both countries in the limelight. But the Abrahamic Covenant does not feature in Friedman's arguments although he does admit there is a 'Super-Story'. The meaning of the Abrahamic Covenant seems to escape him.

Six and a half million warring American Jews are camped opposite five and a half million warring Israeli Jews with the Atlantic Ocean and Mediterranean Sea separating them. They are not united although they crowd under the umbrella of being Jewish. And there is a battle raging.

And it is a 'RELIGIOUS BATTLE', a 'BATTLE IN THE DENIAL OF EACH OTHER'S BRANDS OF JUDAISM'?

In summary

The American Jews admire the State of Israel and since 1967 are bursting with pride because of its perceived strength. The Israelis look to American Jews to aliya. An increasing number of Israelis are leaving for America to chase the 'American Dream'. But American Jews are reluctant to come and live in Israel. The majority of American Jews are Reform and Conservative and do not fit in with the powerful Orthodox Jews in Israel. American Jews sacrificially support Israel financially. So the strongest of bonds encircle them because money has power. The religious differences however are so divisive they could explode from within. This situation must be resolved as unity is vital to avoid another slaughter and diaspora of Israel. The threat to Israel's security is much greater than any potential threat to the comfort and wellbeing of Jews in America. The Israeli Jews are satisfied to have repossessed their LAND. The American Jews are happy in diaspora, happy to stay in 'exile'. America is too comfortable to leave. They have become American to a degree that they are much more American than they are Jewish although many of them would deny it. They continue to feel responsible for Israel but are only willing to provide their money rather than themselves. Their motto is that they are 'One With Israel' but prefer to be separate, so Jews constitute a divided people. Thomas Friedman was of that opinion when he wrote that American Jews are ashamed of the behaviour of Israel's treatment of the Palestinians. His sensitivity in this matter appears triggered by Israel's management of the two intifadas. He is willing to cede the West Bank to the Arabs, although he hedges about splitting Jerusalem with them. He feels the Arabs will be totally and completely and finally appeased when a Arab Palestinian state becomes a reality. He gives the impression that a lack of progress toward a two state settlement has been Israel's reluctance to give up land. If the Jordan River becomes Israel's secure eastern border, Israel will be in great jeopardy with an armed Palestinian state existing west of the Jordan River. Control of the entire Jordan River will not be easy. The existence of such an Arab state would be a source of constant harassment. But Friedman sees a rosy future for both states with all the American know-how to be dispersed. He feels that American foreign policy and the sensibilities of American Jews are being hurt by Israel's reluctance to cooperate with the creation of a Arab Palestinian state within its borders[238]. But American Jews do not live in Israel and will not bear the physical brunt of Arab aggression.

Apart from the above, the religious divide is greater than the political distance that separates American Jews and Israelis. Politics in Israel irritate the sensibilities of

American Jews but the religious divide is the greatest threat for their collective future. Why? Because the Abrahamic Covenant is not being honoured. It is the only divine reason for Israel's existence in the Promised Land. God has allowed them to be decimated when they have not honoured that Covenant several times in the past and it could happen again. The religious rift is very great between the ultra-Orthodox Jews and the Reform Jews. Nobody appears to be doing anything about it in either place. The 'confused' Torah, which Jews revere, and Messianic expectation in Israel, are not fully understood by either group. This is divisive. Both groups get their confused information from sources other than the Tanak and cannot come together.

There is a move in the Knesset to enforce a stereotypical 'Jewishness'. Friedman has written about this:

"... for the past 15 years the Israeli Orthodox parties have been trying to force the Israeli parliament to amend the Law of Return, which stipulates that any Jew in the world can come to Israel and automatically be granted citizenship. The so-called 'Who-is-a-Jew amendment'—which Israel's Orthodox parties have been pushing—would, in effect, define as Jewish, and hence eligible for Israeli citizenship, only those persons born of a Jewish mother or converted to Judaism by an Orthodox rabbi according to Jewish law (halacha)"[239]. Others would be excluded. If the 'Who-is-a-Jew Amendment' ever gets passed, Friedman contends that Reform and Conservative rabbis would not be considered Jewish. However he overlooks the discrimination against followers of Messianic Judaism, which was already in place, when the Supreme Court of Israel ruled in 1989 that Messianic Judaism constituted another religion and that Jews who had become Messianic Jews were not therefore eligible for aliya under the law. This ruling was challenged. On April 16th 2008 a case was brought by a number of people with Jewish fathers and grandfathers whose applications for citizenship had been rejected on the grounds that they were Messianic Jews. The argument was made by the applicants that they had never been Jews according to halacha, and were not therefore excluded by the conversion clause. This argument was upheld in the ruling, and the government agreed to reprocess their applications. Messianic Jews may now have aliya if their father is Jewish, but between 1989 and 2008 they could not[240]. One wonders hypothetically about the future fate of a converted husband of a previously Orthodox Jewish woman who had, along with his previously Orthodox wife, both turned Messianic Jews. Would they be able to aliya? So all is not well in the definition of Jewishness between Orthodox Jews, Reform and Conservative Jews and Messianic Jews. And what of the status of Jews born in Israel who become Messianic Jews? They may all have Jewish mothers. Name-calling and discrimination is rife, even in the Knesset and Supreme Court. Messianic Jews are convinced that their Jewishness is the Tanak. They allege halacha, which is Talmudic is elevated above the Tanak by Orthodox Jews. They insist the Talmud is not canon.

Jewishness in the Tanak comes from the claim that Abraham is the father of the Jews and the acknowledgement of the Abrahamic Covenant. Can the current diasporic Jews remaining out in the world fulfil the Abrahamic Covenant if they are not living in Israel? They seem to think so. American Jewish communal solidarity alone will not sustain American Jews in exile. But it would indeed be difficult to accommodate six million American Jews in Israel in the near future if all sought aliya. Therefore Jews must come to a proper understanding of the Abrahamic Covenant even while living in America and elsewhere in diaspora. It is the best deterrent to assimilation in diaspora. Communal solidarity is good but by itself is not the Abrahamic Covenant. The Abrahamic Covenant defines a mission, and links it to the hallmark of male Jews, which is circumcision.

Jewishness may also be viewed through the eyes of anti-Semitism. This is a negative approach but it reveals a lot, especially in the diaspora, and now in the way some in the world may have come to view Israel as a 'defensive warring nation'. In the pre 1948 diaspora Jews were misfits in Eastern, Central and Western Europe. In Eastern Europe persecution and pogroms were rife killing hundreds of thousands of Jews. Central Europe murdered over six million of them. America and Britain were kinder, but anti-Semitism was still a perception and restrictive. This is best expressed by Nordau's suspicion of Socialism as he had already been suspicious of Liberal philosophy: "If we should live to see Socialist theory become practice, you'll be surprised to meet again in the new order that old acquaintance, anti-Semitism. And it won't help at all that Marx and Lassalle were Jews . . . The founder of Christianity was a Jew too, but to the best of my knowledge Christianity does not think it owes a debt of gratitude to the Jews". His prediction for Socialism was so correct in post 1919 Russia. Nordau saw also the western Jew as rootless, who "was excluded with varying degrees of politeness from the clubs and gatherings of his Christian fellow countrymen . . . . He fled from his Jewish fellows because anti-Semitism had taught him to be contemptuous of them . . . He had lost his home in the ghetto, yet the land of his birth was denied to him as his home. He had no ground under his feet, no community to which he belonged. He was insecure in his relationship with his fellow man, timid with strangers, and suspicious even of the secret feelings of his friends". The Moritz Goldstein article was published in 1913 titled 'German-Jewish Parnassus'. Laqueur aptly summarises it: "Goldstein argued that the Jews were dominating the culture of a people which denied them both the right and the capacity to do so. The newspapers in the capital were about to become a Jewish monopoly. Almost all directors of the Berlin theatres were Jews, as were many of the actors . . . and the study of German literature was also to a large extent in Jewish hands. Everyone knew it; only the Jews pretended it was not worthy of notice. For what mattered they claimed, were their achievements, their cultural and humanistic activities. This, said Goldstein, was a dangerous fallacy, 'for the others do not feel that we are Germans'"[241]. So Jewishness has a negative quality perceived by both Jews and gentiles, which has gotten Jews in a lot of trouble.

This chapter has dealt with the Jewishness of Jews. But the Jewishness of the LAND must also be considered. God talked of "healing the land". If Arabs are residing in Israel they must understand that they are living on JEWISH LAND. That is an extremely important reality of the Abrahamic Covenant—The Land is Jewish because the sacredness of the pronouncement of the Covenant wills it. Abraham's migration there at God's specific request makes the land sacred. It is important to the eschatology of the Tanak. Abraham could have continued to live in Ur of the Chaldees and pioneered a religious influence there. But that was not a divine option. The land must be possessed and cannot be traded away if the Torah is to be obeyed and the Messiah is to be proclaimed. The land is thus defined as Jewish. Jerusalem is indispensably Jewish. The Torah and Messiah also need unity of definition in Israel's immediate future. To be away from the Land as a nation for two thousand years has been Israel's folly. Being back is Israel's strength and legitimacy.

Land or territory is required in a definition of nationhood. Stalin and Lenin specifically referred to the Jews in such a definition. The Jews may be plentiful in diaspora but could not be regarded as a nation. Stalin scoffed at the idea that the Jews in the Soviet Union constituted a nation. Laqueur quotes Stalin: "What kind of race, whose members lived in different parts of the world, spoke different languages, never saw each other and never acted in concert? This was not a real living nation; it was something mystical, amorphous, nebulous, out of this world.... But no one could seriously maintain that petrified religious rites and vanishing psychological traits were stronger than their socio-economic and cultural surroundings, which were inevitably leading to assimilation"[242]. Diasporic Jews could therefore not demand national status or autonomy. Stalin railed against Zionism. He unwittingly underscored that land was sacred to the cause of Zionism, and that "petrified religious rites" should be interpreted by Zionists as 'cast in stone': The Land bequeathed to Abraham in the Covenant with God is indispensable and sacred. Biro Bidzhan or Uganda never could be divine substitutes. Ur of the Chaldees was not a site chosen by God. But Canaan and Jerusalem were. The Land, the Torah and Messianic expectation absolutely define Jewishness.

NOTES

[224] 'Who are the True Jews According to the Bible'? Posted by Zadok. Wikizine 'Israel Rejects Black Hebrews as Jews'. See Race and History News and Views November 2002.

[225] 'Against Zionism: True Jews are Against Dispossessing People of their land and homes'. See Peace and Collaborative Development Network, posted by Patrick Mac Manus, January 2011 in Peace, Conflict and Development.

[226] 'Traditional Jews are not Zionists'. Posted by Michael F Blume
True Torah: 'Jews Against Zionism'. See writings of (i) Satmar Grand Rebbe Joel Teitelbaum, and (ii) Rabbi Stephen Wise

[227] "Korelitz (1996) shows how American Jews during the late 19th and early 20th centuries abandoned a racial definition of Jewishness in favour of one that embraced ethnicity". It is alleged that this was advocated between 1915 and 1925 by the Menorah Movement in their 'Menorah Journal' and largely adopted by American Jews. See Wikipedia in Jewish Self Identity.

[228] See Hasidic Judaism on the internet.
Founded by Ba'al Shem Tov (Rabbi Esrael ben Eliezer). Considered the strictest Jews with reference to their piety. The founding ideal was to restore spirituality and joy to a religion that had become largely academic and buried in Talmudic study.

[229] See Wikipedia: Conservative Jews (Masorti Jews) are traditionalists who want to conserve Jewish traditions.

230 Orthodox Jews are defined as Jews who adhere faithfully to devotion and study of the Torah, synagogue attendance, strict observance of the Sabbath, religious festivals and the dietary laws.

231 See 'Who is a Reconstructionist Jew'? Jewish Virtual Library. There is an appeal to tradition as well as to the search for "contemporary" meaning. True Jewish life encompasses worship and study and full participation in secular life.

232 Reform Jews—See Jewish Virtual Library. The major feature appears to be the acceptance and encouragement of pluralism.

233 See writings of Hazzan Yochanan Zaqantov

234 For Haredi see Thomas Friedman's Beirut to Jerusalem pages 287, 288.

235 Ibid page 470

236 Ibid page 471

237 Ibid pages 474, 475

238 Ibid Pages 496-502

239 Ibid page 476
See also Israel: In Search of an Identity by Nissim Rejwan.

240 Israel Today Magazine April 25, 2008: 'Jerusalem Institute for Justice'.

241 Max Nordau and Moritz Goldstein quoted in Walter Laqueur's book 'History of Zionism' pages 388-391

242 J.V. Stalin's Marxism and the National Question', page 6 quoted in 'A History of Zionism' by Walter Laqueur, Schocken Books, New York, pages 426, 427.

CHAPTER 22
THE CONSTITUTION OF ISRAEL

odern Israel is a democracy and does not have a single-document Constitution as such. The numerous conquests of Israel as a nation since its establishment by Abraham have been debilitating. These fluctuations in its nationhood have kept its nation status in a weak and unstable state. It started as a theocracy where the spoken commands of God were passed mouth to mouth as oral Torah. Following slavery in Egypt, Moses became its great leader and he produced the expanded written Torah. As a theocracy Israel continued to the time of Samuel when it changed to a monarchy. In a long and divided line of monarchs, after the glorious kingdoms of King David and King Solomon, the history of Israel followed a disastrous pattern. Despite the commissioning of the judges and the prophets who tried to lead Israel, multiple lapses into idolatry occurred. Israel's record of nationhood could be summarised as periods of weakness or vanquished status. In AD 70 Israel began a 2000-year lapse in nationhood until 1948. We may arbitrarily divide Israel's nationhood to ancient and modern. Ancient Israel's Constitution was unquestionably the Torah, which will be defined as the Tanak, based solidly on the Abrahamic Covenant. Out of the Tanak and the Talmud grew the Halacha or body of laws. This consisted of the moral law and the system of rituals and ethics, which governed the behaviour of its citizens with each other and with its neighbours. There continues to be a plethora of religious rules without universal application to Jews. The reason to include a discussion of the Constitution of Israel in this book is that it governs anyone living in Israel.

In 1948 Prime Minister David Ben-Gurion after declaring the State of Israel unilaterally settled down to govern. Wisely he did not produce a single-document Constitution of Israel. The Declaration of the Establishment of the State of Israel became "the consensual basis on which the state rests". In essence, it is modern Israel's founding covenant[243]. Subsequently there was a tussle between the secularists and the religious population in referencing God

172

and a compromise was reached to use Tzur Israel (Rock of Israel) as a substitute. If this is recognized as a synonym for Yahweh, so be it. Mizrahi ideology is a compromise between the extreme of secularism and primitive Judaism: "... that the Jewish nation without religion is a body without a soul, that religion and nation constitute an indissoluble unity". The Constitution however must not infringe on religious freedom by legislating the religious practice of citizens. Therefore the Constitution regulates the individual's behaviour as a citizen in the maintenance of an orderly state while religion regulates the behaviour of the individual in his expression of his love to God and his neighbour. Church and state can be kept separate. Daniel Elazar's erudite article on the Israeli Constitution is most comprehensive. He patterns Israel's piece-meal and developing Constitution after the British model. Its scope is outlined well by Elazar in relation to the Knesset and the Courts[244].

Israel's Orthodox view that Ancient Israel's Constitution cannot be ignored in uttering the developing Constitution of the modern State of Israel is valuable. Modern Israel's Constitution should be firmly based on the Abrahamic Covenant of LAND, TORAH and MESSIAH. But the Constitution will be preoccupied with law and order in the land and not seek to legislate religious practice. Israel's religious practice will emanate solely from the Tanak where Torah and Messianic hope reside. The Land caters to the body and breath of life. The Torah and Messianic hope inspire the soul, and make life satisfying and worthwhile.

In the early years of the modern State of Israel the World Zionist Organization and the Jewish Agency had considerable power and influence and succeeded in the Knesset's enacting that "the State of Israel see itself as the creation of the Jewish People in total ...."[245]. In other words there is a Jewish NATION across the globe and a Jewish STATE embodied in the State of Israel. Elazar concludes that "Subsequent agreements have transferred other functions to the state and have altered the structure of the Agency to make it more representative of the Jewish people as a whole, but a basic constitutional framework remains the foundation of the federal pattern which Israel and its diaspora partners are fostering as a means of unifying world Jewry"[246]. A great lesson was learned from the disunity of world Jewry in the crucial years of 1937 and 1938 prior to Hitler's declaration of war and the inability to prevent the Holocaust catastrophe. While the State of Israel needs solidarity with diasporic world Jewry, world Jewry and the State of Israel cannot qualify as a federation. In a federation there is a central government, which binds the units of the federation together. These units are subject to central control, which requires their allegiance. This cannot happen as Israel's current 'constitution' cannot have jurisdiction in the diasporic countries. Only the Abrahamic Covenant can bind diasporic Jewry with Israel and not the temporal, political and judicial segments of the Jewish state. It is incumbent on diasporic world Jewry to secure solidarity with the state of Israel as its protector. Aliya should be achieved by world diasporic Jews to subject them to the state of Israel as citizens. Until then they owe allegiance to the countries they live in as diasporic Jews. Dual and multiple citizenships, are allowed in Israel to Israeli citizens, but must be subject to the Israeli Security Service Law and to a mandatory military service according to that law. As well they are subject to the Penal Law and the Rabbinical Courts Jurisdictions Law regarding marriage and divorce. Those elected to the Knesset may not hold dual citizenship[247]. Dual citizenship has its problems as in the Jonathan Jay Pollard spying case.

Since Israel is multiracial and has a plethoric expression of Judaism, Christianity and Islamism, Israel's 'constitution' will have jurisdiction over all racial and religious divides. But other than religious tolerance and personal freedoms the minority races or religions cannot be permitted any temporal, political or judicial autonomy. Progeny of intermarriage will be treated as individuals who must choose where they want to be racially and religiously. The Moslem component in Israel will be quite large, but despite this there can be no autonomy afforded to them. Moslems and Christians must be governed by the same temporal, political and judicial elements of the 'constitution'. It is understood that the Christians and Moslems choosing to be citizens of the State of Israel will not be allowed to have any kind of separate and independent power as could be accommodated in a federation. Christians and Moslems living in Israel must respect the Abrahamic Covenant. They are welcomed to share in the vision of LAND, TORAH, and MESSIAH.

All citizens of Israel should know about their 'constitution'. Elazar has conveniently and accurately documented Israel's Constitutional Framework[248]. Briefly it consists of:

Table I
1. Declaration of Independence (1948)
2. Legislation of Constitutional Import
3. Basic Laws

Table II
1. The Foundations of the State:
   A. The Constitutional Force of the Declaration of Independence.
   B. Continuity of pre-state legislation
   C. The Territorial Integrity and Boundaries of the State (Basic Law: Jerusalem, enacted 1980)
   D. Official Languages and their use
2. Basic Constitutional Principles:
   A. Israel as a Jewish State (Declaration of Independence; Law of Return, enacted 1950)
   B. Religion and the State
   C. Citizenship, Nationality and Immigration (The Law of Return)
   D. The Rule of Law
   E. Separation of Powers
   F. Basic Laws
3. Basic Political Institutions:
   A. Elections
   B. The Knesset
   C. The Government
   D. The Presidency
   E. Local Government
4. Other State Institutions:
   A. Israeli Defence Forces
   B. State Comptroller
   C. Israeli Lands
5. The State Economy
6. The State and National Institutions
   A. The Jewish Agency and the Zionist World Federation
   B. Specialised National Institutions

Personal Comment

Christians and Moslems must recognize and respect the abiding foundation of the reason for Israel's existence, which is the Abrahamic Covenant and its commitment to Land, Torah and Messiah. Then they must submit to be governed by the above constitutional pronouncements. Their loyalty to the Jewish State must be solid or they must be advised to emigrate.

NOTES

[243] Jerusalem Centre for Public Affairs, Daniel Elazar Papers Index, Constitution, Government and Politics, 'The Constitution of the State of Israel' by Daniel Elazar

[244] See Berthold Lewkowitz, Der Weg des Misrahi, Vienna 1936, cited by Walter Laqueur In his book 'A History of Zionism' Schocken Books, New York.
See also Daniel Elazar Papers Inde, as above.

[245] Ibid.

[246] Israel Nationality Law, Wikipewdia, the Free Encyclopedia.

[247] Dan Eden: Dual Citizenship—Loyal to Whom?

[248] Jerusalem Centre for Public Affairs, Daniel Elazar Papers Index: Constitution, Government and Politics.

CHAPTER 23
NETANYAHU'S SECOND TERM

W hat mandate did Benjamin Netanyahu obtain in the last election to become Prime Minister? His Likud Party had won one seat less than Zipporah Malka "Tzipi" Livni's Kadima Party. Before answering this question it is vital to consider Tzipi Livni's position. Her Kadima Party had government under Ariel Sharon and Ehud Olmert prior to the last election. After Netanyahu formed government Livni became the first woman opposition leader. She is considered pragmatic, a valuable qualification. She is the nation's leading voice today for a second two state solution. But her stance is validated by only a paper-thin support in her party. She won the leadership of the Kadima Party by only 1.1%[249]. Livni could not form government because she would have been defeated immediately in the Knesset by the majority who do not support her pragmatism. So Netanyahu came to power presumably on the understanding that another two state solution would not be immediately embraced. Despite Livni's compromise to support another two state solution she has significant insight which wars against her own inner pragmatism.

Hezbollah has entered into Lebanon's democratic process[250] and Hamas into the Gaza elected government[251]. World opinion could be that this process legitimises Hezbollah and Hamas. But both are motivated by the express aim of wiping Israel off the map. Livni said: "With more accountability, such groups would be tempted to abandon their military approach in favour of a purely political platform. But this analysis ignored the possibility that some radical groups sought participation in the democratic process, not to forsake their violent agenda but to advance it"[252]. The question must be asked: "If al Qaeda were to become a political party winning electoral endorsement, say in Turkey which is considered a democratic country, or Yemen where it has considerable power already, would the EEC and the US accept it as a legitimate democratic cause"? Livni supported Israel's invasion of Hamas-run Gaza. The warrant issued for her arrest by a court in Britain on the basis of possible war crimes charges embarrassed Britain's Labour Government[253]. These outrageous sentiments are felt to expose dangers to Israel's existence. Israel has learned that it cannot trust public and judicial opinions even in her so-called allies. This illustrates how vulnerable the security of Israel is to pragmatism and so-called logic. Livni may never form government if she runs on the policy of giving away land. Israel's security is seen as based on the foundation of land, guaranteed by her own strength besides the reliance on her allies. The number and friendliness of the foreign embassies in Tel Aviv or Jerusalem is comforting but not security enough on which to base survival.

What is happening in the Netanyahu Government today? Governments must have a guiding philosophy but they cannot spend all their time in philosophising. To govern rightly is to look after the welfare of all the inhabitants of the state. Netanyahu has to concern himself, not only with the future but also the present. His first term in government was exemplary in his handling of the economy. No state prospers if the economy is not growing. His second term is proceeding well. Underneath his 'pragmatism' is the understanding that the reason he is Prime Minister, and not Livni, is because the base of his parliamentary support includes the parties who are in opposition to giving away significant land necessary for Israel's defence.

A brief look at Israel's current economy is revealing. The economy expanded an annualised 4.7% in the first quarter of 2011 as exports and investments climbed. This is part of a continuing upward trend since Netanyahu took power. Housing is expanding with no mortgage crisis. Unemployment is expected to drop to 6.1% by the end of 2011. The shekel has gained 7% against the American dollar. Inflation has slowed to 4% [254]. American aid to Israel is 3 billion dollars a year in cash besides loan guarantees. Israel spends more of its GDP on defence (double) than any other western country. The global economic crisis was faced by Israel with increased taxes and not by stimulus spending. This has worked according to the Finance Minister to diminish the global downturn's adverse effects in Israel and the success of this policy is obvious[255]. Netanyahu is certainly doing well.

In September 2010 Israel qualified to and joined the OECD (Organization for Economic Cooperation and Development). In 2010 the Bank of Israel was ranked first among Central Banks. As of 2010 Israel ranked second among foreign countries in the number of its companies listed on the US Stock

Exchanges. In 2010 the Leviathan Natural Gas Deposit was found estimated at 16 trillion cubic feet. It is not in production yet. Currently 64.7% of Israel's electricity comes from coal while 32.6% comes from natural gas. The latter is expected to increase sharply. Tourism is a major source of income. In 2010, 3.4 million foreign tourists visited Israel[256].

The other vital element of Israel's security is her foreign policy, as it exists today in the Netanyahu regime. A discussion of the evolution of the foreign policy of Israel since 1948 would fill volumes. It is beyond the scope of this book. Israel's future is tied up with it and together with the economy forms the cornerstone of Israel's security. The dialogue between Prime Minister Benjamin Netanyahu and President Barak Obama and the vital decisions they make or do not make will determine the outcome for some time, at least in the near future. Netanyahu will only act in accordance with the will of the population of Israel. At this time of writing it is yet to be determined wither the 'Arab Spring' is heading. The existence of stable democratic Arab governments in the Middle East will certainly bring prosperity to the Arab world. The banishment of poverty is the ultimate bulwark against strife. But since Israel is living within a 'Sea of Arab States' a new Arab atmosphere will be a boon.

Israel's foreign policy issues today have been aptly headed as follows[257]:

> United States Aid
> Washington's pressures for peace talks.
> Military sales to China
> Maintenance of contracts with Venezuela
> Jerusalem
> Public opinion
> Population trends and immigration
> Strategic cooperation
> Espionage.
> The Arab Spring

A detailed discussion of the above is beyond the scope of this book and is not necessary to arrive at several conclusions. Netanyahu needs to clearly ascertain where the Israeli majority stands with regard to the issue of giving away LAND. He can only then act on that decision. It has to be clearly understood that not only is US aid to Israel important to Israel's survival, but also important to the standing and future of the United States in the world and its position in the Middle East. The presence of Israel as a nation represents the strength and resolve of the United States. US aid should not be used as a stick to force compatibility with what may appear to be in the best interests of the US alone, especially if it is a policy determined by what is best for the US-Arab relationship. And it certainly is not what may be concocted as best for achieving "Peace in the World". Questions arise: Has the World lined itself up against China to wrest away Tibet in the interests of "Peace in the World"? Does the US have a two state settlement policy to impose on China and Tibet? Is the violent threat of extremist Moslem terrorism to be appeased by the destruction of Israel?

So what does Netanyahu face and what is he saying? As stated already above he is facing tremendous pressure from outside Israel to a two state solution. And it is also coming from Livni and the 'Knesset Caucus', which is originating from the Kadima Party. The next election will test Israel's resolve to keep the post 1967 borders or will see them give away LAND which is seen as vital to Israel's existence. So the big question is: "If Israel will not allow a second two state solution what shall be done with the Palestinians in the West Bank and Gaza"? This is the real question facing Netanyahu and Israel. To face this question Israel needs reformation and unity. It needs to understand the Abrahamic Covenant, which is basically LAND, TORAH AND MESSIAH. How does the Abrahamic Covenant translate into a viable political process? Israel cannot divest itself of the Abrahamic Covenant and simply come to a secular pragmatic 'peace at any cost' decision. Plainly speaking: The Arabs came during the hiatus of Israel's devastation and diaspora and a clear plan is necessary to accommodate them. Just as there was a streaming back of Jews to Israel there could be a streaming back of Arab Palestinians to Arab countries. Israel should and must facilitate this transition if it becomes a reality. If Israel is not going to be a partner to the formation of a Moslem state within its borders a viable alternate plan is vital. Facilitation of another Arab State in Palestine is deemed to always threaten Israel's security. Hezbollah and Hamas will not go away. Iran will not seek an embassy in Jerusalem once a Arab Palestinian State is established. The evolution or devolution of Israel's relationship with the 'new Egypt' and indeed with all the new Arab Spring countries remains indeterminate at present. The vast amount of Arab land possession in the Middle East is expected to come into the equation.

Benjamin Netanyahu is a very able man and knows the aspirations of the Jewish people. He will be wise and circumspect. Netanyahu has told Obama that return to pre 1967 borders will not happen. His address to the US Congress was masterful[258]. He demonstrates strong leadership. His address to the US Congress is on the Internet but I will repeat some of his statements:

1. In a region of shifting alliances, Israel is America's unwavering ally.
2. Support for Israel's security is a wise investment in our common future, for an epic battle is now underway in the Middle East between tyranny and freedom.
3. Of the 300 million Arabs in the Middle East and North Africa only Israel's Arab citizens enjoy real democratic rights.
4. But while we hope and work for the best we must also recognize that powerful forces oppose this future. They oppose modernity. They oppose democracy. They oppose peace.
5. A nuclear armed Iran . . . would make the nightmare of nuclear terrorism a clear and present danger throughout the world . . . . The threat to my country cannot be overstated.
6. No distortion of history could deny the 4000-year-old bond between the Jewish people and the Jewish land.
7. . . . our conflict . . . . has always been about the existence of the Jewish state.
8. . . . the Palestinian refugee problem will be resolved outside the borders of Israel
9. Jerusalem must never be divided again. Jerusalem must remain the united capital of Israel.
10. . . . in the Middle East the only peace that will hold is the peace you can defend. So peace must be anchored in security.
11. . . . if Israel simply walked out of the territories. The flow of weapons into a future Palestinian state would be unchecked . . . .
12. . . . it's vital, absolutely vital—that Israel maintain a long-term military presence along the Jordan River.
13. . . . . no one can guarantee that our peace partners today will be there tomorrow.
14. Hamas remains committed to Israel's destruction and to terrorism.
15. All people who cherish freedom owe a profound debt of gratitude to your great nation. (the United States of America).

Netanyahu has taken a strong stand. The security of the State of Israel is his prime concern. He sees it through survival right wing eyes.

Thomas Friedman's opinions are valuable and he should update his book. His Americanism sometimes overcomes him. In the New York Times of 17th September 2011 he wrote an OP-ED article entitled: 'Israel: Adrift at Sea Alone'. He laments the recent events in Israel's diplomacy, which include the 'collapse' of the relationships with Turkey and Jordan and the deteriorating relationship with Egypt in the Arab Spring and the further destabilization of the relationship with the Syrian Arab Spring. The latter two are really unknown quantities at present under no predictable outcome and control. Friedman also views the refusal by Netanyahu to accept Arab Palestinian statehood at the UN and the painting of Obama into the corner of a veto at the Security Council, which he states Obama is struggling to avoid, as very serious backward steps. He feels Netanyahu and his foreign minister are the obstacles to a more peaceful life for the Israelis. Friedman may be wrong in his current views. His conclusion: "Unfortunately, Israel today does not have a leader or a cabinet for such subtle diplomacy. One can only hope that the Israeli people will recognize this before this government plunges Israel into deeper global isolation and drags America along with it". This is a dire opinion to hold and undercuts the confidence in Israel's democratic governing parties. In Friedman's opinion there appears to be no one of 'stature' in Israel to take up Friedman's 'cause'.

This opinion is a very shaky one and is not helpful to Israel. One has to wonder whether Friedman has considered making the ultimate sacrifice by achieving aliya and perhaps aligning with Tzipi Livni, running for the Knessett, and convincing the Israeli electorate of his views for the future of Israel. He has supporters in Israel and could be a desirable leader. He understands the dynamics of diplomacy and government. It is reported that he has advised the Obama Presidency. He would be an excellent candidate to secure the perpetuity of Israel. A 'Prime Minister Thomas L Friedman' should then negotiate a Palestinian State, and secure Israel's future by emphasizing the Abrahamic Covenant. Security of the LAND of Israel, reformation of the TORAH, and realization of the MESSIAH will be his overwhelming challenge. It is possible that he has "come to the kingdom for such a time as this". But he must act to achieve his convictions. In the interim he is undermining Netanyahu's government with his journalism. Is he taking an anti-Zionist stance similar to the liberals in the early 20th century?[259] In another recent article in the New

York Times Friedman has stated in commenting on the resounding ovation Netanyahu received in the US Congress when he spoke there in May 2011 that it had been: ". . . bought and sold by the Israel lobby"[260]. Prime Minister Netanyahu's senior advisor Ron Dermer has adequately replied.

Recently severe criticism of Prime Minister Netanyahu has come from David Remnick, editor of The New Yorker[113]. Remnick grew up in a secular Jewish home and if he has any understanding of the Abrahamic Covenant, he has not expressed it. He severely criticizes Avigdor Lieberman, Netanyahu's foreign minister as "wildly xenophobic", without recognizing the nature of the Israeli government to be a coalition. Lieberman, as an ultra orthodox Jew, may have some extreme ideas but Netanyahu needs him in the coalition. That is why this book calls for a reformation of Judaism to the centre, which is Tanak inspired, and where the religion of Abraham, Moses and Jacob is based. Extreme ideas will not be shed in Israeli thinking without the reformation called for by this book.

NOTES

249 Israel News, 17th September 2005: 'Tzipi Livni Wins Kadima Leadership by Narrow Margin' (1.1%)

250 World News on msnbc.com: 'Coming Out Party For Hezbollah in Lebanon' by Jim Maceda

251 BBC News, 28th January 2005: 'Big Hamas Win in Gaza Election' (75 out of 118 seats)

252 MK Tzipi Livni, Leader of the Kadima Party and Leader of the Opposition in the Knesset.

253 CBC (Canadian Broadcasting Corporation) News: Israel Upset After UK warrant Targets Politician, 15th December 2009.
     Guardian.co.uk News: British Court Issued Gaza Arrest Warrant for Tzipi Livni' Article by Ian Black and Ian Cobain, 14th December 2009

254 Bloomberg May 16th, 2011.

255 'Explaining Israel's Growing Economy', Newsweek March 2010.

256 See Wikipedia: Tourism in Israel

257 See Wikipedia: Israeli Foreign Policy

258 Transcript of Prime Minister Netanyahu's Address to the US Congress, The Globe and Mail (Canada), 24th May 2011.

²⁵⁹ See chapter of this book on Zionism.

²⁶⁰ See Jerusalem Post breaking news "PM advisor's letter to 'New York Times;' 12/16/2011 Senior Advisor Ron Dermer replies to the NY Times' request for Netanyahu to write an OPED piece.

CHAPTER 24
WHITHER AMERICAN FOREIGN POLICY?

The support of the United States for the existence and safety of Israel has been apparent since the formation of the United Nations. It will not be easily rescinded. Israel recognizes its semi dependence on the US and is grateful. It is therefore important to know where Israel stands with the changing face of US politics. Essentially, this is a discussion of the policies presidents of the US have advocated since 1948 and into the present and future. Significant activity did not take place till after the 1967 Six Day War. The frenzy of attempts to bring peace was motivated because Israel came to be seen as a 'occupying power'. This placed Israel in 'aggressor and bully' roles. How did this affect American attitude toward Israel? How did this attitude translate into positions of strength or weakness? How should Israel react and behave towards these attitudes or stances? Has the changing face of the Middle East placed Israel in a stronger or more vulnerable position? Has America's standing in the world affected Israel's strength or vulnerability?

US diplomacy in the Middle East has been complicated by America's need for oil and therefore placation of the Arab states that have oil. Even though the Americans have had an innate desire to defend Israel (apart from the presence of the Jewish lobby) there is the realization that America is inordinately dependent on oil and its economy is intertwined with the motor vehicle industry, which is a major consumer of oil. The price of oil soars when there is a disturbance in the Middle East. The OPEC (Organization of Petroleum Exporting Countries) cartel came into being as a pressure tactic to enforce Arab wishes. Despite American dedication to bringing democracy to the Middle East it has been forced to befriend the despots in the oil rich countries, which have not been using their oil riches to relieve poverty and promote the aspirations of their peoples.

US diplomacy has also been affected by its own vulnerability to the changing face of Islam. Three factors have been cited as being causative. One is the friendship of the US with Arab despots governed by the US appetite for oil. Another is its friendship with and protection of Israel. The third appears to have been retired after the time of President Reagan: competition in the global balance of power with communism. The disintegration of the Soviet empire and the changed face of Chinese communism into a global 'capitalistic' economic power brought amelioration. President Nixon was the giant who engineered the inevitable inclusion of China in world affairs. President Reagan, Prime Minister Thatcher and President Gorbachev managed the inevitable collapse of Soviet communism. American diplomacy no longer has to cope with communism. But Islamic Jihad took the place of communism by threatening the security of the United States.

Islamic Jihad has arisen for two reasons. First the perception of sponsorship of Arab despots who were keeping the Arab masses in poverty. This began with the suppression of the rise of Iranian democracy. Mossadeq was crushed in favour of the Shah Pahlavi. This gave power to the Ayatollahs and created the current pariah state of 'theocratic' Iran. The US befriends the Saudi Royal family's grip on power. It initially supported Saddam Hussein. It supported the Hashemite dynasty, the Egyptian and Pakistani military regimes, and tolerated the Syrian despot. Al Qaeda was spawned in opposition to the presence of American troops on Saudi soil. The other reason advanced is the creation of Israel in the guise of a two state solution, twins conceived in an inhospitably small womb. The League of Nations left a midwife in charge who could not deliver twins. One twin was born by abruptio. The other twin remains unborn. There is no qualified doctor able to perform Caesarean section. The British Mandate engineered the first two state settlement creating Jordan but failed to shift the Arabs east of the Jordan River although they prevented Jews from settling east of it. Had Britain moved the small number of Arabs in the West Bank (in 1920) to east of the Jordan River, there would have been no problem today.

Islamic Jihad continues to haunt US diplomacy in Iraq, Afghanistan and Pakistan, and elsewhere, while constantly threatening the US mainland and US allies. A world wide clandestine network of the al Qaeda with a 'home-grown' constituency still threatens even though bin Ladin is no more.

The Afghan and Iraqi wars and the unreliable Pakistan are impoverishing the US and controlling its foreign policy. And now another force has surfaced. The Arab Spring started a modern element in Iran where it was crushed but is belatedly now in full theatre west of that country. It has complicated US and NATO foreign policy in the Middle East.

With this backdrop for the whirlpool that is the Middle East, the democratic State of Israel is America's only bastion there. The Arab Spring cannot yet be counted upon. It would be the height of folly to weaken and destabilize Israel by insisting on a two state solution without safeguards. A properly negotiated settlement that ensures Israel's security must take place.

A brief look at the policies of the US presidents since Israel's inception in 1948 is valuable. They were all ignorant of or did not acknowledge the roots of Judaism and the Abrahamic Covenant:

1. **Franklin D Roosevelt** 1933-1945. He supported Jewish immigration to Palestine and took measures to increase Jewish migration quotas to the US. It is alleged he could have done more to prevent Hitler from perpetrating the Holocaust[261]. His Evian Conference was a failure in saving Jews from Hitler. But he did assist modern Israel's inception despite his making the same promises to the Arabs who he wanted as allies. There was significant duplicity in his negotiations with Jews and Arabs.

2. **Harry Truman** 1945-1953. He concluded World War II. He supported statehood for Israel. His promises to the Jews were not followed by solid action. His most significant move was to request that 100,000 Jews from the post-war refugee camps in Europe be admitted to Palestine. This was highly irritating to Clement Attlee's Labour Government and Ernest Bevin, the Foreign Minister. They had no intention to carry this out because of their promises to the Arabs. But it was the delayed fulfilment of this request that led to the whole matter being referred back to the United Nations Organization where a study was commissioned. The UN Study Committee recommended that the 100,000 Jewish immigrants from European refugee camps be transferred to Palestine and the British White Paper that had replaced the Balfour Declaration be rescinded. This eventually led to the UN vote, which resulted in the revoking of the British Mandate and the eventual withdrawal of the British from Palestine and

the unilateral declaration of the State of Israel[262]. The United Nations' Partition Plan of the 29th November 1947 came into being.

3. **Dwight Eisenhower** 1953-1961. He wanted Israel to return to the 1948 borders but he did nothing to further an agreement[263]. Because of this any policy he may have formulated would not have helped Israel. He was too preoccupied by Suez, Iran, and communism to clarify a succinct policy toward Israel. He was however willing to help any nation that might be threatened by the Soviet Union.

4. **John Kennedy** 1961-1963. He was pro-Arab in his Middle Eastern policy[264]. This interpretation is because he tried to maintain a balance of power between Arabs and Israelis and prevent Israel from being strong militarily and having nuclear weapons. Kennedy exerted pressure on the Israeli government to inspect Israel's nuclear facilities. Ben-Gurion's government was thus weakened leading to his leaving office. During Kennedy's tenure and his successor's tenure the surrounding Arab nations secretly prepared for war to annihilate Israel. US intelligence had to know that but they let it progress unchecked. This would eventually culminate in the 1967 Six Day War. Winning the 1967 Six Day War during Levi Eshkol's tenure greatly strengthened Israel.

5. **Lyndon Johnson** 1963-1969. Managing competition with the Soviet Union's influence in the Middle East was Johnson's motivation. He was preoccupied with Vietnam and tried to prevent the 1967 War by negotiation with Eshkol, Nasser, Kosygin, and U Thant, with backing from Britain and France. As usual the US was seeking multilateral support for intervention abroad. While Johnson dithered Eshkol, Eban, and Dyan acted. The Six Day War was to be the most decisive action Israel had taken and provided its perceived current borders. After the war was over Johnson emphasized negotiation and initiated the "Land for Peace" ideology as a negotiating tactic[265]. This negotiating ideology was echoed by Israel. Giving away Israeli possessed soil has not ensured Israel's peace and security. Lyndon Johnson's dithering and Eshkol's decision to act pre-emptively to the Egyptian-Syrian-Jordanian war machine has worked mightily in Israel's favour. The British sponsored UN Resolution 242, which followed the war was not implemented fully. It could not obtain Israel's long-term security.

6. **Richard Nixon** 1969-1974. Nixon was preoccupied with Soviet Union détente, Vietnam, China and finally Watergate to be able to bring a concerted peace to the Middle East. The Soviet Union backed Egypt and

Syria with arms and personnel. Nixon was bound to grudgingly balance this with arms and moral support to Israel. But his main motivation was to prevent confrontation with the Soviet Union. In Nixon's mind détente was more of a priority than Israel. Golda Meir and Rabin had to be strong against the initiatives of Secretary of State Rogers and the US State Department, in their attempts to force one-sided Israeli concessions to the Arabs. Occupation of the Sinai was the cause of enmity with Egypt and also the position of the strength of Israel. Possession of the Golan Heights was Israel's strength in the face of Syria. The Jordanian king's vulnerability to the Arab Palestinians and their support of the Syrian incursion into Jordan led to a significant pledge by the US and Israel in Jordan's support. US-Israeli ties were strengthened and benefited from arms shipments to Israel, which had been slow in coming. Henry Kissinger, Nixon's National Security Advisor, played an active role during this time. When he became Secretary of State he advocated a slow resolution to Israeli-Arab disagreements. This was labelled "stalemate" balance of power and "standstill" diplomacy. It led to Israel's strength in consolidating the gains of the Six Day War. Nasser's replacement by Sadat who was willing to expel the Russians also helped. But Sadat's demand that Israel withdraw to pre 1967 borders was bluntly met by Meir's reply: "Israel will not withdraw to the pre-June 5, 1967 lines". The Yom Kippur War ensued which by Arab initiation was meant to enforce the withdrawal of Israel to pre-1967 borders. This war was won decisively by Israel with US arms support in the face of massive support to the Arabs by the Soviet Union. Nixon and Kissinger strengthened Israel's hand indirectly with their intention to keep the Soviet Union at bay. Israel benefited from American money and arms. Kissinger's diplomatic efforts achieved disengagement lines between Israel and Egypt and Israel and Syria after the Yom Kippur War but not much else. The Geneva Conference of 1973 was only a public relations exercise[266].

7. **Gerald Ford** 1974-1977. The Kissinger diplomacy continued into the Ford presidency. Ford attempted to pressure Israel into concessions to Egypt. He threatened to review the US-Israeli relationship in terms of money and arms. He feared another oil embargo. But the US Congress was opposed to this and he backed down. Kissinger achieved the Sinai II further disengagement peace between Israel and Egypt[267].

8. **Jimmy Carter** 1977-1981. Carter was perhaps the most religious of all recent presidents. But he had no professed knowledge of the roots of Judaism. His basic ignorance of the Arabization of the Middle East led

him to believe that there was a historic 'Palestinian Homeland' to be established in Israel. He felt that the Arabs' predisposition to not recognise Israel till there was a return to pre 1967 borders was justified. He ignored Israel's 4000-year history in favour of his presumed Arab ownership of Palestine. His 'crowning achievement' was the Camp David Accords, which eventually led to diplomatic peace between Israel and Egypt. This was largely due to Sadat's willingness to recognize Israel than to Carter's persuasiveness. Sadat saw that what Carter and Vance were preparing to take to another Geneva Conference would never get off the ground under the planned co-chairmanship of the US and the Soviet Union. Besides, the Arab states were not united in their aims. Sadat was responsible for getting the Camp David Accords motivated and Begin was the victor in preventing it from resulting in a commitment to an unjust two state result. Carter's efforts for a two state settlement failed. When the Iranian 'hostage crisis' occurred he was distracted[268]. Carter's bias to the Arabs was very apparent. It is eminently exposed by his actions since he left the presidency. His comparison of Israel's control of the West Bank and Gaza to apartheid is exaggerated and calumnious and has not helped Israel's cause[269]. It takes no account of the actions Israel needed to take to prevent the unpredictable Arab Palestinian suicide bombings and their other clandestine guerrilla tactics within Israel's borders. Arab Palestinians in the West Bank today have a thriving economy. Stable management of the West Bank by Israel is the supporting framework for this prosperity. It is unfair to label this apartheid.

9. **Ronald Reagan** 1981-1989. He regarded a strong Israel as a strategic asset[270]. But he failed to treat Israel as such. He did not immediately pursue Carter's initiatives to establish a Arab Palestinian state. His foreign policy was preoccupied with communism and the cold war. He came to the presidency highly concerned about the Soviet invasion of Afghanistan. Reagan did not understand Israeli besetment, that is to say, Israel was trying to defend against Iraq and Jordan on their east flank, Syria and Lebanon on the northern flank and Egypt on the western flank. And in all three flanks the PLO was subversively attacking Israel instead of seeking a negotiated peace. He made sure the withdrawal from the Sinai was completed after Sadat was assassinated, which Israel intended anyway. He failed to see Begin's bombing of the Iraqi nuclear reactor as of value. He supplied the Saudi's with Airborne Warning and Control System aircraft, which was perceived as detrimental to Israel's security. He saw Israel's

incursion into Lebanon as a disturbance of the balance of power with the Soviet Union. Despite this Israel was able to drive out the aggressive PLO leadership from Jordan, then from Lebanon to Egypt from where they were evicted to Tunis. Reagan's plan to annex Gaza and the West Bank to Jordan was vehemently opposed by Begin and declined by Jordan. Again Reagan failed to treat Israel as a strategic asset by trying to give away land, which would have weakened Israel. His involvement in Lebanon also failed when Syria perpetrated the bombing of the American embassy in Beirut and the devastating loss of three hundred American servicemen who were peacekeepers there. Reagan's foreign policy in the Middle East was somewhat 'confused' later in his presidency with ambivalent loyalties in the Iran-Iraq War, and with the emergence of terrorism suffered by Americans abroad from radical Islamic elements motivated and financed by Libya, Iran and Syria. He bombed Gadhafi, countenanced the Iran-Contra Affair, and then tried to reconvene a peace conference to achieve an Arab-Israeli settlement co-chaired with the Soviet Union. When the first Intifada started Israel recognized its vulnerability and Shamir appealed to Schultz. After Schultz arrived on the scene the Camp David Accords blossomed again but did not come to fruition. In the waning days of Reagan's presidency, Schultz persuaded Arafat and the PLO to recognize the State of Israel and its right to exist and Arafat also renounced terrorism. This cleared the way for Israel to have direct talks with the PLO with the US as convenor or supervisor[271].

10. **George H. W. Bush** 1989-1993. The Soviet Union collapsed during this presidency although it started happening in Reagan's tenure. This removed serious competition with the Soviets for influence in the Middle East. Bush became preoccupied with the Gulf War—Operation Desert Storm to free Kuwait and he prevented Israel from retaliating to Iraqi SCUD missiles much to Israel's chagrin. Arafat sided with Sadam Hussein, which led to his increased disfavour. In the aftermath of the Gulf War, Baker conceived the Madrid Peace Conference. This was to be co-chaired with Gorbachev. This also widened representation from the Arab world and included other Arab Palestinians, weakening Arafat's own PLO representation there. In his attempt to bring peace to the Arab-Israeli scene Bush based his efforts on UN resolutions 242 and 338. He pressed Israel to freeze Jewish settlement activity linking it to aid to Israel. Shamir's refusal to talk directly to the PLO, freeze settlement activity, link Jerusalem to the talks or compromise territorially led to the US with-holding of the $10 billion loan

guaranty for Israel. This aid was very necessary to accommodate the great influx of Soviet Jews into Israel at this time. Bush was clearly anti Israel in his attitude regarding the loan guarantees. This was thought to cause Shamir's defeat at the Knesset election that followed, at which Labour defeated Likud. Several factors for this were considered. Possibly the large majority of secular Jews saw that preservation of Israel lay in some sort of compromise. Possibly the secular electorate viewed the right wing religious parties as too protected by Shamir. Possibly the right wing parties saw Shamir as weak in not responding to the Iraqi SCUD missiles. Perhaps he was seen as too easily acquiescing to Bush. With Rabin as Prime Minister, Baker restarted negotiations to achieve an Arab-Israeli peace. Rabin made a half-hearted concession in cancelling some settlement housing starts but did not call a freeze. He was granted the $10 billion loan guaranty. With Bush's defeat in the US presidential election and the increase in violence in Israel, which caused Rabin to be more hardline in dealing with it, the peace process went nowhere. The Oslo Accords were conceived without US involvement starting in 1991 during Bush's tenure[272].

11. **William Clinton** 1993-2001 He entered the Arab-Israeli dialogue with his advisors firmly believing that Rabin's pragmatism would win them success. Rabin pursued separate negotiations with both the US and the Norwegians. But they merged in the White House as the Oslo Accords, signed by Rabin and Arafat in the presence of Clinton. Rabin was talking to the PLO renamed 'Palestinian Authority' offering them limited self-government in Gaza and Jericho, and talking indirectly to the Syrians offering them Golan as land for peace, all with conditions and under the umbrella of US supervision. On October 26, 1994 Israel and Jordan signed a Peace Treaty after secret talks between Rabin and King Hussein. Clinton officiated at the signing. Subsequently further agreements between Rabin and the Palestinian Authority became known as Oslo II and again signed under Clinton's auspices. Not long after the signing Rabin was assassinated by Yigal Amir. Peres became Prime Minister and elections were held in the West Bank and Gaza giving Yasser Arafat's Palestinian Authority electoral legitimacy. Yossi Beilin and Mahmoud Abbas held talks outlining further arrangements. Violence then erupted perpetrated by Hamas and other Palestinian militants with multiple suicide bombings in Israel. Israeli retaliation occurred and further peace talks ended. In the ensuing election of the Knesset, Likud was returned and Netanyahu replaced Peres as Prime Minister. Clinton was more popular with both Israelis and Arabs than any

other previous president was perceived to be. But his efforts are considered more passive in motivation, allowing the parties involved to come to terms of their own rather than to blazing a settlement from a master plan of his own[273]. In his second domestically troubled term when impeachment was a possibility, Secretary of State Madeline Albright took the initiative to push Netanyahu. But Netanyahu was not cooperative and Oslo II did not succeed. The Wye Agreement provided some redemption for Clinton, but that too failed. The election of Barak brought some hope to the waning Clinton presidency. At what was dubbed Camp David II Barak could not deliver Arafat's demands despite the marathon session energized by Clinton. Sharon's visit to the Temple Mount appeared to incite the Second Intifada, which led to bloodshed and Barak's resignation, which forced new elections. Clinton called a summit at Sharm al-Sheik to call a truce to the mayhem. A last ditch effort by Barak to work out a peace with Arafat did not succeed. Al Qaeda attacked the USS Cole killing seventeen sailors. Ariel Sharon was elected Prime Minister of Israel. Since leaving office Clinton appears strongly supportive of the two state settlement. He recently stated: "An increasing number of the young people in the IDF are the children of Russians and settlers, the hardest core people against a division of the land. This is a staggering problem". This statement is perceived in Israel as unfair. To Israel, defence of its land cannot be a staggering problem to peace? The Clintons are currently hand in glove with Obama in US attitude to Israel.

12. **George W. Bush** 2001-2008. Bush came to the presidency with a bias towards Israel. The reason for this may have been religious. Sharon was as yet an unknown quantity but Bush was biased in his favour. He believed in a strong Israel. Secretary of State Powell met with Arafat and Sharon and urged them to achieve peace. He told Sharon to stop building new settlements in the occupied territories. Clinton had commissioned George Mitchell to investigate the start of the second Intifada and Bush endorsed the findings of the Mitchell Report[274]. Violence continued, incited by Palestinian suicide bombings. And then al Qaeda struck with the attack on the Twin Towers of the World Trade Centre and the Pentagon. Three thousand people died. Bush began his war on terrorism and became preoccupied by the battle with Islamic Jihad. He started two wars in an effort to bring security to the United States. Bush decided also to pursue Arab-Israeli peace resorting to the 'two state solution'. However when a shipment of arms from Iran bound for Arafat was intercepted Arafat was isolated in his Ramallah compound and Sharon re-established a strong

military presence in the West Bank and moved to crush the Intifada. Prince Abdallah of Saudi Arabia brought forth a plan that all Arab states would recognize Israel if the pre 1967 borders were resumed. At this point a suicide bomber claimed twenty-nine Israelis. Bush stated that America recognised Israel's right to defend itself from terror. He classified Arafat as a terrorist and refused henceforth to deal with him. This led his mother to call him "The First Jewish President" of the US. He conjured up the Road Map for Peace. He continued strong support for Israel. With Arafat sidelined the Palestinians named moderate Mahmoud Abbas to the new post of Prime Minister. Sharon and Abbas then engaged in the Road Map for Peace. Sharon stated that he was prepared to make difficult concessions. But the suicide bombings continued and the 'Road Map' did not go anywhere. Mahmoud Abbas resigned. Sharon then began his policy of 'unilateral disengagement'. First he built the wall to protect Israel from infiltration by suicide bombers. Then he removed seven thousand Jewish settlers and withdrew the IDF from inside Gaza. This was dubbed 'Sharon's Folly'. Gaza remained blockaded by land and sea to prevent Iranian arms flowing in. Sharon also planned to separate the area of the West Bank occupied by the Jewish settlers from the rest of it. Bush appeared to sanction these moves and in addition Bush allowed Jewish settlements to continue in the West Bank. Arafat died at the close of Bush's first term[275]. Sharon's stroke felled him and Ehud Olmert took his place.

14. **Barak Hussein Obama** 2008—His Nobel Prize for Peace was deserved in that he decreased the tension and anti-Americanism in the world. He has the staggering job of concluding two wars started by the second Bush and dealing with Pakistan and Iran. His presidency is bearing the brunt of the world economic downturn. He is dealing with the Arab Spring, which can have major consequences in Egypt, Tunisia, Yemen, Libya, Syria and other Arab countries. Although he favours a freeze of Israeli settlements and a two state solution he has advocated a 'land swap' method for the solution to the post 1967 war borders. He has been challenged by Prime Minister Netanyahu's visit to the White House. What Obama's subsequent two speeches mean is unclarified for detail. His second speech was more conciliatory towards Israel's security concerns. He has repeatedly stated that he is strongly supportive of Israel and is committed to current levels of aid. He is against a unilateral declaration of an independent Palestinian State at the United Nations, which he claims will not get anywhere without Israel's input. He appears poised to veto any motion at the UN Security

Council that supports a unilateral declaration of a Palestinian state. He appears to want a peace between Israel and the Palestinians to tie in with the changes he hopes for in the Arab Spring[276]. Obama is viewed as a great statesman and hopes are high that in a second presidential term he will achieve an Arab—Israeli peace.

In a recent speech before 5000 listeners at a conference of the Union of Reform Judaism, and at which Israeli Defence Minister Ehud Barak was present, Obama stated: "I am proud to say that no US administration has done more in support of Israel's security than ours. None. Don't let anyone else tell you otherwise. It is a fact". (Reported by Newsmax.com 17ᵗʰ December 2011).

William B. Quandt has written analytically about the Peace Process and Arab-Israeli negotiations. The American participation is outlined well by him. In the introduction to his book cited here he shows how obtuse and cyclic US foreign policy toward the Arab-Israeli conflict can be. He has also shown how Presidents can change in their attitudes during and after their tenures in office. He has shown that the positions over the years have evolved, and are not the same as in 1948 and again in the post 1967 outlook. He has continuing high hopes for the US ability to resolve the conflict. His ability to distinguish 'procedural peace efforts' from 'what has to be done in substance' to achieve peace is valuable[277]. But his analysis does not show an understanding of the Abrahamic Covenant.

Peres, Rabin, Sharon and Olmert have been perceived as soft by their compromise leading to relinquishing of land. But it did not happen. Begin, Shamir and Netanyahu had been adamantly against the ceding away of land. Shamir's words in 1991 are significant:"I don't believe in territorial compromise. Our country is very tiny. The territory is connected to our entire life—to our security, water, economy. I believe with my entire soul that we are forever connected to this entire homeland. Peace and security go together. Security, territory and homeland are one entity"[278]. It is possible that he saw monetary compensation and technology going to the Arabs and not land. He may have been ready to accommodate all the Arab Palestinians on Israeli soil on Israeli terms. On the other hand he may have been seeing their alternatives of choice to live on Arab soil in Jordan, Syria, Lebanon, and Egypt. Was he thinking of a 'Palestinian Spring'?

Overall, the pro-Israel stand of US foreign policy in the Middle East has gotten stronger over the terms of the US presidents mentioned above. George W. Bush supported Israel very strongly. The recent Netanyahu meeting with Obama in Washington DC has led to a strong Israeli stand, which was voiced by Netanyahu's speech in the US Congress. Netanyahu is to be considered the strongest of all the Prime Ministers of Israel since Ben-Gurion, especially in his second mandate. The security of Israel has been the prime concern in his negotiations. Begin and Shamir could not cope with a land for peace solution. Barak thought he might be able to do it but when he got to the table he had difficulty. Most of the US presidents envisaged a land for peace final solution, but they do not understand the impossible task it would be to defend Israel in such a milieu without negotiation and compromise. The majority in Israel want peace without the further ceding of land. It must always be remembered that Israel is only one lost war away from annihilation. American presidents are insufficiently aware of this in their relations with the Arabs, and more importantly with Israel.

Many analysts, Quandt included, start their thinking and assessments from 1967. They should go back, at least to AD 70. They should clearly see Arabization of the Middle East as a displacement, disintegration, assimilation and eventual annihilation of those people who lived in those countries before the Arabs. In particular, they have difficulty seeing the Arabization of Palestine for what it was, the opportune occupation of the homeland belonging to the Jews, which Arabs are now proclaiming is their birthright. Analysts fail to see that in the case of Palestine, Arabization has now been reversed by conquest by a people taking back their homeland. Alternative thinking that blames the Middle East turmoil and worldwide terrorism on the foreign policy of the US with regard to aiding Israel is perceived as an excuse to allow continued Arabization of the world by an Islamic extremism. Bin Ladin's motivation came first from the presence of US troops on his home soil. He retaliated with terrorism. Now there is a bunching of anything that offends Arabs as being anti Islam and pro Israel and analysts continue this thinking. Meanwhile the Imams preach hatred to the 'home-grown' Moslem youth in western countries. The conclusion is that these countries are paying the price of the freedom given to the spread of Islamic extremism, and Israel is being blamed. American foreign policy must not be forced into the straitjacket of appeasing Arab extremism, which is threatening the existence of Israel. Israel is very dependent on the

US for the foreseeable future. Therefore American foreign policy is extremely important to Israel.

NOTES

261 'Historical Perspectives on Franklin D. Roosevelt, American Foreign Policy, and the Holocaust' by Joseph J Plaud. FDR American Heritage Centre.

262 'President Harry S Truman and US Support for Israeli Statehood' by Ami Isseroff: Truman wrote in his memoirs, "The question of Palestine as a Jewish homeland goes back to the solemn promise that had been made to the Jews by the British in the Balfour Declaration of 1917—a promise which had stirred the hopes and the dreams of these oppressed people. This promise I felt should be kept ...."
See also Cmd. 6808, London, 1946, page 11—Cited by Walter Laqueur in 'A History of Zionism' page 571, Schocken Books, New York
See also Ibid, the chapter titled 'The Struggle for the Jewish State'.

263 'Decade of Transition: Eisenhower, Kennedy and Origins of the American-Israeli Alliance' by Abraham Ben-Zvi, New York: Columbia University Press, 1998
See also "Eisenhower Foreign Policy' Rad Essays by Bailey, Cohen, Kennedy

264 'Mossad and the JFK Assassination' See John-F-Kennedy.net

265 'Lyndon B. Johnson—A Righteous Gentile' by Lenny Ben-David in the Jerusalem Post, September 2010
Also see 'Peace Process: American Diplomacy and the Arab-Israeli Conflict Since 1967', Third Edition by William B. Quandt.

266 'Peace Process: American Diplomacy and the Arab-Israeli Conflict Since 1967' by William B. Quandt, Third Edition Nixon and Foreign Policy-AP Study Notes Gerald Ford's Foreign Policy Legacy by Stephen Zunes

267 'Peace Process: American Diplomacy and the Arab-Israeli Conflict since 1967' by William B. Quandt, Third Edition

268 Ibid. The Peace Treaty between Israel and Egypt had been built on the confidence gained by Kissinger's achievements. In Quandt's words: "Peace between Egypt and Israel would not make war impossible in the Middle East, but it would dramatically change its nature. The danger of US-Soviet confrontation would be reduced as well. On these grounds even a separate peace

had immense strategic value for the United States" (Page 236). This admission underscores Begin's constant contention that his so-called 'hardline' negotiating skill was achieving the security of the US as well. Israel's existence is of great importance to the western world.

269 Miller Centre, University of Virginia, An Online Reference Resource: American President, Jimmy Carter.

270 Ronald Reagan, "Recognizing the Israeli Asset", Washington Post, August 15, 1979, p. A25 quoted in Peace Process: American Diplomacy and the Arab-Israeli Conflict since 1967, William B. Quandt, Third Edition

271 'Peace Process: American Diplomacy and the Arab-Israeli Conflict Since 1967' by William B. Quandt, Third Edition
See also 'Politics, Jewish Journal.com: Ronald Reagan'

272 'Peace Process: American Diplomacy and the Arab-Israeli Conflict Since 1967' by William B. Quandt, Third Edition Slate: Politics. 'The Bushes and the Jews—Explaining the President's Philo-Semitism' by Anne E. Kornblut, April 2002
See Beirut to Jerusalem by Thomas Friedman page 536

273 'Peace Process: American Diplomacy and the Arab-Israeli Conflict Since 1967' by William B. Quandt, Third Edition
The Cable (Reporting inside the Foreign Policy Machine): 'Bill Clinton: Russian Immigrants and Settlers Obstacles to Mideast Peace' posted by Josh Rogin

274 'Peace Process: American Diplomacy and the Arab-Israeli Conflict Since 1967' By William B. Quandt, Third Edition

275 Occidental Observer: George (H.W.) Bush: "The First Jewish President" Michael Kinsley's review of Bush's memoir, posted December 2010
See also Foreign Policy of the George H.W. Bush Administration, Wikipedia
See also 'Peace Process: American Diplomacy and the Arab-Israeli Conflict Since 1967' by William B. Quandt, Third Edition

276 Jewish World Review: 'Obama's Altruistic Foreign Policy' by Caroline B. Glick. *See also* 'What Have Obama and Netanyahu Wrought'? posted by Henry Siegman in the Middle East Channel, Foreign Policy

277 'Peace Process: American Diplomacy and the Arab-Israeli Conflict Since 1967' Third Edition by William B. Quandt. Quandt is Professor of Politics at the

University of Virginia. He was senior fellow in the Foreign Policy Studies Program at the Brookings Institution and then on the National Security Council in the Nixon and Carter Administrations. He was actively involved with the Camp David Accords and the Egyptian-Israeli Peace Treaty (Wikipedia)

278 Linda Gradstein, 'Shamir Bars Losing Territory', Washington Post, July 25, 1991 p. A27. Quoted in 'Peace Process: American Diplomacy and the Arab-Israeli Conflict Since 1967' by William B. Quandt, Third Edition

CHAPTER 25
WHITHER THE ASPIRATIONS OF WORLD JEWRY?

These aspirations are labelled as synonymous with the yearnings of Jewish hearts. What do Jews want for the future? After searching around for long-term wishes we arrive at the simple basics. Jews want the LAND of Israel to be intact and secure. They want the TORAH to be honoured and understood to give them guidance for their temporal and spiritual lives. And they want the MESSIAH to be real and to be their leader. This is not simply my opinion. After careful introspection the most secular Jew will agree with the most Orthodox Jew that considering their history, their future must be based on the secure foundation as outlined above. Otherwise, Israel's history will be repeated. Reformation must come in all three spheres. The over-riding factor in all thought for the future should be: ISRAEL IS ONE LOST WAR AWAY FROM ANNIHILATION AGAIN. Therefore it behoves all Jews to be cognizant of the Abrahamic Covenant, which is LAND, TORAH, and MESSIAH. There must be no idolatry in the land and Israel must be a good neighbour. Idolatry is more than bowing down to idols. Anything that would prevent Jews from the worship of the true God is an idol, be it wealth, comfortable living, humanism or secularism. Being a good neighbour is helping the Arabs without compromising Israel's security. This is eminently possible.

In his outstanding book 'Beirut to Jerusalem' Thomas Friedman has eloquently portrayed time and events up until October 1994 when the Peace Treaty with Jordan was signed. A lot has happened in the nearly twenty years since. When Friedman wrote, Rabin and Arafat were still alive, and Hamas had not yet taken over Gaza. Friedman added a new final chapter to his book for its 1998 printing. He labelled this final chapter "Buying a Ticket". This chapter contains what I call 'The Lamentations of Thomas Friedman'. He is at times optimistic and at times his pessimism is massive. His lamentations are directed at several different aspects of the Middle East dilemma. The most serious lamentation in my opinion contains his assessment of the relationship between Israel and American Jews. His assessment of this deteriorated relationship is correct but the cause he cites is incorrect. He wrongly attributes the root cause of the poor relationship between Israel and American Jewry to the Israeli-Palestinian failure to come to terms with a two state solution as the goal. The real reason for the doldrums is what follows in his book. It is extremely depressing. He cites his attendance at Rosh Hashanah and Yom Kippur services in Washington. He found them:

> ". . . *strikingly flat. At various lunches and dinners after the services, I asked different friends about their rabbis' sermons. Everywhere I inquired, people seem to be dissatisfied with what their rabbis had to say. My rabbi asked the question, Why be Jewish? Another talked about homosexual rights. Another spoke of the need for more community volunteerism. Nobody talked about Israel. As I thought about this, I realised that the American Jewish community, in my lifetime, had been held together and motivated to action by four vicarious experiences—all of which were fading away in the 1990s. The most important of those experiences was Israel*"[279].

This is a staggering observation by Friedman. When American Jews saw Israel making peace with Egypt, Jordan and the Arab Palestinians, and there were signs also of thawing of the relationship with Syria, the challenge to American Jews faded. The risk to Israel's security was disappearing. Begin, Peres and Rabin had all scored Nobel prizes. (There will no doubt be a rethink of the situation now that Egypt, Syria and Jordan are in a state of flux). Friedman also cites:

(i) The visitation of American Jews to Israel as tourists going there simply to enjoy the Eilat beaches and the fish restaurants in Jaffa, (he obviously prefers these visits to be religious pilgrimages).

(ii) The disappearance of the "Fiddler on the Roof Judaism" of the grandfathers who had died off.

(iii) Repatriation of the majority of the Russian Jews.

(iv) Secularisation of the Holocaust remembrance: The Holocaust Museum in Washington had become a tourist attraction instead of a religious shrine.

(v) Proliferation of Pizza Huts, Toys Are Us, and Ace Hardware Stores in Israel.

He found these causing weakening of the bonds between Israel and American Jewry.

As a result Friedman sees American Jews increasingly assimilating into American society, and Israeli Jews increasingly assimilating into the Western world[280]. This insight is realistic. For prevention of this deterioration there must be a return to the Abrahamic Covenant, which embodies Land, Torah, and Messiah. There must be reformation. It is a massive task. Over 6 million American Jews and over 5 million Israelis need reformation. Spirituality and dedication to a religious life that is not extreme or indifferent must prevail. The religious needs of the Jews must come into focus and must be realistic.

What can be done? Conferences should be held in Israel and America and elsewhere to resolve the religious impasse. These must be calls to prayer and worship but at the same time there must be the adoption of compromise between the two extremes. All left wing and right wing religious ways of life and worship must meet in the centre. That centre is where Abraham, Jacob and Moses stand. The blueprint is in the Tanak. The Reformists must see that dancing with the Scrolls of Torah is only symbolic. They must move to a belief structure based on the Abrahamic Covenant. The Orthodox Jews must move away from the severe extremes of halacha stemming from a confused and misplaced reverence for the Talmud. The Abrahamic Covenant must be resurrected and accepted as the secure cornerstone foundation. The Tanak was closed as canon long ago by the inspired leadership in Israel. The Talmud and all rabbinic utterances must be subordinated to the Tanak. Abraham, Jacob and Moses did not have or bequeath the Talmud and halacha to Israel. The Tanak must suffice. Defensible LAND must be retained. The TORAH must be defined as Tanak and only Tanak, and must be supreme. The MESSIAH must be defined by the Tanak and unity reached in that understanding. This is a formidable and daunting task. But it must be achieved. Abraham, Jacob and Moses would want this if alive on the planet today.

It is essential that Israel make provision for the Palestinians within their borders. This should be the major task in any further negotiations with the Arabs and Arab Palestinians. Land for peace is a difficult policy, thus far unsuccessful in achieving lasting peace. Israelis are reluctant to cede land. Any path forged by Israel's negotiations should be subject to dual confirmation by the Israeli population in a referendum and ratified by the Knesset. But an education and reformation of all Jewry must take place.

The MESSIAH as part of the Abrahamic Covenant needs serious attention. The LAND and the TORAH have had most of the attention of the Jews thus far. The definition and identification of the MESSIAH should come only from the Tanak. It is the only Jewish canon in existence. No other source material should be used as an inspired standard. To repeat, the Talmud is not canon. All Israel from the extreme right ultra Orthodox to the Reformist and Conservative factions on the left, need to focus on MESSIAH. The ostracized Messianic Jews must also be included.

They all must abide by the Tanak. The Talmud, no matter how much esteem it may have accumulated over the centuries, is not part of Torah. Halacha must be reoriented to the Tanak. The Tanak must be the basis for the unity of all Jewry, Israeli and American and other diasporic Jewry. THIS WILL DEFINE THE TRUE JEW. Jewish aspirations must be prayerful and repentant. The worship of the God of Abraham, Jacob and Moses must be supreme. It must become deeply personal. Extremism, both secular and ultra orthodox, has given Judaism a bad name and has enveloped world Jewry in a state of confused disunity. It thus has become virtually impossible for an Israeli government to negotiate successfully with the Arab Palestinians. The fragmentation of representation in the Knesset attests to this.

There is work to be done in Israel with reformation of Torah and definition of Messiah. Land is paramount[281]. The fair dinkum Jew is the one who is faithful to the Abrahamic Covenant. The aspirations of all Jews must be oriented to the Abrahamic Covenant and this requires a sensible middle of the road Judaism.

NOTES

[279] Beirut to Jerusalem, pages 365,366
[280] Ibid: page 567,568
[281] See Survey of Israelis after the Six Day War, quoted in '1967—Israel, the War and the Year that Transformed the Middle East' by Tom Segev page 665

Chapter 26
The Palestinian Spring

The Palestinian Spring is defined within the scope of Eretz Israel, an inclusion of the West Bank and Gaza in an Israeli state. It is being related to Israel's current possession of the West Bank and Gaza. The majority of Israelis claim that these are parts of their ancestral homeland. As a preamble a discussion of some attitudes and prevailing sentiments would be relevant.

In a recent reprinting of Hannah Arendt's 'Eichmann in Jerusalem, A Report on the Banality of Evil' the Introduction is written by Amos Elon. It is titled 'The Excommunication of Hannah Arendt'. In it he states: ". . . under the governments of Golda Meir and Menachem Begin, the Holocaust was mystified into the heart of a new civil religion and at the same time exploited to justify Israel's refusal to withdraw from occupied territory"[282]. Taking that statement out of the context in which Elon used it, it still stands as a belief that Elon obviously held. Exploiting the Holocaust to justify refusal to withdraw from 'occupied territory' was not the intention nor conviction of either of the Prime Ministers named, on the evidence available. Elon is far from the truth. The justification for refusal to withdraw for both Meir and Begin was the concept that Judea, Samaria and Gaza belong to Israel from the gift of God and the right of conquest. In Elon's time the demands of the Arabs were in excess of the ability of the Israelis to deliver. Ehud Barak offered them all of Gaza and most of the West Bank but Arafat had refused. The prevailing sentiment was that if the Arabs take the responsibility for dispossessing the Jews of the Holy Land by conquest, Israel has the right to take it back. Since the Arabs had not, the Arabs are labelled opportunists in Palestine. Elon is willingly ignorant of the Abrahamic Covenant, which embodies LAND, TORAH, and MESSIAH. And all who agree with Elon and feel that the Arabs have a right to live there ahead of the Jews are themselves ignorant of the Abrahamic Covenant and what is the significance of Jewish male circumcision. They have not been schooled in the Tanak[283]. One cannot have a Jewish State that denies the Abrahamic

Covenant[284]. The world needs to know that the establishment of the State of Israel was not a revenge for the Nazi Holocaust, nor to shield the Jews from future holocausts. It is for the fulfilment of the Abrahamic Covenant. Without Abraham in the equation, the Jews have no legitimacy or lasting future.

Hannah Arendt was magnificent in her chronicling of the Eichmann trial and has the best analysis available of Hitler's Final Solution and its orchestration in Europe, of which Eichmann was a part. Her unpopularity with many Jews resulting from her book stems from her bitterness that Jewish leaders in Europe 'cooperated' with Hitler's regime by providing enumeration lists of Jews and failing to organise a defence. It is not anti-Jewish to recognise that this happened. The circumstances faced by those Jewish leaders in Europe were very complex and are not within the scope of this book. Perhaps they lacked the 'paranoia' that is obvious retrospectively. Amos Elon's ideology is in error but sympathy for Arendt's bitterness is called for, though not for all her conclusions. Walter Laqueur cites Hannah Arendt's fearful statement in connection with Herzl and Zionism. In 1946 she wrote: "The parallels with the Shabtai Zvi episode have become terribly close". Shabtai Zvi was a false messiah who perpetrated a scandal in Jerusalem in 1664 that threw many Jews into confusion and could have brought a slaughter of Jews by the Sultan in Constantinople who ruled Palestine. It appears she was fearful that there would be a backlash causing another slaughter of the Jews caused by Zionism, as well as another unnecessary confusion of unfulfilled Jewish expectation and terrible disappointment. This was a legitimate worry of an intellectual.

The word 'Judenrein', originally coined by the Nazis, envisioned the total eradication of Jews from Europe. It has now been ascribed to Zionists, and to the current State of Israel in relation to Arab Palestinians, by twisting of statements made by certain Jews[285]. Israel has never had a policy defined to "cleanse" Judea, Samaria and Gaza of Arab Palestinians. The Jewish settlements are not intentioned to "cleanse" current Israel of Arab Palestinians. The pre 1967 borders of Israel contained Arabs living peacefully as citizens of Israel with democratic representation in the Knesset. Arabs in Israel have freedom and a better life if they live peacefully and are not subversive. It is the violent Arabs who vow annihilation and plant suicide bombers to kill Jews in Palestine that are to be excluded from Israel. The IDF responds with force to Arab Palestinian belligerence. Arab Palestinians and their sympathisers refer to 'international law' in trying to exact their aims, but 'international law' and

UN resolutions dealing with Israel are in the main developmentally flawed and biased against Israel. To imply that Israel has an 'Eichmannian final solution' for the Arab Palestinians is false and absurd. On the contrary it is extremist Jihadi movements like Hamas that vow to kill every Jew on the planet. Hamas has a well-outlined publicly stated 'Eichmannian final solution' for Jews on the planet. This is clearly stated in its charter. Israel has a duty to defend itself against such open threats. The Abrahamic Covenant will never be wiped off the planet. Hitler made a ignominious attempt to do this but Jews have prospered despite having partially paid his high price by suffering the effects of his hate and venom. That venom was clearly voiced in the circular sent out by the Nazi Party Chancellery in 1942: "It is the nature of things that these, in some respects, very difficult problems can be solved in the interests of the permanent security of our [German] people only with ruthless toughness"[286]. That ruthless toughness was Hitler's Final Solution. Sensitive Israelis see the Hamas Charter containing the same Nazi venom with the wiping out of Israel clearly stated. Hamas and Hezbollah vow Judenrein in Palestine.

Leviticus chapter 19 has a lot to say about the current situation where peaceful Arabs live on Israeli soil. In the same dissertation in which Moses forbade idolatry and exhorted care for the poor and destitute in Israel, he laid down clear and implicit rules about the treatment of non-Jews living in Israel. Actually it is God speaking the words. Verses 33 and 34: "And if a stranger sojourn with thee in your land, ye shall not vex him. But the stranger that dwelleth with you shall be unto you as one born among you, and thou shalt love him as thyself; for you were strangers in the land of Egypt; I am the Lord your God". Humanly speaking this command of God looks like a very tall order to Israelis who dislike Arabs. It is what God requires. Israel is a very open society and is capable of doing this. God has commanded peaceful coexistence with strangers (non-Jews) who he wants Jews to love as friends. This includes Arab Palestinians. This can take place without compromising the Abrahamic Covenant.

Israel has something to offer strangers. It is a relationship with Israel's God. It is very easy to become Jewish despite not being born Jewish. Conversion smacks of assimilation but is offered as an inclusive option. It is noted that the current extremes of Jewish religious thought and practice have made this option very difficult for many to convert to Judaism. American Reform Jews have difficulty realizing desires to achieve aliya because the powerful rabbis in Israel are ultra-Orthodox. Israel must heed the call for reformation and take the practice of Judaism back to where Abraham, Jacob and Moses stood. The desired religious practice of Judaism should be in the centre of the current extremes in worldwide Jewry. The majority of American Jews belong to the Reformed and Conservative schools and are not very deep in their understanding of primitive Judaism. In Israel over fifty percent of Jews are secular and not religious. A small percentage of world Jews are on the extreme right as ultra Orthodox Jews. All must come together in the centre to the religion of Abraham, Jacob and Moses. This centrist position is yet to be defined by reformation for which a call has been made. This centrist position lies in the lives of pre-Talmudic Abraham, Jacob and Moses. A centrist Judaism will be a much more attractive religious experience to offer strangers. When this centrist position is achieved Jews must proselytise. Arabs have spread Islam throughout the Middle East, so why cannot Israel spread Judaism? This will open the door to "the stranger" being referred to above. The 'Ruth and Naomi experience' will be multiplied. Palestinians must be convinced that Judaism is a satisfying way of life with a great future. Abraham, who they claim as father, had a Covenant with God offered through Jacob. This offers blessing to all nations, bringing rewards for all. Jews must realize that what the IDF cannot do, the Torah and Messianic expectation can. The IDF cannot convince Arab Palestinians of the mission of the Abrahamic Covenant but the power of the spirit of God in the Tanak and the Messiah can. How many rabbis in Israel have such a conviction? How many have seen the Messianic mission in the happiness of all nations? The circumcision of the Arabs should be linked to the Abrahamic Covenant. Ishmael carries Abraham's genes and should return from the wilderness into Abraham's household where he belongs, by acceptance of Abraham's Covenant. Civilization marches on blindly from crisis to crisis. God offered the world through Abraham blessedness and happiness, through the Messiah. Eden awaits restoration through Israel.

If they do not wish to unite with Israel as the children of Abraham, who they are through Ishmael, they can still dwell among Israelis and be loved and belong as those 'born among us'. They can practice their religion peacefully and still vow secular allegiance to the State of Israel. This is a radical idea but it will bring peace into the borders of Israel and into the Middle East. Those who still vow annihilation of Jews should and must leave Israel. This is not a call for an ethnic cleansing. The Burghers of Sri Lanka were in a similar plight. They were stateless in the country of their birth but accomplished an exit. They felt themselves to be misfits in the country in which they were born. They decided that they wanted no part of the native scene. So they voluntarily left to live in the countries where they felt more at home. This happened at tremendous personal cost. So the Palestinians who do not wish to live on Israeli soil on Israeli terms of government may exit. But they can stay and be joined to Israel and enjoy all the benefits available through the Abrahamic Covenant.

Jews have a record of peaceful coexistence throughout the 2000 years of the diaspora throughout the world. Despite the pogroms, Nazi enforced ghettos, death marches, starvation and gas ovens, as a people they have survived through their own peaceful initiatives. They have been exemplary citizens who have participated in the affairs of the host nations with positive lives and have made outstanding cultural, political and scientific contributions. Their philanthropy is genuine and charitable. They have not been subversive in the host countries. They are champions in the cause of justice, eg. in the civil rights struggle in the US racial divide, and the support given to the blacks against apartheid in South Africa. Jews have made it abundantly clear that they are more than willing to be good neighbours. But in Israel where their existence as a nation is under the constant threat of annihilation, the borders must be strongly defended. Zionism was a just cause, which helped to bring them back as a nation. Allied help, military might, being good neighbours, and being a good host nation are great defences. They have a great offering to the world through the Abrahamic Covenant. There is nothing sinister about Jews.

Israel had established good neighbourly relations with Sadat's Egypt and with King Hussein's Jordan. There is no need for these relations to be discarded by the occurrence of the Arab Spring. Jordan's current monarch has made significant contributions to the 'Arab Spring' aspirations of Jordanians with his reforms. Israel welcomes the Arab Spring that is occurring and encourages the democratic changes and relief of poverty and backwardness in these awakening countries. And Israel is ready to offer the Palestinians within their borders a 'Palestinian Spring' of their own. Within Israeli jurisdiction and within the vision of the Abrahamic Covenant, this can be accomplished. What is Israel offering? First of all a sense of belonging as Israel is ready to follow God's command to love the stranger that dwells with them. They remember that they have been strangers during the 2000 years of the diaspora and they have survived. They welcome the Palestinians to be as close as good neighbours, and closer by offering them conversion and oneness with the Jews. They could live peacefully and prosperously within Israel's borders even without conversion.

This will assure a secure and happy life. Arab Palestinians within Israel's pre 1967 borders enjoy full citizenship and political freedom and seats in the Knesset. This can be extended to Arab Palestinians in Judea, Samaria and Gaza if they wish to be a part of Israel.

And so Israel is offering the Arab Palestinians within the post 1967 borders the hand of friendship, a Palestinian Spring. But it must be on Israeli terms and within the bounds of Israeli law. This cannot be in the form of a 'Palestinian State' within the borders of the new Israel. And what of the aspirations of the Arab Palestinians who do not wish to embrace such a friendship? They must voluntarily emigrate. Voluntary emigration will not be easy and therefore Israel has a duty to help them emigrate without loss of value of land and property they hold. Like the Burghers of Sri Lanka who did not wish to embrace the native scene, they can respectfully sell up and leave in order to fulfil their aspirations elsewhere. A Jewish majority in Israel must be preserved.

The Arab Spring should reach the Arab Palestinians on Arab soil, but not on Israeli soil. These Arab Palestinians are situated in Egypt, Lebanon, Syria and Jordan. Israel's policy appears to be that because of the passage of time the majority of them have been born in those countries and have never known Israel's pre or post 1967 borders. Israel is a foreign country to them, no matter how much they desire to come to Israel. They are considered part and parcel, citizens by birth, of the countries named, which are Arab countries. They no longer have a birth claim to Israeli soil. Their parents left voluntarily or in fear because of the wars the Arabs started. They can only come back through religious conversion. Aliya can be theirs. Israeli Arabs, the ones who remained, enjoy all the freedoms and comforts of a democracy. The Arab Palestinians living in Judea, Samaria and Gaza could enjoy the same benefits of democracy should they remain in Eretz Israel. What will be their status? In Hannah Arendt's 'Eichmann in Jerusalem' she cites Carl Friedrich Goerdeler's characterization of Jews living in Europe as having an ". . . unseemly position as a more or less undesirable 'guest nation' in Europe"[287]. His reasons for this conclusion are not elaborated. Certainly European Jews were not behaving unseemly or undesirably. Israel will not offer this type of 'guest nation' status to these West Bank and Gaza Arab Palestinians. They will be bona fide Israeli citizens with the same rights and responsibilities as all Israeli citizens. They will not be undesirable as long as they are not subversive. They will be incarcerated after trial and conviction as any ordinary citizen of Israel for any subversive behaviour.

In his vision of the future State of Israel Theodor Herzl, the father of political Zionism wrote in 1895:"We shall try to spirit the penniless population [Arab] across the border by procuring employment for it in the transit countries, while denying it any employment in our country . . . . Both the expropriation and the removal of the poor [Arabs] must be carried out discreetly and circumspectly[288]. Despite the crude and objectionable language used by Herzl, this shows the compassionate consideration for the Palestinian Arabs who would be displaced if they chose not to live in an Israeli state. Herzl did not plan to herd them militarily across the border nor did he nightmare up an 'Eichmannian final solution' for them. Jordan, Syria, Lebanon and Egypt should and could accommodate all the Arab Palestinians who wish to live in a sovereign Arab state. The others who do not wish to leave could live peacefully in Israel. The recent opening in the Egyptian border with Gaza is to be welcomed as an exit site for Gaza Arabs who want to leave. It has been noted that large numbers of them have moved into Egypt. Gaza has long felt an affinity with Egypt. Many West Bank Arab Palestinians have felt that they were part of the state of Syria and envisage unity with Syria[289]. Others would prefer to be part of Jordan, which administered the West Bank for many years.

Envisioning an inclusion of the West Bank and Gaza within Israel, and a voluntary emigration of Arab Palestinians from the post 1967 borders of Israel is a 'revolutionary' idea. But it is not new. The 'International Post-War Settlement', London, records that in April 1944, the national executive of the Labour Party in Britain stated: "Let the Arabs be encouraged to move out as the Jews move in. Let them be compensated handsomely for their land, and their settlement elsewhere be carefully organised and generously financed". Abba Eban, in his book 'Tragedy and Triumph' records Churchill as stating to Weizmann on 4th November 1944:"If you could get the whole of Palestine [west of the Jordan River and including the Negev] it would be a good thing, but I feel that if it comes to a choice between the White Paper and partition—you should take partition"[290]. These ideas are practical and possible. One wonders how many will choose to emigrate. Given the possible realization that there will never be a Palestinian state established within the borders of Eretz Israel if this scenario occurs, many may opt to do so. This seems to be a SIMPLISTIC solution to the aspirations of people who call West Bank and Gaza home. But

210

it is the REALISTIC solution. The US would never consider the formation of a independent and hostile American Native Indian state within its borders. Neither would Australia allow a sovereign hostile Aboriginal state within its borders. Neither is Israel forced to allow a sovereign hostile Arab Palestinian state to be established within its borders should this scenario take place.

This plan to facilitate the voluntary emigration of Arab Palestinians will require expensive compensation. All those Arabs owning land, houses and assets in Judea, Samaria and Gaza will sell to Israelis or other remaining Arabs who wish to buy these at market prices. The Israeli government can buy up assets unsold to the public. Those who do not own land and assets will also be compensated with a basic amount to be able to make their exit comfortable and purchase or build homes elsewhere. Compensation will also be made to all bona fide Palestinians in refugee camps wherever they exist within Israel's borders or in Jordan, Syria, Lebanon and Egypt. There will be established a GRAND MASSIVE FUND for this compensation[291]. The contributors to this fund should be the Israeli Government, World Diasporic Jewry, especially American (who are usually very generous), European Union and Australian Jewry. All Arab countries with oil, and all other governments disposed to do so including China should be contributors. All the countries, which regularly support the Arab Palestinians in the UN should feel obliged to do so as this will be aid to the Arab Palestinians. This should be viewed as a boon to Egypt, Lebanon, Syria and Jordan since reasonably well-heeled Arab immigrants will enrich these countries. Immigrants who enter any country with capital quickly enter the economic well being of that country creating wealth and stability.

This plan may look silly and unrealistic to some. Consider what another one or two wars between Israel and the involved Arab states would cost. Just add it up. The costs for war are massive in terms of money, and lives, and destroyed homes and infrastructure, and the care and compensation of the bereft and wounded, and the displaced, and the loss of productivity. There is always a large amount of humanitarian aid that flows into a war torn area donated from various personal and social charities. Add it up. It will exceed expectations and will form a massive compensation fund. Just add up the cost to the US to conduct the wars in Iraq and Afghanistan. Wars cost massive amounts. The idea for a massive compensation fund is not so stupid when considered thoughtfully. Peace can be bought when the money benefits those who need and deserve reparations. Peace can be bought honestly as a measure to prevent war. THE ARAB PALESTINIANS WHO EMIGRATE FROM ERETZ ISRAEL MUST BE COMPENSATED. Such a planned and successful outcome would be quite a contrast to what usually happens to a conquered people. Compensation has been previously offered by Levi Eshkol and Ehud Barak and is not a new idea.

And what will be the fate of the aspirations of those Arab Palestinians who decide to remain within Israel's post 1967 borders? They will be Israeli citizens and live in harmony with a Jewish state[292]. Think of all the Christians who live peacefully in Arab states, despite being attacked sometimes by extremist bigots, for example the extremist Islamists who attacked the Coptic Christians in Egypt. There should be laws in place to punish people who prevent religious freedom, unless that freedom exceeds reasonable bounds and there is an agenda of subversion with attempts to take over the state. Imams who preach hatred and violence cannot be tolerated. Jihad will have no place. The suppression of women and the use of Sharia Law in Moslem communities will not have a place. There will be no independent relations allowed with foreign Arab countries. Any aid or support to foreigners who vow the destruction of Israel will not be tolerated. Arab Palestinian citizens of Israel will have their grievances addressed by Israeli courts.

If the West Bank and Gaza are incorporated into the State of Israel, Israel must offer such a 'Palestinian Spring' to the eligible Arab Palestinians living within its post 1967 borders. Israel has the directive for this from God. Arab Palestinians living in Israel are entitled to be happy and to have dignity and a true sense of belonging in Israel since they have chosen to dwell there. Israel is already offering this to those Arab Palestinians who wish to be their peaceful in house neighbours.

The major alternative to this scenario is for the Arab Palestinians in the West Bank and Gaza to reach a negotiated 'second' two state settlement with Israel. But such an alternative has to be peacefully negotiated and is the mountain still to be climbed.

NOTES

[282]   Eichmann in Jerusalem, A Report on the Banality of Evil, Introduction, page xviii.

283   Quoted by the New York Times 'Middle East' May 25, 2009.
Amos Elon wrote provocatively for the New Yorker and in his many books.
He cited Israelis to be too religious and having a heightened focus on military
power. He drew attention to himself blaming the Zionists who had embarked
on "a national and social renaissance in their ancient homeland" for being "blind
to the possibility that the Arabs of Palestine might entertain similar hopes for
themselves". Amos Elon had been a controversial figure in Israel. He had no
acknowledged concept of the Abrahamic Covenant. He had retired to Tuscany in
Italy.

284   'Interview with Amos Elon' cited in "America's Best Political Newsletter" Out of
Bounds Magazine, Counterpunch, December 27,2004, "Zionism Has Exhausted
Itself", An Interview with Amos Elon, by Ari Shavit, (Ha'aretz)

Excerpted:
Question: "In your view, the Jews are not a nation?"
Answer: "I don't think they are one nation. I don't think so. It's a religion".
Question: "If so, the problem is even worse. A Jew who isn't religious is basically
lacking an identity".
Answer: "Why must a person constantly define himself? Only doctrinaires
demand that you present your identity card all the time. I don't want Judaism to
be a tattoo on my forehead. And I can't say that I'm a Jew because I am a secular
person".
Question: "Let's leave the matter of identity aside. The possibility that in
the future there may not be a Jewish people or a Jewish nation or a Jewish
civilization doesn't bother you?"
Answer: "If people want to assimilate to the point that they disappear within the
general society without a trace—that's their right. I don't think it's a tragedy. It's
not the end of the world".

See Walter Laqueur's 'A History of Zionism' page 404.

285   The Hasbara Buster, The "Judenrein" Canard, April 20, 2010
Strategic Affairs Minister Moshe Ya'alon in the Jerusalem Post: "If we are talking
about coexistence and peace, why the (Palestinian) insistence that the territory
they receive be ethnically cleansed of Jews? Why do those areas have to be
Judenrein? Don't Arabs live here, in the Negev and the Galilee? Why isn't that
part of our public discussion? Why doesn't that scream to the heavens?"

The discussant alleges: "There's no equivalence, and Ya'alon knows it well, between the Arabs who were already living in the Negev (and) in the Galilee when Ya'alon's ancestors roamed the Pale of Settlement . . . ." This is patent nonsensical falsehood, as King David's kingdom included the Negev and Galilee long before the current Arabs' ancestors moved into the areas.

[286] Quoted in 'Eichmann in Jerusalem—A Report on the Banality of Evil' by Hannah Arendt, page 161, 2006 printing

[287] 'Eichmann in Jerusalem—A Report on the Banality of Evil' by Hannah Arendt, page 103, 2006 printing

[288] Quoted in 'The Lemon Tree: An Arab, a Jew, and the Heart of the Middle East' by Sandy Tolan, page 18. (This book is well worth reading for its description of the pre 1948 life in Palestine).

[289] See 'The Case for Israel' by Alan Dershowitz page 7: "Between 1880 and 1967, virtually no Arab or Palestinian spokesperson called for a Palestinian state. Instead they wanted the area that the Romans had designated as Palestine to be merged into Syria or Jordan. As Auni Bey Abdul-Hati, a prominent Palestinian leader, told the Peel Commission in 1937, "There is no such country . . . . Palestine is a term the Zionists invented . . . . Our country for centuries is a part of Syria".

[290] Cited in "A History of Zionism' by Walter Laqueur, Schocken Books, New York page 542

[291] Prime Minister Ehud Barak was perhaps the first to officially offer a fund of $30 billion for compensation of Arabs as part of a two state solution—cited by Alan Dershowitz in his book 'The Case For Israel' page 9.
See also page 50 where Dershowitz cites the Peel Commission as making large amounts of money available for reparations, eg 2 million English pounds being donated from the British Treasury to Transjordan, and other unspecified amounts from unspecified sources, for loss of territory.
See '1967—Israel, the War and the Year that Transformed the Middle East' by Tom Segev published by Abacus, pages 627,644-647.

[292] See Israel Jerusalem.com: 'Israeli Soldiers'—"In Israel, Jewish soldiers guard the Jewish shrines while Arab Catholic and Arab Orthodox Israeli soldiers guard the Islamic shrines like the al Aqsa Mosque". This illustrates that Arabs can be part of the Jewish state.

CHAPTER 27
RESOLUTION OF THE CONFLICT

At the end of Part I where I outlined my personal history I posed the question "Am I a True Jew?" With parents who were Christians despite some Jewish ancestry I will not achieve aliya unless I become formally converted to Judaism through an Orthodox Rabbi. This is unlikely at present with my conviction that only Tanak is Torah thereby rejecting the Talmud as Torah. So aliya is 'on hold' but my anxiety for Israel's security is acute. My only authority to be heard is the Abrahamic Covenant, which is the main structural component of the Tanak. The Tanak is not a complex document. It is a record of the history of Israel in dialogue with their God. I hold it as a vital, dynamic and living document containing the human expression of God's desires. It is for all ages and for all civilizations. Of those who accept the Tanak as such, the attitude of A J Jacobs is brilliant and illuminating. He is a New York Times Bestseller, and wrote "The Year of Living Biblically". Jacobs is a Jew who in my estimation is 95% assimilated into American society and not practicing any prescribed form of Judaism. He could be classified as a Judaeo-Christian from the attitudes he takes. He may not agree with this assessment. But one has only to read his book to realize his value judgements of extracts of both the Tanak and B'rit Hadasha as evidence. This, despite his sometimes half-hearted endorsements of the beautifully phrased ideas of the Tanak he so eloquently discusses. I rejoice in his perspective and sincerity, which are convincing and thrilling. He would be an ideal choice for chairman of the committee to bring both extremes of the Jewish gulf together in the centre in the reformation so necessary in current Judaism. I would like him to have theologically parsed every verse in the Tanak to make a full assessment of him, but I am willing to trust him on the available evidence. On page 316 of his book he states: "The Bible may have not been dictated by God, it may have had a messy and complicated birth, one filled with political agendas and outdated ideas—but that does not mean that the

215

Bible can't be beautiful and sacred". See also pages 200-201 for an explanation of the documentary hypothesis: "The challenge is finding meaning, guidance, and sacredness in the Bible even if I don't believe that God sat behind His big oak desk in heaven and dictated the words verbatim to a bunch of flawless secretaries". The very disappointing feature of his book is his ignorance of or calculated exclusion of a discussion of the Abrahamic Covenant on which the whole Tanak hinges. He gives circumcision ample space in his book but does not link it to the Abrahamic Covenant in which dwells the plans of the eternal God for the redemption of mankind through the Jews. How would A J Jacobs interpretively parse Genesis 17:9-14? I quote:

> "And God said to Abraham: as for you, you shall keep My covenant, you and your descendants after you throughout their generations. This is My covenant which you shall keep, between you and Me and you and your descendants after you: Every male child among you shall be circumcised; and you shall be circumcised in the flesh of your foreskins, and it shall be a sign of the covenant between Me and you. He who is eight days old among you shall be circumcised, every male child in your generations, he who is born in your house or bought with money . . . . My covenant shall be in your flesh for an everlasting covenant".

Circumcision is not the Covenant but is the sign of the Covenant. The entire story and purpose of the Tanak is integrated in the Abrahamic Covenant. Will A J Jacobs subscribe to the idea that God gave Israel a job to do? If they do not do that job they get punished. Reformation and rededication bring them back. And the cycle is repeated. It is now high time for Israel to break that cycle and finish the job.

Recognition of the fair dinkum Jew has been difficult. The Jews link their existence to the creation of the universe. This is not a literary endeavour even if one takes the stand that the story of creation is a great piece of literature and nothing more. The beginning of Israel's history clearly starts with creation and communication with their God. Considering the course of that history the lineage from Adam to Abel to Enoch to Noah to Abraham is very real to Jews. Their ethnicity starts with Abraham who was given a mission in the form of a Covenant to bring back a perfect state of existence, the Edenic state. The

Abrahamic Covenant is about LAND, TORAH and MESSIAH. This mission has been defined and established by Moses and the great writers and characters of the Tanak. Rather than wipe the Jews off the earth for their waywardness and idolatry as he did with the antediluvian civilization God chose to let them in and out of captivity. Unfortunately these punishments were almost annihilations. But he always brought them back, this last time rather belatedly after 2000 years of punishment. But they are back and still have the Abrahamic Covenant to fulfil. Every male Jew acknowledges that duty by his circumcision. It is incorporated in his flesh. Collectively, Jews must acknowledge the will of God enshrined in the Torah, and embark on the mission of the Messiah.

It is very distressing today that prominent Jews in the world discuss the status and fate of Israel without reference to the Abrahamic Covenant. Many have taken the stand that their religious history is quirky and extreme and not to be taken seriously. It may not be the right moment to start rebuilding the Temple, but it needs to be spoken about in public and planned. A J Jacobs fears it might be tantamount to the end of the World to rebuild the Temple at this present time. The greatest reason for the existence of Israel and the retention of Jerusalem is Messianic and calls for the rebuilding of the Temple.

The Jews are back in their homeland. They are there by reconquest and the post 1967 borders are current. Although the original tract of land was from "the river of Egypt to the great river, the River Euphrates", they have settled for loss of the current land areas of Jordan, southern Syria and Sinai. They now occupy Judea and Samaria, Gaza, and the Golan Heights. And they have Jerusalem in its entirety. The post 1967 borders represent a miniscule of land in comparison to the vast amount of land occupied by the Arabs following Arabization of the Middle East. Displaced Arab Palestinians are the new reality. Gaza and the West Bank are home to them. Their future needs also to be considered.

Mahmoud Abbas has delivered to the United Nations the request for a declaration of the new Palestinian State of the West Bank and Gaza. President Obama has addressed the General Assembly and his decision to veto the application in the Security Council has been voiced. This is on the basis that the statehood of Palestine will not be a reality without Israel's input and cooperation. Obama wants to get Israel and the Palestinians back to the negotiating table. Obama is a great statesman and his links with the Jews preceded his political life and solidified in his political life. David Remnick has pointed this out. Remnick labels Obama a 'Philo-Semite'. He quotes a statement from Obama: "The dream of a Jewish and democratic state cannot be fulfilled with permanent occupation" [of the West Bank and Gaza][293]. Here is a warning from Obama that a Jewish state cannot be a democratic one if it includes millions of Arab Palestinians. Therefore, if a 'Palestinian Spring' as outlined in this book does not take place, a Palestinian State will need to be created, with a loss of land.

Israel is faced with lessons to be learned:

1. God has a plan for this planet, which must be respected. He wants the Edenic state of perfection to be restored. He intends to do this via the covenant he made with Abraham that cannot be ignored by Israel at any time in their past, present or future.
2. The causes of the devastations, decimations, and captivities of Israel outlined in the Tanak are clearly related in the Tanak to Israel's idolatry as a nation. Idolatry takes many forms, all denying the existence and worship of the one true God. The Egyptian, Assyrian, Babylonian and Roman devastations inflicted on Israel have only one root cause.
3. The returns of Israel to the Jewish Homeland have also one root cause: That of repentance, reformation, and return to the Abrahamic Covenant and its fulfilment becoming the purpose for the existence of Israel. There is no room for secularism, humanism, religious superficiality or extremism. A return to the Tanak as their guiding light must be supreme.
4. Because of Israel's current predicament of having a large population of Moslems in its territorial homeland it must be kind to them, short of their taking over the state. A method for this has been outlined in the chapter named 'The Palestinian Spring'. If this method does not become a reality a Palestinian State must be negotiated. Driving the Arab Palestinians out by brute force is not an option.
5. Israel is wary of United Nations resolutions and 'International Law' expositions, which are presumably endowed with great authority. Those affecting Israel are considered biased in favour of the Arabs because of the alleged false claims made by the Arabs and their supporters. Arabs may have been in Palestine for centuries but Israelis have been there for millennia.

6. Propagation of Judaism in terms of Land, Torah and Messiah as a unity has never been magnified and accomplished thus far in the history of modern Israel. This must be undertaken. Torah and Messiah have application for all humanity because God has willed that all nations of the earth be blessed by access through the gates of Eden. This cannot be ignored. God wants to restore access to the Tree of Life for all humanity, not just the Jews. The Jews cannot sidestep this responsibility.

Israel must negotiate with the displaced Arab Palestinians because of their reestablishment of the Jewish homeland. In these negotiations the following will be prominent:

1. The post 1967 borders of Israel are current and real. Land for peace as a policy has not brought peace thus far. Compromises are needed.
2. Israel will not allow Palestinians living outside the post 1967 borders to return to the area within those borders. Compensation will be needed.
3. Jerusalem is the capital city of Israel and is not subject to any division or internationalisation. It is the focus for Messiah's reign. This must be steadfastly negotiated.
4. The Golan Heights will continue as an inviolable part of Israel. It is a major defensive strategy.
5. Gaza, Judea and Samaria are viewed as part of Israel and Arabs living there can continue to do so if they live peacefully as Israeli citizens. Compensation will be necessary if they desire to relocate outside those borders and in fact are encouraged to do so if they wish to live in an Arabic Islamic State. Notwithstanding, land swaps will be necessary if a Palestinian State is negotiated.
6. If a Arab Palestinian State in Gaza and the West Bank becomes a reality its borders and conditions of independence will be difficult to negotiate to the satisfaction of the security of Israel, and the aspirations of the Palestinians. But it will be imperative.

Because God has allowed Israel back into their homeland
1. They are to renew their vows to the Abrahamic Covenant:
2. They are to hold the negotiated borders of the LAND steadfastly and defend it from any external or internal attack. This involves being

219

good neighbours and showing kindness to the strangers within their gates, besides employing military might in defending the borders.

3. They are to enter a period of reformation with regard to the TORAH and recognize the Tanak as the sole guide to live by and relate to their neighbours.

4. The Temple must be rebuilt on Mount Moriah where Abraham 'sacrificed' Isaac, the holiest spot in Israel. It is not Mount Gerizim. Jews will weep and pray no longer at the Western Wall but will worship and rejoice in the rebuilt Temple.

5. Israel must identify the MESSIAH as defined by the Tanak and hasten the establishment of his kingdom as defined by the Tanak. The rebuilt Temple will facilitate the worship and honour of the Messiah.

6. Jerusalem will be the sole capital of Israel under Israeli control. It is Israeli territory but may be accessed by Moslems, Christians and others. It is the seat of the Messiah's kingdom. The eschatology of the Tanak ends in the Messianic Kingdom being proclaimed and established in Jerusalem. It is eternal.

7. Jews are to remember that if they become idolaters and turn away from the worship of the one true God their enemies will vanquish them. The Tanak predicts such an outcome. Israel is only one lost war away from another devastation and scattering. The Abrahamic Covenant must be kept. God is as patient as he is eternal.

8. Israel must always have the best IDF in the world. To repeat for emphasis, Israel is only one lost war away from another devastation and scattering. But Israel can be positive and hopeful. Theirs is the "Super-Story" because it is in God's plan that the Abrahamic Covenant will be kept.

There are still some imponderables. Israel must stay a democracy[294]. Does that call for the ascendancy of a secular state? Israel cannot become a theocracy or be governed by the religion called Judaism in the affairs of state until Messiah appears. It is still important to keep church and state separate until Messiah appears because of the fragility of democracy and the high price attached to free will. The current milieu does not fit into the Moses template in respect to political and civil government. Stoning homosexuals and Sabbath breakers (Jewish) is similar to cutting noses off of adulterous women and hands off thieves (Moslem). A J Jacobs will agree that these are archaic remnants of an excessively extreme religious zeal. The maintenance of a 'state' which is obedient to the Abrahamic Covenant and which is not dictatorially influenced by an extreme Orthodox Judaism is the desirable option. The Land and its governance can be maintained on a level as is seen in the model of the US and Great Britain. That is why a very strong IDF must be maintained to protect Israel from its enemies. This does not imply that the state must be sponsored by a majority of godless people who give not a thought to Torah and Messiah. The religious fervour of the Israelis in worship must continue in terms of Torah and Messiah. That bridled religious fervour needs to be a moderate and centrist Judaism, based only on the Tanak, which all Israelis will be able to joyously embrace. So there will be no room for a 'ayatollah style' governance of Israel in the current situation. A personal godliness is important in all Israelis. Idolatry must be shunned. The personal involvement in Torah and the Messianic mission is essential. Reformation is called for in order to restore Israel to this status.

NOTES

[293] See The New Yorker March 12, 2012 'Threatened' by David Remnick. Remnick has also written a biography of Obama entitled 'The Bridge: The Life and Rise of Barak Obama' published by Knopf and Doubleday, 2010

[294] Theodor Herzl had expressed what kind of government was suitable for the Israel he envisioned in his Judenstaat. According to Laqueur "He preferred a democratic monarchy, or an aristocratic republic. Nations were not yet fit for unlimited democracy . . . . Herzl was opposed to any form of theocracy. The priests would receive the highest honours but would not be allowed to interfere in the administration of the state. They would be kept within their temples, as the army would be kept within barracks". See 'A History of Zionism' by Walter Laqueur, Schocken Books, New York, page 93.

CHAPTER 28
REFORMATION

S eventh-day Adventism originated in the North American Protestant revival of the first half of the 19th Century. William Miller predicted the end of the world with the return of Jesus Christ in October 1844 AD[295]. This was on the basis of an eschatology built on the prophecies in the Book of Daniel. When that did not happen, a reinterpretation of the 1844 event became the commencement of a celestial Investigative Judgement[296]. In the Heavenly Sanctuary (which was the blueprint for the wilderness Tabernacle and Solomon's Temple) Jesus Christ had moved from the Holy Place to the Most Holy Place, in his Day of Atonement ministration as High Priest, to commence this Investigative Judgement. This judgement is to decide who on earth is worthy to be saved. Several SDA scholars have challenged this doctrine repeatedly over the years since 1844, as being unbiblical. But since the doctrine was blessed and authenticated by SDA prophetess Ellen Gould White, these scholars have been ejected from the church. The most recent scholar to be ejected in 1980 was Desmond Ford who for fourteen years had been the Chairman of the Theology Department of Avondale College, the prestigious SDA University in Australia. Desmond Ford found that the doctrine was conceived on an untenable and non-contextual interpretation of Daniel's prophecies. It was also incompatible with the Pauline doctrine of salvation by faith alone in Jesus Christ. Besides, Desmond Ford showed an erroneous and manipulated interpretation of world history underpinning the doctrine[297]. The doctrine has since become fossilized and is hardly ever mentioned in the churches according to reports[298]. But the administrators of the church will not change in view of the challenge change would pose to Ellen White's authority. In addition, around 1980, researchers and ministers of the church Ronald Numbers and Walter Rea[299] exposed the extensive and un-acknowledged dependence Ellen White had on contemporary writers. She credited her visions as the sources of her writings. Both Numbers and Rea were ostracised and ejected. The SDA Church lost an estimated 300 ordained ministers and over 200,000 members worldwide over these issues in the immediate aftermath. A greater falling away has continued over the years[300].

All movements both secular and religious, at some time or other in their history, are faced with the need for change. Some accomplish change well, while some do not, often rejecting logic and truth. This is a human failure. Non-acceptance of necessary progressive change leads to fossilization, decay and irrelevance.

This book stridently calls for a change in the current disunity in Judaism. The reformation being sought is attention and re-orientation to the Abrahamic Covenant, which underpins the whole structure of the Tanak and primitive Judaism. Taking the Tanak as the sole and only authoritative foundation and guide, JUDAISM IS A REDEMPTIVE RELIGION. No matter what point of origin is taken, it is redemptive. The Pentateuch represents the religion of Moses, Israel's greatest guru. The foundation he laid is redemptive. The entire sanctuary service outlined by Moses in the Aaronic priesthood is redemptive. Judaism is not a philosophy. It is a live communication between God and humanity. There is no Judaism without Moses. He gave us the Creation story and this tells of a condition of perfection, which was tarnished by disobedience to the Torah. The redemptive plan was initiated outside the Gates of Eden with Adam and Eve, clothed in animal skins, looking longingly to get back into Eden. But the Messiah was needed to accomplish this re-access and God gave the promise of the Messiah at the Gates of Eden. A symbolic animal sacrifice was instituted to atone. This was the promise of the coming Messiah. Adam, Abel, Noah, Abraham, Jacob and Moses, all offered animal sacrifices, symbolic of what the Messiah would do for them, to help them to get back into Edenic perfection and immortality. Moses received the Ten Commandments, built the tent tabernacle and ordained the Aaronic priesthood to carry out the symbols of Messianic salvation. The Day of Atonement also signified the Messianic provision. This was all given at Mt. Sinai. Messianic sacrifice had been enacted already on Mt. Moriah, the fact that deity was to be the propitiation. This is the whole basis of primitive redemptive Judaism. Judaism is incomplete and non-functional without this Messianic Hope. But the structure and practice of current Judaism has strayed far, far away from this purity over the centuries, so that it is no longer a functional religion. Perhaps it is not necessary to bring animal sacrifices back, but the maturity in Judaism is capable of realizing the Messianic provision of redemption.

A Jewish nation cannot be a completely secular state without the total renunciation of primitive Judaism. Assimilation has already occurred if the Jew is separated from the practice of primitive Judaism. The state must have the same ethics as primitive Judaism. This should not be seen as a union of church and state. Without the Abrahamic Covenant Judaism is a purposeless religion. Primitive Judaism legitimises the Jews as a nation and there is an obligation to embrace the Abrahamic Covenant. Judaism in its purest primitive expression is the preservative of the Jews, the resistance to assimilation, and the hope of the world. This was God's contract with Abraham and must be honoured. It is Israel's pillar of cloud by day and pillar of fire by night. It is the Shekinah. Israel's God wants to live with them. "Let them make me a sanctuary that I might live among them".

The Rabbinic Judaism of the European ghettos was mostly Talmudic and extreme. The Tanak had been deserted and confusion was rife. Walter Laqueur describes the early 19th Century AD Judaism as "an ossified religion based largely on a senseless collection of prohibitions and equally inexplicable customs elaborated by various rabbis in the distant past . . . . a moribund religion"[301]. Laqueur notes that the European Jews sought to correct this ghetto mentality of the prevailing corrupted Judaism by responding to the Enlightenment that followed the French Revolution. He points out that Moses Mendelssohn tried desperately to reform this corrupted Judaism. Mendelssohn ". . . saw no contradiction between the essentials of a Jewish religion and his own moral maxims such as 'Love truth, Love peace' (Jerusalem) . . . . But even those who were deeply convinced of the values of Judaism, its traditions and its contributions to civilization, regarded it more as an impressive fossil than a living faith"[302]. Laqueur also cites Moritz Steinschneider, another would be reformer of Judaism: Pressed by a student who was enthusiastic about Zionist activities ". . . he looked longingly and sadly at his great collection of Jewish books and said 'My dear fellow, it is too late. All that remains for us to do is to provide a decent funeral'"[303].

The call for reform in Judaism is not rare. Calls for reform of ethnic Judaism started with Abraham himself who cleansed his own father's house of idolatry. Moses had the task of extensively reforming a people steeped in Egyptian Sun-Worship and idolatry. The Judges in Israel and every prophet who contributed to the Tanak were all reformers. God made an impassioned call through Isaiah: "Come now and let us reason together, saith the Lord: though your sins be as scarlet, they shall be as white as snow; though they be red like crimson, they shall be as wool. If ye be willing and obedient, ye shall eat the good of the land. But if ye refuse and rebel, ye shall be devoured with the sword; for the mouth of the Lord hath spoken it" (Isaiah 1:18-20). Judaism is indeed a redemptive religion. Now that Israel is ensconced in Canaan, powerful reformers are needed. There is no need to identify Jews as Ashkenazi or Sephardic. They are all of the Abrahamic Covenant. One looks to the Prime Ministers to be the dispensers of reform. Visionary rabbis could be instruments of reform. A conference called for all the factions in Judaism could provide a stage for discussion, reformation and renewal. The Judaism of Moses of the Pentateuch and the prophets of the Tanak needs to be reinstated. The fossilized religious foundation built on the Talmud needs to be demolished.

The voices of Thomas Friedman, Alan Dershowitz, Walter Laqueur, A J Jacobs, David Remnick and many others call for reformation in the religious life and political consensus in Israel in order to bring peace to Jewry and strength and vitality back into Judaism. Isaiah adds his voice again: "And it shall come to pass in the last days, that the mountain of the Lord's house shall be established in the top of the mountains, and shall be exalted above the hills; and all nations shall flow unto it. And many people shall go and say, Come ye, and let us go up to the mountain of the Lord, to the house of the God of Jacob; and he will teach us of his ways, and we will walk in his paths; for out of Zion shall go forth the law, and the word of the Lord from Jerusalem. And he shall judge among the nations, and shall rebuke many peoples; and they shall beat their swords into ploughshares, and their spears into pruning hooks; nation shall not lift up sword against nation, neither shall they learn war anymore. O house of Jacob, come ye and let us walk in the light of the Lord" (Isaiah 2:2-5). It is high time.

Existence upon this planet called Earth is to be summed up in three words: Creation, Redemption and Glorification. Jews grasp the meaning and import of all three. Judaism is summed up in the Abrahamic Covenant where God wants Land, Torah and Messiah to be enacted in order to restore the perfect Edenic state of existence, his original plan. The possession of Land has been accomplished but needs to be sealed and protected. The absolute Torah of the Tanak needs to be restored. And the Messianic vision must be embraced. This restored existence is to be achieved for all humanity through the government of the Messiah, who is the healing of the nations. This is the fair dinkum purpose for the preservation of the Jews and the fulfilment of their mission, the Abrahamic Covenant. History bears out that there have been many extinct peoples. There are many indigenous people in subjugation to stronger powers in the world today, perhaps facing extinction. But for the Jews, extinction is not in their future.

THE END

NOTES

[295]   Google: William Miller and 1844

[296]   'Foundations of the Seventh-day Adventist Message and Mission' by P. Gerard Damsteegt. Grand Rapids, Michigan: William B. Eerdmans Publishing Company

[297]   Good News Unlimited: Daniel 8:14—The Day of Atonement and the Investigative Judgement

[298]   The Adventist Forum discusses this aspect in their meetings. They are independent of the organized hierarchy of the church and consist of rank and file SDAs. There is no actual research data on the frequency of sermons preached in the SDA Churches on this doctrine. But it is the impression that ministers stay away from this topic in the churches.
See also 'Good News For Adventists'—Inhouse Problems With The Investigative Judgement.

[299]   See 'Prophetess of Health' by Ronald Numbers. William B. Eerdmans Publishing Company See also 'The White Lie' by Walter Rae. M & R Publishing

[300]   See nonsda.org—Honest Answers for Real People: Seventh-day Adventism—Why Are So Many Leaving?

[301]   'A history of Zionism' by Walter Laqueur, page 18.

[302]   Ibid page 16

[303]   Ibid page 17

BIBLIOGRAPHY

1. The Tanak. Several translations are used: The King James Version and the New King James Version (NKJV) are used predominantly.
2. 'From Beirut to Jerusalem' by Thomas Friedman, Harper Collins Publications, 1998
3. 'Exiled' by Serpouhi Tavakdjian
4. 'The Case For Israel' by Alan Dershowitz, John Wiley & Sons, Inc., 2003
5. 'Eichmann in Jerusalem—A Report on the Banality of Evil' by Hannah Arendt, Penguin Group Inc. (Originally published 1963 by the Viking Press Inc.)
6. 'Peace Process—American Diplomacy and the Arab-Israeli Conflict Since 1967' by William Quandt, Third Edition, The Brookings Institution, 2005
7. 'The Year of Living Biblically' by A J Jacobs, Simon & Schuster Paperbacks, 2008
8. 'History of Zionism' by Walter Laqueur, Schocken Books, New York.
9. 'Daniel 8:14: The Day of Atonement and the Investigative Judgement' by Desmond Ford, 1980. Available on line
10. 'Colonial Mixed Blood—A Story of the Burghers of Sri Lanka' by Allan Russell Juriansz, (To be published shortly). Genealogy sources are cited here.
11. '1967' by Tom Segev, 2008 published by Abacus
12. Numerous other sources are used and these have been carefully footnoted.

GLOSSARY

1. Achdut Ha'avoda Party—Early left wing labour party in Palestine
2. Aliya—Immigrating to Israel
3. Ashkenazi Jews—European Jews
4. Betar—Now defunct Youth Movement
5. Eretz Israel—Land of Israel
6. Etzel—synonymous with Irgun Zvai Leumi—Jewish Military Organization
7. Haganah—Early Jewish Armed Force in Palestine
8. Halacha—Body of Jewish Religious Law
9. (Hareshima) Hamamlachtit Party—Formed by Ben Gurion in 1968 when his Rafi Party decided to amalgamate with others to form the Labour Party of Israel
10. Harel Brigade—Reserve Armoured Brigade of IDF
11. Hashomer—Guild of Watchmen founded in 1909 to defend Israeli settlements
12. Herut Party—Freedom Party founded by Menachim Begin
13. Histadrut—Federation of Jewish Trade Unions
14. Irgun Zvai Leumi—Jewish Military Organization
15. Jewish Agency—Officially created in 1929 to assist Jewish immigrants to Palestine. Was philanthropic and apolitical. But in 1948 it became the organ of government on the Unilateral Declaration of Independence
16. Kibbutz—Communal Agricultural Settlement with common ownership and where children live separately from parents
17. Knesset—Israeli Parliament
18. Lehi—Israel's Freedom Fighters
19. Likud Party—Right wing 'cohesion' party emanating from several parties, mainly the Herut Party
20. Mapai Party—Early 'Party of Israel's Labourers', forerunner of the Labour Party
21. Mapam Party—United Workers Party of the early years

22. Mizrahi—Oriental Jews but distinct from Sephardim or North African Jews, although sometimes included with the Sephardim.
23. Moetzet HaPoalet—Jewish Working Womens Group
24. Mossad—Israel's Intelligence Agency
25. Palmach—Armed Strike Force functioning within Haganah, active pre 1948
26. Poalei Zion Party—Jewish Socialist Party associated with Communist Paolei Zion. The latter was dissolved in 1928
27. Rafi Party—Party coming out of Mapai Party led by Ben Gurion when he left it in 1973
28. Sephardim—Jews emigrating from North African Arab countries to Israel. They are sometimes included with Oriental Mizrahi Jews
29. Shlomzin—Organization providing help to Israeli families
30. Tanak—The Old Testament
31. Yerida—Emigrating from Israel
32. Zohar—Jewish mystical thought also known as Kabbala

INDEX

Likud 83-4, 94-6, 98-9, 177, 192, 229

M

Maccabeans 69
Machpelah 38, 40, 58, 60, 150
Mahinda 3
Mahmoud Abbas 114, 141, 192, 194, 217
Malachi 29, 41, 43
Man-Child 56
Manna 72, 78
Martin Luther 6, 8
Masara 122
Max Nordau 20, 149, 151, 171
Mecca 108
Melchizedek 33, 35, 37-8
Midrash 53
Mishna 47, 53
Mohammed 108, 123
Monotheism xv, 31, 37
Moses 19-21, 23-4, 26-7, 30, 39, 41-5,
    53, 57-8, 65-7, 69-73, 147-8,
    159-60, 202-3, 206-7, 223-5
Mossad 92, 95, 197, 230
Mount Moriah 28, 32-4, 38, 57, 101,
    108, 123, 220
Mount Sinai 34, 42, 45, 58, 60, 73
Muslim Brotherhood 114, 117, 140, 144
Mystical 148-9, 169, 230
The Myth 148-9, 154

N

Nasser 91, 123, 188-9
Nazis xiv, 12, 205
Nebhiim 44
Nebuchadnezzar II 65, 67
Negev 42, 45, 89, 101, 130, 210, 213-14

Nehemiah 117, 150
Neil Armstrong 34
Netanyahu vi, 84, 95-102, 124, 161,
    177-84, 192-6, 198
Nile Valley 121-2
Nixon 186, 188-9, 197, 199
Noah 20, 27, 29, 31-2, 37, 216, 223
Nobel Prize 55, 101, 194
Noel Clapham xiii

O

Obama 115, 125, 141, 179, 181-2,
    193-6, 198, 217-18, 221
Olmert 97, 99-100, 102, 131, 138,
    177, 194-5
Ondaatje 5, 15-16
Onomastikon 15
Organization of Petroleum Exporting
    Countries 185
Oriental Jews 230
Oslo Accords 93, 96, 100, 113, 132, 192
Ottoman Empire xv, 76, 109, 117-18,
    122, 127

P

Palestinian Spring vi, 125, 134, 138,
    146, 195, 204, 208-9, 212, 218
Passover 51, 53, 58, 60, 72, 78, 83, 85,
    155, 160
Patriarch 27, 39, 53, 147-8
Patriarchs 27, 29, 31-2, 41, 48
Pentateuch 19, 41, 44, 53, 67, 147,
    223, 225
Peres 95, 100, 102, 119, 131, 192,
    195, 201
Pharaoh 66, 70, 72, 78

Y

Z